To Wayne,

Roadie

◆

I hope you enjoy Reading this as much as I enjoyed writting it.

Stay LOUD!

Karl K

7/8/02

Roadie

A True Story
(at least the parts I remember)

———————— ◆ ————————

Karl Kuenning RFL

Writer's Showcase
San Jose New York Lincoln Shanghai

Roadie
A True Story (at least the parts I remember)

Writer's Showcase
an imprint of iUniverse.com, Inc.

For information address:
iUniverse.com, Inc.
5220 S 16th, Ste. 200
Lincoln, NE 68512
www.iuniverse.com

Cover design by Jean Boissonneault

ISBN: 0-595-18526-6

Printed in the United States of America

This book is dedicated to all Roadies, Ex-Roadies, or anyone who ever dreamed of being a Roadie

Contents

◆

Foreword xi

Acknowledgements xv

How did I become a "Roadie"? 1

My First Gig 4

Roadie School 11

The Big Apple 14

Hell must have stairs 18

The show must go on? 19

False Arrest 23

Harry 27

The Hurricane 29

Low Bridge 31

Human Target 33

A really hot show 35

Very funny 39

Bad vibes 41

Elvis has left the building 44

Rock Candy 46

Be Prepared 50

Shocking Experience 53

Get Down Tonight 54

Attempted Murder 57

Garden Party 61

Luck of the Irish 63

No Checks Please 65

Gimme Three Steps 70

Heartless 77

Class Acts 80

Hello Dolly 82
My First Tour 83
Rosie 95
A Day in the Life 98
Ode to Mary Jo 113
Bonnie Raitt's shower 117
There's no place like home 121
Cultural Exchange 123
Oil's well that ends well 127
Just for Openers 129
How Much Wood Can A Woodchopper Chop? 132
California Dreaming 134
Viva Las Vegas 138
Truck Driver's Daughters 142
Road Etiquette 145
Quickies 148
The Politics of Opening Acts and Load outs 155
Rarely Tour the Earth 160
Hay, you must be Buck Owens 162
Carole King 163
Let there be light 166
My Fall during the Spring Tour 169
Mistake by the Lake 173
The Fix 175
Cold Shower 179
Turn it up 183
Do Not Disturb 186
If this is Tuesday, this must be Cincinnati 189
Hot fun in the Summertime 191
Road Clichés 193
Turning Japanese 194
A Familiar Journey 197
More Quickies 199
Parlez-vous Français? 204
My Paris Vacation 206
Very Nice 209
The British are Coming! 210

Border Crossing *212*

Yugoslavia *215*

Iron Curtain Call *217*

Scandinavia *220*

The Rainbow at the end of the tour *222*

Lana *225*

Breakfast in Canada *231*

The Final Tour *239*

Home Grown *240*

Union Dues *242*

The Palladium *246*

The Cleveland Massacre *250*

Epilogue *255*

About the Author *259*

Appendix *261*

Glossary *263*

References *277*

Foreword

◆

Why I am writing this book

Whenever somebody finds out that I used to be a "roadie" they almost always ask me one of two questions. (Well, actually three if you count "What's a roadie?") But let's assume for a minute that they know what a roadie is, the first words out of their mouth are usually, "How did you get into that?" or "Why did you get out of it?" This book will answer both questions (for me, anyway) and will fill in the details of my life on the road in between those two events. Whenever I tell one of my "roadie stories", it has a strange effect on people. They almost always want to hear more. Their eyes get wide, and their mouth opens slightly. They get very quiet and rarely interrupt or try to change the subject. Maybe it's the vicarious thrill of imagining for just a split second that it's them backstage about to call for the curtain, or up on the scaffolding arcing their Super Trouper, the headphone crackling in their ear in anticipation of the start of the show. They are telling themselves that if the stars had lined up just a little differently, if there had been a minor change in history, one twist of fate, they could have been the one to be controlling the sound heard by 20,000 screaming fans, designed the lighting for the show, mixed the monitors, tuned the guitars, or handed the drummer a brand new stick after he shattered the old one (without missing a beat).

I've had the idea of writing this book for almost 20 years. It took a variety of unrelated events to coax me to start. First, I have become something of an internet junkie in the last few years and I recently started finding websites of bands I had worked with and e-mail addresses of musicians and technicians I had known. As I read the postings of old fans and new fans not even born when I toured, I saw this intense fascination people have with music, musicians, bands, concerts, and yes, even roadies. While surfing, I found that a production manager that I hadn't thought about in over 20 years was living in Australia and began sending me e-mails. A drummer I thought was probably long dead showed up alive and well in Branson, Missouri. I found myself pulling out old posters, albums, T-shirts and my old Anvil briefcase. I found myself bathed in a sea of reminiscence.

About this time I heard a radio commercial while driving home from work that featured an actor playing an old burned out roadie. What was said in the spot or what was being sold isn't important, what stuck in my head was the realization that Madison Avenue was using a roadie to sell something. The baby-boomers were responding to the memories of the concerts of their youth and the ad agency was capitalizing on that. Could I leverage that baby-boomer fixation into a roadie story worth telling?

The final consideration was simple—TIME. As I write this book in 1998, I am 41 years old. I was 23 when I left the road. According to standard insurance mortality tables, I should live to be about 85, so my life is almost half over if I don't get hit by a bus (a distinct possibility since I used up a large amount of my allocated luck during my roadie years [more on that later]). If I was going to write the book, it needed to be now.

I have been working on this book in my head for two decades, reliving the events, trying to remember the details, separating the fact from the fiction, telling and retelling the stories over and over to one or two people at a time. Most of the actual evidence is long since gone. There are very few photos, an occasional itinerary, backstage pass, or poster, no autographs, and all the old friends that I could ask questions of have long since been misplaced. I make no absolute guarantee as to the accuracy of any of the details contained in this book. I probably have some of the dates mixed up and some of the names wrong. What's important is that this is how I remember these episodes and it makes up who I am during that period of my life. Only one thing was certain—the book's format. You see, the road is a series of disjointed scenes, the book should be written the same way. A tour has a beginning and an end, but everything else in between is a blur. It is like your memories are in a blender. There are big chunks of individual memories floating around in a sea of blackness. Since my memories are not in chronological order, neither is the book. The only thing I can promise is a beginning and an end, and a roadie smoothie (chunky style) in between.

At this point you're probably wondering what bands I worked with. Did I work with your favorite? Do I have secret backstage details about your number one artist? The answer to those questions is, "It really doesn't matter". The stories contained in these pages are true, however they are also representative of millions of other stories, from tens of thousands of other roadies working with thousands of other bands. My suggestion is to not get too hung up on who the story is about, but rather focus on the story itself. Chances are you could replace the names of who is involved and change a few of the details, and it would be a story about your favorite group or artist. I worked with over 200 artists during more than a five-year period, some famous and some not so famous. A sampling of some of those artists includes Lynyrd Skynyrd, Dolly Parton, B.B. King, KC and the Sunshine Band, Jean-Luc Ponty, Bonnie Raitt, Supertramp, Talking Heads, Ray Charles, Carole King, Sly and the Family Stone, The Spinners, Patti Smith, Pat Metheny, and Blue Öyster Cult..

The range of music styles is diverse, so there should be something for everyone's taste.

Acknowledgements

◆

I wish to thank the hundreds of Roadies who visit www.roadie.net and gave me the motivation to publish this book. Many of those Roadies also contributed to the glossary located at the back of the book.

Thanks to Richard Tyler for being my mentor.

Lastly, thanks to my wife Chris for tolerating this three year project, even though she didn't really understand my passion for it.

How did I become a "Roadie"?

◆

I have to make the assumption that you must at least have some kind of idea what a roadie is or you wouldn't have picked up this book. However, if you are like most people you probably have some preconceived notions about who roadies are, what they do, how much they are paid, how they live on the road, how they "hang" with "the band", the drugs, the groupies, motorhomes, trashed hotel rooms, backstage passes, and did I forget to mention the drugs and groupies? Well, this book will change forever the way you look at that faceless guy bathed in amber light sitting in a block of 24 of the best seats in the house blocking your view while he controls the sound you are listening to. I'll get more into roadie job descriptions later in the book, but first the beginning.

"Karl, How did you get into being a roadie?"

Simple, I had a valid driver's license.

Actually, like most stories there is a lot more to this one than my having a driver's license, so let's back up a little. I was an unpopular geek in high school (I know you're asking yourself how a cool ex-roadie could be a geek, but it's true). Since I wasn't a "jock", a "head", or a "motorhead," I had to find my niche to survive school, and I chose "AV nerd". Actually it was a cool gig. I had permission to wander around the school at will, while running movie projectors, overhead projectors and filmstrip projectors. The dirty little secret of the "AV Nerds" is that we are a very powerful group in the politics of a high school. If the principal in my school wanted to have an assembly, he had to see me. I had the secret knowledge to make the lavaliere microphone pop to life and fill the room with his voice. I knew how to make those big stage lights burn brightly by throwing those big scary levers that everyone was convinced would cause electrocution if touched. I even knew how to run a spot light (very handy when the drama club wanted to do South Pacific or The Music Man). And the absolute coolest thing was that they sometimes paid me for skipping class! Ok jocks, aren't you sorry you all made fun of me? No? Ok, back to the story. During high school, I bought a Super 8 camera and won second place in a national contest, the 1972 Kodak Teenage movie awards, for a 3-minute and 20-second film featuring my younger brother, Keith, in a weird dream sequence (this could be done by a 5-year-old on a good computer now, but at the time a mix of humans with frame by frame animation was very cool). This was a critical junction in my life (stay with me, I'm getting to the roadie stuff) as I decided I was going to go to photography school, and be a filmmaker. So where does one go to be a filmmaker? Since I won a Kodak award I focused my search there. It turns out there is a college in Rochester, New York associated with Kodak called R.I.T. (Rochester Institute of Technology). Some say it's the best photography school in the world, so I went there. What I didn't know was that they were going to make me take still pictures for two years before I ever touched a movie camera (and the first year in black & white only). In hindsight, I probably should have gone to U.C. Berkeley or The Brooks Institute of Photography and studied film, but if I had, I never would have become a roadie (I told you I was getting to the roadie stuff) and you wouldn't be reading this book. At R.I.T., I joined the "Tech Crew", which was the university equivalent of "AV Geeks". However, instead of overhead projectors we did mostly stage stuff, including state of the art sound reinforcement and theatrical lighting. It was here on the R.I.T. Tech Crew that I became more and more disillusioned with photography and more and more enamored with stage work. My first year in school I focused on the classes, the second year I lost my focus, (a really bad thing for a photographer). Then it happened, my first gig. NOTE: For those of you keeping score at home: Here comes the beginning I have been promising...

My First Gig

◆

It was October of 1975 and I knew that some of the Techies also worked part-time for a local sound and light company. This was partly due to the fact that the guy that ran the tech crew (Dan) also owned the light company. I always knew that eventually they would have enough confidence in me to ask me out on a "road trip" too, so I waited for my chance. It came on a Thursday; J.C. (an old timer on Tech Crew, I think he had been a student at R.I.T. 6 or 7 years) approached me and asked me the big question, "Hey Karl, do you have a driver's license?" "Sure, why?" My heart was racing. Was he playing a joke on me, or would I finally be included in this secret brotherhood that got to go to far away exotic places, and do concerts with famous rock stars? J.C. spoke, "I lost my license last week, and if you can drive a six-wheel truck, and if you can be gone from campus for a couple of days you can come with us to do sound for a couple of shows." Could I? Would I? Of course, of course, what do I do? Mix the sound, place the mikes, and maybe introduce the band? What? Well actually you'll just be driving the truck. You see J.C. and Dick (the other Techie on this gig) were both rather large and it turned out they picked me not only because of my flawless driving record, but because I was small. Back then I was 5' 9 ½ " and weighed 145 pounds soaking wet. If you've ever been in the front seat of an old six-wheel truck there is barely room for two big men and a stick shift, never mind adding a third person. I swallowed my pride (certainly not the last time I would have to do that on the road) and said yes.

We left at four in the morning for Poughkeepsie New York. My very first road gig would be Brian Auger and the Oblivion Express. Like a lot of you, I had never heard of him before, but the ride up the New York Thruway was nice (albeit a little cramped) and before I knew it we were at "the load in". I didn't really know what I was doing, but I tried to help J.C. and Dick, along with some eager but easily distracted student stage-hands, get the PA unloaded and stacked. Then I pretty much just watched. I watched as the lights that were ingeniously mounted in racks were lifted into the air via a hydraulic tube called a genie lifter. Once air-borne these "par lamps" were aimed at key positions on the stage in preparation for the show. The band didn't have a light man, so the light guys just improvised and washed the stage in several colors planning on using the spot lights for specific accents. I watched the band roadies set up, and I watched every detail with amazement during the sound check. I remember thinking how good this band sounded. I got my first real back stage pass that day, and I took advantage of it by watching the show from backstage. J.C. or maybe it was Dick suggested that I get some sleep since we had a show in Cleveland the next night. Sleep? How could I sleep? This is great! I was still a photo major at that point and I did bring a camera along. It was something that I rarely did again since there were times you had to do certain things or had to be certain places and keeping tabs on a $500 camera was not possible. Also I soon learned that roadie etiquette only allowed band pictures at specific times and under very specific circumstances. I don't really remember the load out except that I didn't really know what I was doing ("Hey you! Which case is next?" "I dunno," I replied.) I also vaguely remember the student stagehands cutting out before the truck was finished, which it turned out was a common dilemma at some college gigs. Many a fight broke out between students and crew over load outs (more on that later). On to Cleveland! Oh by the way did I tell you that the band we were doing sound for in Cleveland was going to be Blue Öyster Cult?

Now before you get all hot and bothered remember your time lines. It's 1975, BÖC hasn't released "Don't Fear the Reaper", "Godzilla", or even "I'm Burning for You" yet. The current album for this tour was "On Your Feet or On Your Knees" Blue Öyster Cult. The live album included "Cities on Flame", "ME 262"(about a German WWII jet plane), and "Maserati GT—I Ain't Got You". Now that I've adjusted your temporal perspective, back to our story. We pulled up to the Agora and cracked the truck door at noon. I was very tired since I had done the lion share of driving the 493 miles from Poughkeepsie to Cleveland (sleep depravation was a condition I would never quite get used to as a roadie). Unlike the college gig the night before this was a professional stage crew, union guys. As I would learn later in my career, the union could be your best friend, or your worst enemy. Right now they were my best friends. They did all the heavy work while we just pointed. They all knew what to do and when to do it, real pros. The band roadies also were all business. Now let me spend a few minutes and explain exactly what a "band roadie" is.

Basically, the definition of a band roadie is simple: a frustrated musician. Now, before all you band roadies get your Manny's Schlepper T-shirts all in a wad, it doesn't apply to all of you, just most of you. Drum roadies tend to be ex-drummers or aspiring drummers, or really, really bad drummers. Ditto keyboard roadies, guitar roadies, violin roadies, and even hammer dulcimer roadies. So what does a band roadie do? Everything. Their responsibilities include the setup and maintenance of the instrument or instruments they are assigned, running to local music stores (like Manny's in NYC) for guitar picks and strings, tuning guitars, keeping the musicians furnished with water or a Heineken or freshly squeezed salt grass juice during the show, and most importantly, "babysitting". Babysitting is a very important duty, and takes complete and intense concentration while the show is in progress. (I'll bet you thought those guys hanging around in the shadows backstage were drinking champagne, and chasing naked groupies, didn't you?) What they are really doing is watching, vigilantly waiting for anything that would interfere with the show, or threaten the band. Minor situations include broken guitar strings (there is always a spare ax at the ready), broken drum heads (ever try changing one while you are wedged upside down under a 250-pound drummer while he's still beating the crap out of the drums that are still functional?), fallen mics, stuff thrown from the audience (have a nice trip!), or Perrier spilling into a Marshall Amp (get the fire extinguisher). More serious items include, drunken idiots trying to jump up on stage to "party with the band!" Pyrotechnic screw ups, electrical problems, PA failure during the show, or even a fan trying to climb up the front of the speaker stack possibly causing it to topple it out into the audience. The band roadies are the last ones to set up for the show, after the light roadies and sound roadies are well on their way to being finished. This is how it works. Lets assume the stage already exists and no assembly is required like here at the concert at the Agora. It is an old hall that was once a movie theatre or perhaps even a vaudeville house. The trucks back right up and unload right onto the stage (a nearly perfect load-in). The problem is that there is very little space, lots of gear, road cases for that gear, and a specific order that it all goes up. Sound is first, so the PA starts to go up. Stacking the PA is an art. Bass cabinets at the bottom, horns higher up, and bullets on top. It resembles the building of a pyramid, and it can take different shapes in various venues. The horns have to be aimed at the various sections of the hall and cords then need be hooked from each speaker down to the appropriate amps. While this is going on the light guys are running their cables and getting the lights "up". Racks of lights go up on Genie towers or suspended from a truss supported by Genie lifters. Once the lights were placed, The soundboard and light board both need to be bull dogged out to the sweet spot in the house (no small task since those dudes are heavy and very fragile), snakes are run to the boards, and empty road cases are stowed literally wherever they fit. Oops, I just realized I am using lots of "road lingo", like PA, snakes, stacks, horns, house, boards, etc. so you may be having a hard time following along. If you find a word and you don't understand what the heck I'm taking about please turn to the glossary and look it up. I'll try to give definitions where appropriate as well. OK. So the sound guys are about to start making noise and the light guys have pulled out the A-frame and are aiming. The band roadies (remember them?) are pulling out the band gear and doing some assembly. They really don't have much access to the stage yet since the light guys are pretty much monopolizing that square footage. Now all this has happened in about one hour or so. By the end of hour two the lights are aimed and the PA is blowing out any cobwebs. Now the band roadies get to place their gear on the marks laid out by the light guys (remember they have already aimed the 80 to 100 Par lamps). Eventually there is a sound check and then the opening act sets up and time permitting, does a check as well. The opening act that night in Cleveland was The Michael Stanley Band (a Cleveland favorite). Everything went well that day; I thought that was how all load-ins and sound checks went. Naïve me.

Now on with the show. I still hadn't slept much, but it didn't matter, this was the most exciting thing I had experienced up to that point in my 19-year life. I hung out stage left near Dick who was mixing monitors with a band roadie assigned to a fog machine. He was heating the water in preparation for the headliner while we watched and listened to MSB. After their set, and one encore, we waited for the main event. I had no idea what to expect, and now over 23 years later, it's still burned into my memory. The lights (all of them) were killed. The dry ice hit the boiling hot water, the blowers kicked in, and the unmistakable smell of stage fog hit my face as the plume exploded out across the pitch-black stage. Then something very odd happened. A flashing red light and a toy siren blared in my ear just to my right. An overweight band roadie who had been standing next to me (I hadn't noticed him because there was virtually no light at this point) strode out onto the dark stage and grabbed the center vocal mike. What seemed like a full minute went by with the only sound being the stupid whining sound of that siren, the only light a rotating red beacon. It was a toy Fireman's hat from Radio Shack! The words still send chills down my spine to this day. At the top of his voluminous lungs he shouted "ON YOUR FEEEEET…OR ON YOUR KNEEZZZZS…HERE THEY ARE…THE AMAZING BLUE ÖYSTER CULT !!!!! Then the band, which had stealthily positioned themselves on stage under cover of fog, broke into a kick ass cover version of "Born to be Wild". It was at that exact millisecond, that instant in time that I knew that this was what I wanted to do. I had to keep reminding myself to take some pictures (remember I still had the camera) and nobody seemed to mind. It was like I was hypnotized. I found out later that taking pictures on stage was a roadie no-no (covered in "roadie etiquette" later in this book). It was either very cold back stage (a possibility), or I was so full of adrenaline that I remember shivering most of the show. By the third or fourth song I was beginning to catch my breath when another life altering event happened. Remember that band roadie I was talking to? The one that had bathed the stage in artificial fog up to everyone's waist? He was drinking a Heineken, communicating with me (mostly sign language, since we were next to the monitor mixer which is one of the loudest spots on the face of the earth), and watching the show. He was babysitting. I was looking at the stage when I saw him jump. He moved so quickly that he seemed to be a blur. One second he was next to me, the next second there was a half-empty green beer bottle suspended in the air. Gravity claimed its prize, and the bottle hit the ancient wooden floor. The blurred roadie had entered the stage and was now clearly visible in the stage lights. Where was he going? What was he going to do? It was happening in slow motion and at triple speed simultaneously. As he neared the apron of the stage, he became airborne. He dove into the audience and I saw two images for a fraction of a second, a young girl's face and then his legs and feet. Then with no warning the band hit a power chord and the stage exploded. Well actually a bank of "flash pots" went off on cue. A flash pot is a theatrical version of the devices the old time photographers held up during the civil war, and then ignited to create enough light to produce a photographic image. These flash devices are about the size of a large ashtray and detonate electrically by remote control by the light guys or a pyro-technician and were very effective in 70's Rock shows. They are also very dangerous. They emit blinding light and great amounts of heat. Now I realized what I had just witnessed. He had noticed out of the corner of his eye that a young girl was climbing onto center stage. In most rock shows this would get you a rude shove back to your feet or perhaps a boot in the face, but this girl was about to get way more for her entertainment dollar. She was about to get her face burned off. She had inadvertently climbed up right on top of one of the devices. He saw where she was and knew that the cue for the pots was about to happen and he instinctively calculated that the only solution, the only way to solve this problem was to sacrifice his body and tackle her out of the way and into the crowd. I never did find out how badly the girl was hurt, but it had to be better than the cosmetic surgery that she avoided. The roadie had some bumps, but was not permanently damaged. He was standing next to me by the end of the next song drinking a new beer like nothing had happened, and again watching the stage out of the corner of his eye. If there was even a microscopic particle of doubt that I was going to be a roadie, this event erased it.

Roadie School

———————————— ◆ ————————————

When I got back to Rochester, I was paid $54. This was the standard roadie pay at the time of $20 per day) plus a $7 "per diem" (a non-taxed expense allowance for food). The fact of the matter was that I would have paid them more than $54 to have experienced what I did that weekend in 1975. I made it very clear to everyone involved that I would go anywhere at any time to do anything (but I really didn't want to keep driving trucks) to go "on the road". I first had to learn my craft so I was sent to "roadie school".

Wait, I forgot, there is no such thing as "roadie school".

The only way I was going to learn the business was the best way anybody learns any business. All you young skulls full of mush out there that haven't figured out what you're going to do next Saturday night, let alone the rest of your life, pay attention to this part since it will be one of the two or three things written in this book that will change your life if you let it. OK ready for the big secret. Watch people that are successful doing something and copy it. That with a little hard work can make you successful too. Pretty darn simple. So, I watched, listened, asked questions, hung out with real roadies, worked as a stagehand, worked lights, worked as third man on sound crews, did sound for all the shows nobody else wanted, and I honed my skills. I learned how to set up lighting systems. I learned how a tri-amp PA system worked, how it went together, how to stack a PA, how to fine tune an equalizer, and what to do if any of it broke. I learned how to run a spot light and instantaneously execute cues for the light man barking out commands in the headphones. I did sound for plays and musicals at the school, I did sound for graduations, I did sound for frat parties, I even did sound for Sunday chapel services (God needs a good sound man too!). I did anything to advance my knowledge of the profession I had now chosen to replace photography. All this work also paid for quite a few rolls of film as well which was nice. At this point I was a sophomore and I could get an associates degree if I completed my second year. Second piece of advice for anyone under 21 reading this book, and it comes in two parts. First, and this is important so I'm going to say it twice. Stay in school, whatever you do, stay in school. With that said though first make sure you have at least some sort of clue as to what you are passionate about before you decide what to go to school for. The most important part of any job you will ever have is that you have a true passion for the job. I had a passion in high school for filmmaking, not photography. I am convinced that if I had done my homework I would be writing this book today about my successful movie-making career. I blew that one, but I got lucky and found another passion, being a roadie. Just in case being a roadie didn't work out, I wanted to get my degree, and you should too. Ok, enough guidance counselor stuff, back to the story. I was working an average of 55 hours a week at school (Tech Crew), going full time to classes, and going out on the road weekends when there was a gig. Most of the gigs were semi local. By that I mean in Rochester, Syracuse, Buffalo, or Cleveland. Many were in New York City, Philadelphia, or even Boston. A lot of these early gigs were at other colleges. Some artists were "regulars" on the college circuit, and the company I was working for was as well. We were known and well liked by most of the student activities directors, and that translated into lots of One-Night Stands. I did more "school" shows than I can count, mostly between tours (or within the short breaks during a tour). Some of these artists were on their way up; some were on their way down, some never made it at all. I think this is a good time to share a few of the memorable ones with you. Remember these stories are not necessarily in chronological order.

The Big Apple

◆

I worked with Talking Heads twice. The first and the most important show for me was November 5, 1977 in New York City at the Loeb Student Center of NYU. Now let me set the stage {pun intended}. The Eisner & Lubin Auditorium holds about 800 people sitting on folding chairs. The stage holds a four piece band quite well, but only if it's a barbershop quartet. A 1977 era "punk rock" band with all their equipment and all my equipment (remember the PA stacks, the monitors, not to mention the monitor mixer (which tonight was me) doesn't fit too well on a postage stamp size stage. To top it off there was an opening act, Max Romeo & Jah Malla, a reggae band with at least 10 musicians including the back up singers. It was sardine time. It was time to invoke Karl's Roadie Rule #4, "When confronted with an insurmountable situation, improvise." So we worked it out, band members went into "club" mode, leaving extra amps in the truck; working with the bare minimum needed to do the show. I'm sure other compromises were reached as well, but I don't remember any specifics about that. The show went on somehow, because it always did.

Wait; before we even get into the show I need to make sure you haven't altered any historical time lines (do I sound like Jean-Luc Picard in a time shifting episode of Star Trek The Next Generation or what?). This is important, like Blue Öyster Cult earlier; the Talking Heads were not a huge success yet. They were well known in New York City and places where so called "punk rock" flourished. They played gigs at clubs like "CBGB's" and the "Mud Club" (which they mention in their 1979 hit "Life During Wartime" where David sings "This ain't no Mud Club no CBGBs I don't know where I come from"). Their only real hit to date was "Psycho Killer"; they hadn't recorded "Burning down the House", "And She Was" or even "Take Me to the River". But this brings us to Karl's Roadie Rule #6, "Anybody can go see a band that's popular, it's only special when you see a band *before* they are popular." An addendum to that rule states that working with a band before they are popular and then getting to work with them again after they become popular is the ultimate gig. The Talking Heads were part of the infamous "big four" bands to go from regulars at CBGBs to national prominence. The other three were Patti Smith, The Ramones, and Tom Verlaine & Television. For all you "punk" and "new wave" fans, I had experiences with all four of these groups. For now it was the Talking Heads.

Mixing monitors for me was always a bigger rush than mixing the mains. You got to really feel the energy on stage, see facial expressions and side-glances between band members that the audience couldn't catch with a pair of high-powered binoculars in the front row. This gig was even more participatory than normal. Why? Because I was clearly visible on stage (nothing to hide behind, the stacks were off to the side perched on some cafeteria tables). I'm sure to this day some of the audience remembers that the Talking Heads had a 5th member playing something that looked like a big keyboard stage right that night. With that perspective, I saw the uncontrollable energy of David Bryne up close and personal. He was unbelievable, the audience was frantic, and the band responded in kind following his lead and putting on an awesome show. I saw the infectious smile of Tina Weymouth when she turned and flashed it to her husband, the drummer Chris Frantz, an obvious silent communication of her approval of how the show was going and how the crowd was reacting to the show. I'm sure they probably played every song off their debut album "Talking Heads 77", which had only been released two months earlier. I do seem to remember them playing "Uh-Oh, Love Comes to Town" and "Don't worry about the Government". When they broke into "Psycho Killer", near the end of the night, the crowd went berserk. "Psycho Killer Qu'est Que C'est Fa fa fa fa fa fa fa fa fa far better. Run run run run run run run away". I thought at the time these guys deserve to make it big, but would the record companies and the album-buying public allow a "punk rock" band from New York City to become stars? They would.

By the way, I grabbed a poster off the wall in the cafeteria that night and threw it in my briefcase during load out. Luckily, I still have it (the ticket prices started at $3.50).

My experience at NYU was actually one of three I had there. Since you have the flavor of the place, I'll go ahead and cover the other two shows now.

The first show was with Loudon Wainwright III. You will probably know him from two events, the release of his novelty hit "Dead Skunk" (in the middle of the road) in 1972 (it was #1 in Little Rock, Arkansas for six weeks) and his three appearances on M*A*S*H (the TV show) in 1975 as Capt. Calvin Spaulding, the singing surgeon. Loudon hated any reference to "Dead Skunk", and he refused to play it at both the shows I did sound for. Aside from his aversion to his "claim to fame" song, in my opinion he is one of the most creative and humorous songwriters ever. He is by far the funniest man I have ever seen on stage, including the several famous comedians I have seen and/or worked with live {included later in the book}. Pretty bold statement? Yes, and I stand by it. To prove me wrong though you have to see Loudon live, or it doesn't count.

I actually sort of knew what to expect that Friday in April 1977, since I had done a show with Loudon (Tom Waits had opened that show) a few months earlier in Rochester. This, however, was completely different. The good news was there was plenty of room relative to the Talking Heads show later that same year. Mose Allison was the opening act on this night. After the changeover, it was just Loudon and I on that minis-cule stage, and just like at the Talking Heads gig, there was no speaker stack to hide behind while I mixed monitors. I became the straight man for his jokes. Loudon is the king of improv on stage. Several times he would have conversations directly with me using my name, like the audience wasn't even there. Then it got worse—I got the giggles. I could not stop laughing. Loudon is a tall man, but as he performs he kind of crouches over forward and utilizes body language to reinforce the humor. He squints his eyes and pokes his tongue out slightly; it just has to be seen. It didn't matter what he said or did that night, I would laugh hysterically. Tears ran down my face uncontrollably, and my face must have been bright red. This went on for the entire show, he was merciless, and I wasn't exactly playing by the roadie handbook. There is an unwritten rule that a roadie stays professional and stoic at all times. I was about as stoic as a drunken clown at a bachelor party. I just hope the students in the audience had as much fun as Loudon and I did that night.

A mere six days later I was back at New York University on that same stage again, but on this night I would share the stage with Peter Allen. Peter played grand piano and sang a variety of show tunes and Caribbean style Latin beat music. The main thing I remember about Peter was his energy standing up at that piano for the whole show, and his uncanny ability to work the crowd. His big song at the time was "I Go to Rio".

An interesting coincidence between these two performers was their mutual attraction to Liza Minelli. Loudon went to grade school with her, and had a huge crush on her in third grade (he even wrote a song about it in 1972 "Liza" on the "Attempted Mustache" album). Peter Allen met Liza through an introduction from Liza's mother Judy Garland. Peter and Liza were married in 1967, divorced in 1973. Peter succumbed to AIDS in 1992.

Hell must have stairs

◆

I forgot to mention that the Loeb Student Center was an elevator load in. Not very desirable as a roadie. Load out tends to bottleneck at the freight elevator delaying that long drive home. It however would be considered a cakewalk compared to the stairs at Ohio Wesleyan University. It was Feb 1977 and I was to do sound for Jonathan Edwards. I really enjoyed the gigs with Jonathan and his band. His upbeat songs made him a favorite on the college circuit. He had one big hit "Sunshine" {Remember? "Sunshine come back another day, I don't feel much like dancing"), but he actually had a whole show full of great songs, and was a real joy to work with. However this was the load in from hell. The entire PA, lights, boards, cables and road cases had to be carried up a significant flight of stairs (that curved if I remember correctly). To top it off there was only a stage crew of 3 or 4 student volunteers. They tried to be helpful but you try moving road cases designed to roll into a gig weighing hundreds of pounds, by lifting up stairs one at a time. Needless to say the sound check was late and very brief since we barely got the equipment up and running in time for the show. But the show did go on, like it always does (most of the time).

The show must go on?

$\blacklozenge$

One of the shows that almost didn't happen was in Binghamton, New York, just a short three hour drive from home base. The show was supposed to be Dr. Hook and the Medicine Show opening for Sly and the Family Stone. Now both of these bands had already "peaked" and were relying on their past reputations to draw a crowd. Sly had a different reputation among roadies. He was notorious for being very late or not showing up at all to a gig. Back at the shop when we were loading there were multiple bets being placed. Show or no show, how many hours late, and show canceled completely, all were wagered on. We got to the Binghamton War Memorial (which is an ice hockey arena most of the time) and set up for the show. I was on monitors that night, a job I had a love/hate relationship with. I loved the excitement of being that close to the action, as close to the performance as any human being not actually in the band. I hated the pressure when things went wrong, and they went wrong a lot on stage mix. Let me take a minute to explain the job of monitor mixer. As I briefly explained in the Blue Öyster Cult section, monitors are for the benefit of the band. The benefit is being able to hear the other musicians and themselves. Good loud clear monitors are critical to a reinforced sound performance of any magnitude. The reason is simple physics. Sound is created by vibrating and moving air. Your vocal cords vibrate and move air, a door vibrates and moves air when you slam it, and a sound reinforcement PA vibrates and moves a

LOT of air. That air moves out away from the stage blowing its way into your eardrums in the audience. This actually causes a vacuum of sorts on stage. You'd be shocked at how quiet it is on stage when the main PA is blasting and the monitors aren't on. It is very disquieting {pun intended}. Now the monitors solve the problem by blasting sound up or at the performers at a higher relative volume than the front PA (and you thought it was loud where you were sitting). Also monitors can be mixed just like the fronts. The difference is that instead of getting everything balanced and fine-tuned to sound great, the monitors are generally balanced and fine-tuned to get louder. Physics enters in again and creates a new problem, feedback. Remember I mentioned that to make sound it moves air and vibrates? Those vibrations don't like to be captured by a microphone, re-amplified again, captured by the microphone again, re-amplified again, captured by the microphone again; OK I think you get the picture. The result is a potentially dangerous (to the equipment and human ears) squeal that cannot be allowed to get out of control. Many tools are used to prevent the dreaded feedback, among them graphic and parametric equalizers. During sound check the roadie identifies the offending frequency that is causing the feedback, and attenuates (turns down) the specific frequency without affecting the surrounding frequencies as much. Several harmonic frequencies may need to be subdued during the course of a sound check depending on the venue acoustics, position of the mic, or phase the moon is in (it's only a semi-precise art form). The more time the monitor mixer has to adjust things the better (and louder) the monitors will sound that night. So here I am in an ice hockey arena (not exactly Carnegie Hall acoustically if you catch my drift) and we were to do a band that typically showed up late if at all. There would probably be no sound check that night. The load in went fine that day; load in was a stage level roll out (primo load in, you just drive the truck into the arena and back it up to the stage). We set up, Dr Hook set up, and you guessed it no Sly. We did a sound check in abstenia. The medicine show played around for over an hour and we all joked that if worse came to worse they could play "An evening with Dr Hook and the Medicine Show" show. Then we waited. We had supper and waited, we watched the cattle (fans) pour into the festival seating after being held outside for an hour past show time, and waited. The promoter was about to announce that due to circumstances beyond our control Sly and the Family Stone would not be appearing tonight when a stagehand yelled "They're Here!" The promoter, with a nervous grin on his face and sweat pouring down his face announced that Sly Stone would be starting soon, and there would be only a brief delay. The "Family's" bobtail was quickly unloaded and the show finally got started about the time it should have been over. The union crew could have stopped the show right there (there are union contractual provisions that forces the show to end by a certain time and that wasn't going to even be close tonight) but they either had an overtime deal with the promoter or feared the crowd that had been waiting so long (probably both) so they said nothing.

The Dr. Hook show was outstanding. They played all their predictable hits including "Cover of the Rolling Stone" "Sylvia's Mother", and "I Got Stoned and I Missed It" with precision and enthusiasm. They never once complained to me about what I considered a sub-standard monitor performance. I don't know how the mains sounded but I was having fits with the stage. The acoustics of the hall had changed dramatically when the several thousand human bodies had padded the floor of the ice arena. Usually this dampening helped prevent feedback; tonight it deadened everything including the stage monitors. Dr. Hook finished their encore and yielded the stage to the headliner. It seemed to take forever to set up Sly (remember the gear is usually assembled in the afternoon, with the lights on, and no audience). The show finally started, and like Dr. Hook they played all the favorites. Sly was one of my personal favorites in JR High School, especially the song "Dance to the Music". I loved the part where as they were adding each musical instrument one by one and as he gets to the trumpet player he says, "Cynthia and Jerry got a message that says"…{Cynthia's voice} "All the squares, blow it out!" I was really looking forward to actually working with Cynthia. Unfortunately, Cynthia wasn't too thrilled with working with me that night. She was yelling at me most of the time she wasn't blowing on her trumpet, letting me know that she couldn't hear her monitor, and that I better fix it. Now I'm not making excuses but a 15-minute sound check would have been nice prior to the show. Since that wasn't possible I did the next best thing, I "tweaked". That's technical lingo for fiddling with the controls trying to coax a decibel or two out of the black boxes at her feet. Either the tweaking worked or she got tired of complaining, but eventually she ignored me and just played. Sly and his entourage (there must've been about 20 musicians on stage) played all their classic favorites and the audience ate it up. All in all the show was considered a success, but we sure did take the long way around to get there.

By the way, I never saw the Dr Hook boys again, but I heard a news story sometime in the early 80's that a few of the band members had been charged with allegedly having illegal relations with some underage girls in an Australian Hotel room (I seem to also remember something about some German Shepherds). I never did hear the outcome of those charges, but I did find it an interesting coincidence that one of Dr. Hook's big hits in the 70's was the song "Only Sixteen".

False Arrest

◆

Then there was "that night" on the New York Thruway. I don't remember what group we did that night. I don't remember which city it was, or even whether we did sound or lights. It was the trip home I'll always remember. It may have been a show with England Dan & John Ford Coley, or Aztec Two Step, maybe The Pousette-Dart Band, Duke Jupiter, or maybe Orleans. I only remember that it was a college gig, it was summertime, and that my partner for the night was an accomplished "Techie" but a novice "Roadie". Al was a reluctant participant that day, but since everyone else was out on this tour, or that tour, we had a show to do. I talked Al into going by telling him, "we'll be back by dawn, and I'll drive". We left the show that I can't remember, from the city that I can't remember, and headed up I-90. Al slept, and I drove, after all, a deal's a deal. Then somewhere that night on the New York Thruway the six wheeler I was driving ("Little Red") sputtered and spit eventually came to a complete stop. Luckily I had sensed something was wrong as I neared a rest stop and I coasted in. It was about 3 in the morning and we were still over 150 miles from home. Nobody to call that late at night, the only logical choice was to try to sleep there in the rest area, and wait for daylight. Why not sleep in the truck? It was too hot. When the truck was moving it wasn't bad, but in its immobile state it was a sauna. The rest area wasn't much better; I spent the hot sleepless night sitting up, leaned against a vending machine wishing the building had

A/C. Nobody bothered us that night which was fortunate since I was carrying about $2,500 cash in my roadie billfold (the payment for the gig the night before). Daylight finally came so I manned the payphone. After several calls, I finally found a tow truck big enough to pull our truck, and willing to do it on a Sunday morning at 7 AM. Money wasn't the problem; it was convincing him that I had money, and that it was worth his while to miss church to come get us. Things began to look up when he finally arrived and hooked up. I have no idea where he took us, but we ended up in a large barn-like structure that was a truck repair facility. A mechanic looked at our truck and announced that we needed a head gasket, or a valve job or something engine related (guess what? I don't exactly remember what), anyway it was going to take about 5 hours to fix it. Al fell asleep in the man's office (air-conditioned!) but I was hungry. I asked the man if there was somewhere I could get breakfast and he laughed. Well you could go to town (sorry I forget the town's name, I think I blocked it out over the years) but that's about 4 miles up the road. I asked him if he could give me a ride or loan me a vehicle. (Like that was going to happen.) He had even made me show him the cash in my wallet before he would start work on the truck. He mumbled something about insurance rules, so I started walking…I was famished. Upstate New York off the beaten path is breathtaking. The endless miles of green trees, rolling hills, and the blessed quiet. I finally made it to the edge of town. It was the kind of quiet small town that has more churches than restaurants, and not a single fast food joint. I walked past a church as it was letting out. I must've looked a sight. I had slept in my clothes, my long hair hadn't been washed or even brushed in more than a day, and I must have smelled not too good. I watched the people stare at me, then change directions to avoid me while herding their children to safety. I saw a small restaurant ahead. It was named "Nell's" or "Betty's" or something quaint like that, and it was filled with church going people eating their late breakfasts. The wonderful aroma of warm bacon and pancakes greeted me as I opened the door. I went in and sat down somewhere in the back ignoring the icy stares of the locals. All I really wanted was a meal. Eventually they waited on me, and I ate the best stack of pancakes I think I've ever had in my life. The waitress looked surprised when I offered a twenty-dollar bill to pay for the meal, she almost acted disappointed. It was like she really wanted to force me to wash dishes or something. I remember thanking her for the meal, and leaving her a generous tip. Although it would be another 15 minutes before I found out, she paid me back by calling the local police. I was making the long walk back to my truck and was well outside town when a siren whelped behind me. With his row of flashing lights blazing, he got out of his cruiser (staying a safe distance from me) and announced that I should stay where I was, and keep my hands where he could see them. He never did draw his weapon, but his hand was conspicuously perched on the grip. "What's the problem officer? I asked, already knowing the answer. "Boy", (yes, he really did call me "Boy") "Boy, you are in a lot of trouble". "Oh" I said, playing along. He continued, "I don't know where you come from but around here we got a vagrancy law that says you better have at least $15 cash money on you, or you're going spend a couple of days in jail". My guess is that the waitress thought the twenty I had given her was every penny I had, and now because of the generous tip, I should have fewer than twelve bucks. "Officer, I am not a vagrant", I calmly professed. "That so?" "Yes I did a show last night in <fill in name of missing city here> and on my way home my truck broke down. It's at a shop just up the road and as soon as it's fixed, I'll be on my way". "What kind of show?" he asked not convinced. "Rock and Roll" I proudly replied. (Oops, that just made it worse, not a big rock fan based on the body language) "Well, he said I'm still waiting to see that $15". "Sir, as I stated I am a technician, I worked a show last night, and we were paid in cash. I would appreciate that you not make me flash this much cash in broad daylight out here in the open. I'd be happy to show you the money in the front seat of your car. May I please do that?" "No, show me here and show me now or go to jail, your choice". I slowly and deliberately pulled out my wallet (I didn't want to be gunned down on the side of the road while going for my weapon that I didn't have) and opened the bulging wad of hundreds, fifties and twenties. "Where did you get that much money, you steal it?" I handed him my card (can you believe that roadies actually have business cards?) and gave him my final offer. "If you give me a ride up to the truck shop, you can verify my story, and if I'm lying, you can lock me up". He said nothing, but he took my driver's license, and left me in the heat while he sat in his car and called in on the radio to make sure I hadn't robbed a bank or something. Boy was he disappointed, I could see the pain in his face as he came back, handed me my license, and said, "you can go". In an attempt to make lemonade out of lemons I said, "Hey, no hard feelings, can you give me a lift to the truck shop? It looks like you are headed that way anyway." "Nope, out of my jurisdiction", and he sped off, his tires throwing gravel at me, as he made no attempt to turn around. I'm pretty sure he then drove right past that shop where my wounded truck was being repaired. Soon after, I settled up with the mechanic, woke up Al, and we got the hell out of Dodge (driving the speed limit all the way home). It was a few years later that Sylvester Stallone would star in the movie "First Blood" which starts the same way my adventure did. The movie does have a happier ending though; Rambo gets to kick everyone's ass in the town. By the way Al never left the Rochester city limits to do a show ever again.

Harry

◆

A bittersweet memory for me was the night I met Harry Chapin. I had worked with Harry's brother Tom on several occasions since he showed up a lot at the university shows. As much as I liked listening to and working with Tom, I was thrilled to work that one time with Harry. It was at R.I.T. in the ice arena while I was still a student there. The venue was way too big for Harry, although it was set up as a half hall and it was pretty full. Once again I was on monitors, and once again it was just the performer and me. You see Harry didn't have his band that night; it was "An evening with Harry Chapin" event. I don't recall if this show was before or after the Loudon Wainwright show but a very similar thing happened, Harry spoke to me several times during the show. I think he was a little uncomfortable with the huge stage, huge stack of speakers, huge hall, and just him, his acoustic guitar two stage monitors and two microphones. My guess is that since I was the only face he could see (due to the lights) he relieved the tension by conversing with me. My expectations of Harry were high dating back to my High School days, and he didn't let me down. His renderings of "Cat's Cradle", "W.O.L.D." and "Taxi" were flawless. He was very loose that night and fooled around on some of the songs by pretending to be the absent orchestra, mimicking them with his voice at the appropriate breaks between the lyrics. The song I heard for the first time that night was "30,000 pounds of bananas." I haven't heard it since, and after 20 years I can still replay it in my head on demand. The song is a humorous rendition of a truck driver with a load of bananas, in a hurry to get back to his sweetheart, driving down a steep hill near Scranton, Pennsylvania. He loses control of the truck crashing it at the bottom. It sounds morbid, but the way it builds and builds as he picks up speed, and the way Harry's words make light of the situation make you actually laugh as this poor slob is on his way to his fate, and Harry is on his way to a crescendo. Harry died in 1981 in a traffic accident on his way to perform in a benefit; no bananas were involved to my knowledge. Harry raised millions of dollars for world hunger before he died, and his work continues through the Harry Chapin Foundation.

Rest in Peace Harry

The Hurricane

◆

Speaking of famous siblings I had the good fortune to work (separately) with both Kate Taylor and Livingston Taylor (the sister and brother of James Taylor). The story I'd like to tell is about one of the shows I did with Liv.

Sometimes I would do shows with affiliated sound companies. What that means is that we had arrangements with several "sister" companies and would frequently work each other's overflow shows. One of these companies was a two man operation in the boonies. Shelton and Richard had a farm and a small but adequate PA and on this occasion for some reason Shelton was not able to do this college gig on Long Island, but Richard could. I was sent from Rochester to "the farm" somewhere in eastern New York, were I parked my car and helped Richard load the trailer. Now this wasn't a tractor-trailer "good buddy", it was a horse trailer. That's right I guess I forgot to tell you that they hauled their gear around the state in a semi open horse rig. We hosed out the trailer (hold your nose) and loaded everything they had (about half of what I normally carried). The gig was all the way out on Long Island at Long Island University at South Hampton. I asked Richard what would happen if it rained (open trailer remember?) and he said not to worry, the tarps would protect the equipment. So we headed down the Long Island Expressway as the weather got worse. First a mist, then a drizzle, finally a downpour. We had run into the front edge of a level 3 hurricane named Belle. Even though it was getting worse by the minute we forged ahead, and made the gig only an hour or two late. If memory serves Liv got there even later (we were all amazed that he made it at all, because by now the weather was bad enough the L.I.E. was closed. I remember there was a debate as to "weather" to cancel the show or not {pun intended}, but we were in a sturdy building, the students had nowhere else to go, and we had everything set up so what the heck. Liv put on an extra long show, and nobody wanted it to end, after all where would any of us go? I slept that night in a vacant dorm room that the school graciously offered. By sometime the next day the worst of the storm had blown over, and we headed home. I picked up my car at the farm and drove home to Rochester. That one gig took me over three days of my life. By the way, in case you are wondering, the sound equipment stayed dry the whole weekend despite the open horse trailer and the rain. Richard was right, the tarps had worked.

Low Bridge

◆

I'd like to change the subject for a moment, and talk for a minute about sleep depravation. It's one of the aspects of the road that I really disliked, and frankly it scared me. An example of this was one night when my partner and I were driving back from a gig in "Little Red". Neither of us should have been driving, we were both way too tired. I was driving along the New York Thruway, the moon was full and provided the only light save the two round pools thrown forward by the headlights. The stars were out and I was fighting to stay alert. I had the window open blowing cold air on my face, while running the heater on full to keep my legs from going numb. I had downed 3 Dr. Peppers (my drink of choice to this day) not because I was thirsty but I thought the caffeine would help. I had also taken two Vivarins (caffeine pills), which had caused a slight nosebleed. I finally resorted to slapping myself (no really, I'm not kidding I was slapping myself) to cause an artificial rush of adrenaline in a vain attempt at consciousness. Kids, like many things in this book, don't try this at home. If you ever have to inflict pain on yourself to stay awake, it's time to pull over and sleep regardless of whether you'll be late to where you're going. Well, that night I didn't take my own advice. My partner was snoring next to me contorted semi-sideways in the available space on the couch like front seat of the truck. The cab was permeated with a smell that was a combination of spilled coffee and high school gym class. We were the only vehicle on the road, cruising along at about 62 MPH (Red's top speed), and then it happened.

You see one of the fears of anyone driving a truck, even a small one like Red, were low bridges. We all had heard stories of the tops of trucks being sheered off by carelessly driving under a bridge 4 inches too short. The drivers in these stories typically were killed after being thrown through the windshield. Now the New York Thruway has bridges that are tall enough for the tallest 18-wheeler. "Red" however, was short enough that an NBA Center could stand on top of her box and we'd never even muss his hair driving under them.

With that said, I was driving along, my eyelids heavy, and all of a sudden I snapped to attention. Danger ahead!! A low overpass, the lowest I'd ever seen. My god, it had to be only about 12 feet, we were sure to hit. I slammed on the brakes and braced for the worse. It was getting closer; I didn't see how I could avoid it. I thought about turning the wheel sideways but I'd probably just lay the truck over on its side and make things worse. No, better to stay straight, and slow as much as possible. OK, ready here it comes, got to stand on the brake, here it comes, here it comes, here it comes, we're gonna hit........

Gone.

Gone? Where is it? There was no low overpass; there wasn't even a normal overpass. I had hallucinated the whole thing and now we are parked in the middle of I-90. My partner woke and said, "What's up?" Not him, as he was mostly on the floorboard at this point. "Low Bridge" I mumbled, as I shifted into first and let out the clutch. "Oh" he replied and returned to his slumber. I was still shaking with the adrenaline rush when we pulled into our destination.

Human Target

◆

I mentioned earlier that I did a show with Tom Waits in Rochester, opening for Loudon Wainwright III. A few months later in April of 1977, I found myself doing an "O.N.S." with Tom and his band again, this time at Kent State University. This story is going to be more about Kent State than Tom Waits (sorry Tom). Tom is a great performer; his raspy voice and satirical lyrics always make him an enjoyable show. For all you Waits fans the set was heavily based on the "Nighthawks at the Diner" album. He played "Emotional Weather Report", Warm Beer and Cold Women", and my favorite song of Tom's "Better Off Without a Wife" (although I personally don't subscribe to that view). My favorite Tom Waits lyric is "Ain't got no spare, ain't got no jack…. I don't give a sh*t…I ain't ever coming back." Great line.

When I got to the campus of Kent State University I couldn't help but re-live history. As you all know in May of 1970, Ohio National Guardsmen killed four students while protesting the Vietnam War. I was 13 when that happened. During the summer before I left for my freshman year in college, I read a book about the incident, and I was deeply moved. Now I found myself at the sight where everything had happened. We must have arrived ahead of schedule because I walked around the campus and recognized some of the landmarks from the photographs I had seen that were taken less than 7 years prior. I wanted to find something to remind me of the day, perhaps a souvenir. After looking in vain for a spent rifle cartridge, or a used tear gas canister, I finally gave up and returned to the student center ballroom. When I got there I saw something so outrageous; I had to have it. A member of the student stage crew was wearing a T-shirt. On the front of the standard pocket "T" was "Kent State University" printed above the pocket. When he turned around there was a large bull's eye that had "student" written near the center. It turns out that he had silk-screened these shirts himself, and he sold me a brown one that afternoon (I think it was $5 which was a bit high for a T-shirt in 1977) He told me the school had recently warned him to stop making or distributing the shirts or he would be expelled. They told me it was in bad taste. I never did find out if he ever got thrown out of school, but at least they didn't shoot him.

A really hot show

◆

One of the great all time southern rock bands is "The Outlaws". I did about ten gigs with them during my roadie years. I worked lights on some shows, and mixed monitors on others. Their biggest hit was "There goes another love song", but that song only accounted for 1/100th of their powerful stage show. Some of shows are vivid in my memory like St John's University and Cape Cod Coliseum; most of them were so equally and consistently powerful that they all blur together. One show that was unique, and is "burned" into my grey matter (literally) was the "Summer Jam" at the University of Louisville. The day started out great, a little bit overcast, a little on the warm side. The show was to be outdoors in the huge Cardinal football stadium. A stage was assembled and we unloaded the PA and lights and watched the sky. One fear of all roadies doing an outdoor job was the weather. Rain could damage the equipment and lightning (if it hit) could be deadly. We were ahead of schedule and had everything ready for the sound check. The Outlaws and the opening act had not arrived yet, and the sky grew blacker. By the time the road manager got there it had become a serious discussion about whether to postpone, cancel or move the show. The weather was degrading, so a command decision was made jointly by the road manager, the student activities manager and several roadies (myself included) to move the show. So the PA came down, the lights came down, and everything got reloaded in the trucks. The stage had to be struck and a large contingent of student helpers started to move it the short distance to Freedom Hall U of L basketball arena. Then we waited until the stage was re-assembled. The wait was made easier when the sky opened up and rain came down in a solid sheet. The correct decision had been made, and now we were fighting two forces that were completely out of our control, "time" and "heat". You probably guessed the "time" part but what you have to understand is that for some reason the air conditioning wasn't working. By the time the show was set up it was approaching 90 degrees. The school was trying in vain to use large fans to cool off the impromptu greenhouse. We were already over an hour late for showtime when we did a token sound check. The opening acts ("Molly Hatchet" and "The Winter Brothers Band" if I remember correctly) got no sound check at all. They opened the house and the wet fans poured in. For those of you with a background in science can you tell everyone what happens when a hot arena has about 10,000 human bodies hovering around 98.6 degrees added? That's right, it gets even hotter. By showtime it was reported (although I never personally saw a thermometer) that the hall had soared to around 105 degrees. There was actually talk again about canceling the show, but this time everyone agreed to "Go". When the Outlaws hit the stage after the break, fans were actually passing out from heat exhaustion, but only a few. The "Florida Guitar Army" started with "Stick around for rock and roll", and went through all their favorites including "Lover Boy", and Breaker Breaker". They had recently released "Hurry Sundown" and played most of the songs off that new album. To the best of my recollection, this was the first show I worked with the band that Harvey Dalton Arnold had replaced Frank O'Keefe on bass. The Outlaws put on the best show I'd ever seen them do (and I had seen them seven or eight times at that point), the heat gave the entire show an urgency and raw edge that I can't attempt to describe. Nobody wanted the show to end, not the heat soaked students, not Jim, George or the rest of the "Cow Chips" (the nickname for the band's roadies), not myself or the other sound and light guys, and definitely not the band. They played and played and played under those lights and kept playing until they ran out of songs to play. Remember that as hot as the audience was the band was even hotter. They had thousands of watts of stage lamps aimed at them. Think of it this way, you're laying in a lounge chair out by the pool on a hot summer day and someone has come along and turned on a large sunlamp just above your body. When they came back for the encore they played their flagship song off the first album "Green Grass and High Tides Forever." For those of you that are Outlaws fans, and especially those of you that were fortunate enough to see them "live" you'll know what I mean when I say that you have to remind yourself to breathe as Hughie starts the song…

> *In a place you only dream of, where your soul is always free.*
> *Silver stages, golden curtains, filled my head plain as could be.*
> *As a rainbow grew around the sun, all the stars I've loved, who died.*
> *Came from somewhere beyond the scene you see.*
> *These lovely people played just for me…*
> <chorus>
> *Green grass and high tides forever*
> *Castles of stone souls and glory*
> *Lost faces say we adore you*
> *As kings and queens bow and play for you*

What is lost on the attempts to capture this song in the studio is the improvisation that took place during the instrumental break between lyrics in the live stage version. The blazing guitars of Hughie, Billy and Henry would add new riffs and wander off into uncharted land. Monte's drum solos always seemed to occupy just a little more time each time I did a show, and the audience would always go insane. Not just a little insane, stark raving nuts! Twenty years later, it's ironic that one of those lines in Green Grass states…

"All the stars I've loved, who died…played just for me."

In 1995 Billy Jones took his own life. A few weeks later Frank O'Keefe died of an accidental overdose. There will never be a true "Outlaws" reunion (at least not in this space-time continuum). The good news is that, as of this writing, the remaining band members are all still playing music. Henry Paul has a successful country band named "The Blackhawks"; Monte Yoho is playing drums in Branson Missouri on the "Branson Belle" riverboat with "The Nelson Family". And Hughie Thomasson, the singer of the haunting lyrics above, has joined "Lynyrd Skynyrd." (More on Skynyrd later in the book).

To Frank and Billy I hope you both have found peace, the rest of you guys, STAY LOUD!

Very funny

———————— ◆ ————————

Not everything on the road was musical; I mixed sound for several non-musical artists. The first one was George Carlin. He was doing his stand up routine for two shows and had no opening act. Pretty easy gig, not much of a sound check. George was doing his now classic "stuff". "Flammable, inflammable, non-inflammable, you'd think two would handle it. Either it flams or it doesn't." "Why do we have to de-plane, we don't de-bus." And of course the 7 dirty words you can't say on radio. He did two shows that night and both were well received (each one was almost an exact mirror image of the other). Before the show in the dressing room he asked me if I could do him a favor, "Could you record the shows for me?" "I like to listen to them later to critique myself". He even gave me a blank cassette tape to use (a good thing since I didn't have any with me); at the conclusion of the show I gave him the tape and he inexplicably reached in his pocket and gave me $15. A tip, I'd never gotten a tip before. "How'd I do?" he asked. "You were great," I said without needing to lie.

In over five years on the road that was the only tip I ever received

Another time I found myself at Saratoga Springs Race Track providing sound for Bill Cosby. It was harness racing season, and Bill was to be the entertainment between the afternoon and evening races. Sorry to keep reminding you of the time, but Bill wasn't America's dad yet. The Cosby show hadn't aired yet. If anything, most people knew him from "I

Spy" where he starred with Robert Culp. Bill was probably as sick as I think I've ever seen a performer that didn't cancel the show that afternoon. He was deep into the worst phase of the flu, but he was determined to do the show. Like George there was no opening act; just a comic, a microphone, and his material. The only difference was Bill sat on a stool and didn't move for the whole show. To this day I think that Bill's performance was one of bravest things I witnessed on the road from any artist. Not to diminish Bill's courage, bravery was almost an everyday thing for roadies.

Bad vibes

———————————◆———————————

Some gigs are just plain strange. The shows with Gordon Lightfoot are a perfect example of that. This was to be a lighting job (I did a lot of lights during the first two years). The first show was at a SUNY college (State University of New York), probably either SUNY Oneonta or SUNY Oswego. It was a medium size hall, pretty basic set-up. We had four genie towers with 16 par cans per (64 total) a couple of floor pars and two "Trouper" spots. The stage was narrow enough and the PA (different company, Gordon was carrying his own sound company) was big enough that we either had to go just in front of the PA or behind it. If we went behind it would be hard to light Gordon down stage, so we set up as far out on the apron as we dared. The sound guys weren't thrilled but they set up just behind the towers. Sound check was a nightmare. The hall had a lot of wood and no drapes, so all the sound kind of bounced around and caused some feedback from time to time. Gordon was distressed. He called the sound guys over and asked them what the problem was. Instead of blaming the room, or their ability to use tools like equalizers to correct the problem they blamed us! My partner Dick and I were speechless. We calmly asked, what specifically is the lighting system doing to screw up the sound? Their theory was that since the stack was 3 feet back from the edge of the stage it was causing feedback on Gordon's mic, our fault. Dick and I tried in vain to convince Gordon that any competent sound company should be able to overcome the placement of the PA. We concluded sound check without a resolution, and awaited the show. Everyone rationalized that when the crowd was let in; there would be enough dampening to buffer the sound. The show seemed to go fine as far as I was concerned; I ran a spot since the college didn't have any qualified operators. I wasn't real good on spot, but I'd been a spot operator since early high school and could hold my own. Gordon was a high school favorite of mine and I really enjoyed the show. It seemed to go flawlessly for everyone involved. Apparently Gordon didn't share my enthusiasm. After the show Gordon summoned Dick and myself to his dressing room. This just didn't happen unless there was a problem, since we rarely received post show accolades personally from the stars. "No offense but I have to make a change for tomorrow night", said Gordon. "Oh?" asked Dick. Gordon continued, "The show just didn't feel right tonight, too many bad vibes." I'm afraid we won't be able to use your lights tomorrow night." "But Gordon, Dick protested, there isn't a house system at Jones Beach, are you going to play in the dark?" "If I have to, but now you guys just figure it out, use those spot lights or something, I can't have bad vibes ruining another show." So the next night we found ourselves at Jones Beach Theatre and all we unloaded were the two trouper spot lights. As it turns out this was probably for the best. Jones Beach is an amphitheater set up with a stage that literally is a barge on the water, tethered to the front of the audience. The problem for us would have been the small size of the stage. Anyway, I think Dick and I had the record that day for quickest and easiest load-in. And to this day I don't think anyone got as much money for two four-hour spot rentals (they paid us the full contracted amount as if we had done the entire Light show). We lit the stage with the two spots that night, one of the worst examples of modern lighting design I've ever seen. One spot would stay on wide angle flooding the entire stage in an attempt to illuminate the band. The other spot was trained on Gordon or the occasional soloist. We tried to be a little creative changing complimentary gel colors in sync with each other but it was still very boring. Gordon made a point of coming up to us during the load out, and thanked us for our flexibility, and basically to say "no hard feelings". Hard feelings? We got paid for doing one quarter of the work, and eliminated the show's "bad vibes" to boot. Hell, that's a good day on the road.

Elvis has left the building

◆

While we are discussing SUNY gigs, there was a one nighter (I think it was at SUNY Albany) with Elvis Costello that also had bad vibes. Some performers are difficult, but this job was out of control from the beginning. The crew for Elvis was very demanding, which is not unusual for Brits, but it meant we were all in for a long night. If we thought the crew was tense, you should have seen the band. The sound check was a rude fest. The sound system was crap; the monitors were crap, why didn't we have better microphones, etc, etc. Needless to say the monitors weren't loud enough for Elvis (they rarely are for some artists). The final blow happened just prior to supper to the student activities director. This is a student volunteer, and is the person who without any pay, had set this whole show up and had even hired the band. I don't remember what the issue was, but he was trying to appease the road manager, maybe the dressing room was too small or the M&Ms were the wrong color or something, when with no warning, no provocation BAM! (Just like in a Batman movie) I saw the Road Manger cold cock the student. WHAP! He crumpled to the ground bleeding badly from the mouth. All the brits circled their manager as he stormed off (no chance for any of us colonists to retaliate). As we picked the AD up off the stained wooden floor he said, "No problem, I asked for it." "The hell you did!" I countered, but he was just fulfilling the oldest rule in our business, that the show must go on. If he pressed charges, or even reported it to school officials the show would likely be canceled and he'd be to blame. So we all pretended it didn't happen and we bit our lips and did the show. The show may have been good; it may even have been great, I didn't notice. I just wanted the show to be over.

Rock Candy

◆

A short series of shows that I didn't want to end happened in 1976. We were to do sound and lights for a short leg (3 shows) with a tour headlined by Montrose, with Ambrosia and Sparks. Sammy Hagar had recently left Ronnie Montrose's band to pursue a solo career. Bob James had replaced him on vocals and they had just released "Warner's Brothers Presents Montrose". The gigs were close to home starting in Buffalo at an old theatre built in 1926 named "Shea's". I was a huge Montrose fan so this one job I really wanted to do. I was on lights for this show. The guys doing sound knew going in that this band was going to need special attention due to their reputation to need maximum dB. I had been playing around with using two SM-57 mics taped together (side by side) and reversing the leads to one throwing it out of phase with the other. The singer would then sing into the top mic and theoretically only his voice would make it to the board. All extraneous noise (the drums, the guitars, and the reflected sounds of his voice) would be canceled. We had no way to field test it but I took the parts I needed to fabricate it just in case. My first impression of Ronnie Montrose was that he was a very quiet, yet generally friendly man. The new lead singer was short, I don't know how else to say it. I guess I was used to seeing Sammy on "Midnight Special" or "In Concert", when I was in High School. I can't help but say I was visually disappointed. The sound check didn't go that well. As anticipated these guys were LOUD. Even though I was on lights I offered them the experimental mics, and they agreed. I spent the rest of sound check soldering adapters to reverse the leads. Try soldering little tiny wires in an XLR connection with "Space Station #5" knocking you over. Finally it was ready. We deployed the new double mics and tried the check again. It worked (partially). The monitor guy was able to get a lot more stage volume, so the band was happy. Unfortunately, their soundman didn't like the way it sounded out front. The out of phase mics were changing the audio characteristics of the signal and (according to him) diminished the "fullness" of the vocal's sound. We scrapped the experiment and went back to normal vocal mics.

The show opened with "Sparks". They were a very strange band. Two brothers Ron and Russell Mael played keyboards and vocals respectively. Russell looked like the all American rock star while Ron looked like a cross between Adolph Hitler and Charlie Chaplin. He scowled the whole show, which was part of the act. The other thing that was different was the bit he did with the piano stool. Now I knew something was up before the show when the band roadie asked if I had any black gaffer's tape he could borrow. Well of course I did, we used it for just about everything, and the black color made it disappear on stage. He took the roll and started to rebuild a piano stool that was in five or six pieces. I remember asking him, "why not just buy a new one, or borrow one from the stage crew?" He laughed and said Ron is a little hard on stools, this one will do fine. During the show Ron would fuss and fidget with the stool from time to time (no wonder I thought it's only taped together with gaffer's tape). Near the end of their final song, he stood up and smashed the stool on the stage for effect. The tape let loose and the stool separated into its five or six component pieces on cue. To this day it was the most cost efficient special effect I had witnessed. If there are any Sparks fans reading this they played songs off of their most recent album at the time "Indiscreet". My favorite song of theirs is "Tits". It's about a man with a new child lamenting the change of status of his wife's breasts from play toys to food source. A lot of the other Sparks tunes revolved around sex, two examples are "Under the Table With Her", and "Without Using Hands".

Ambrosia was, like Montrose, a big favorite of mine. They had recently released the album "Somewhere I've Never Traveled" which included "Dance with me George", and "Can't let a Woman". They were a "keyboard oriented" quartet that had a harmonic sound similar to "Yes" or "Emerson Lake and Palmer". An earlier hit of theirs was "Nice Nice Very Nice", which has lyrics based on Kurt Vonnegut Jr.'s "Cat's Cradle" novel. They were very easy to work with and the show (although somewhat over produced) came off well. The feeling I got that night talking to the promoter and the record guys were that they were the ones to watch. They could be the next super band of the 70's while Montrose had already peaked and was on their way down. (See Karl's Roadie Rule #5 "All headliners started out as opening acts, in most cases, they will be opening acts again someday" That was to be the case for Ronnie)

On their way down or not, Montrose, with the new short lead singer rocked. They did all of the Montrose classics, including "Rock Candy", "Space station #5" and "Good rockin' tonight" and the crowd was not disappointed (I think they had an unwritten agreement with Sammy that they wouldn't do "Bad Motor Scooter"). He cleverly mixed the new material in with the old so there was never more than a song or two before you heard a familiar favorite. It was LOUD that night at Shea's, and I vaguely remember the Buffalo fire Marshall snooping around in the audience during the show with a dB meter. Only once or twice in my career did someone in authority order us to turn it down, tonight wasn't one of those nights. The other event I remember about that mini-tour was that we were experimenting with a white backdrop (called a scrim) lit from behind with different color gels. It gave the stage a surreal cartoon look. It was extremely effective, and we used a version of it on one of the J.L.P. tours coming up later in the book.

As far as Ambrosia being the next big super group, that didn't happen, but we were right that Montrose was in for some re-tooling. Ronnie Montrose started over as a solo jazz-rock band with no vocals. He released one of the best jazz-rock albums ever recorded in my opinion "Open Fire" and toured as an opening act for Journey in 1978 (Rule #5). My path was to cross both Ambrosia's and Ronnie Montrose's again later during my roadie years {stay tuned}.

As of this writing, I understand that both the bands, Sparks and Ambrosia, are still working together in some form or another, while Ronnie Montrose continues to be one of the premier jazz-rock guitarists in the world today.

Be Prepared

$\blacklozenge$

When a roadie is not on the road he has to stay busy or starve. Band roadies find temporary gigs, or work on studio gigs if the band is recording, and even do personal stuff for the band if they are on retainer (e.g. wash their cars, baby-sit their kids, etc.). If you're a not so lucky Band Roadie you get laid off and hopefully collect unemployment. This is why Karl's Roadie Rule #2 states, "Never work directly for a band". Sound and Light roadies do maintenance on the equipment at the shop, preparing it for the next trip. There are also in town jobs like small PA gigs at schools or public events like ribbon cutting ceremonies, installing small sound systems at clubs, or even servicing bar band equipment and PAs. During one of these down times I was in the shop trying to justify the minimum wage I was earning when a regular came in for some parts. It was Lou, the short stature, and blue eyed lead singer of the local Rochester band "Black Sheep". He was excited because he had just been offered a chance to join an English band that had the backing of a major record label, and was going to hit "big". "What's the name of this new super group someone asked?" "Foreigner", he proudly replied. I remember mumbling under my breath, "They'll never make it, Lou Graham will be back with Black Sheep by spring". Karl's Roadie Rule number 13, "Never try to predict which artists will be stars, you will be wrong well over half the time". As you all know by now, I had that one very wrong.

The one good thing that happened in the shop was "tour prep". It meant you (or some other crew) were about to hit the road for anywhere from one day to six months. It was an exciting time, anticipating what would be needed, coming up with new ideas for staging or lighting design. The amps had to be checked; a process where the Crown amplifiers were taken apart one by one and every screw and bolt had to be tightened by hand due to the constant rattling it had been subjected to in the air ride trailer on the previous tour. It didn't matter what we tried (even gluing the nuts in place after tightening them), they would always come loose. If this was not attended to, the circuit boards, and heat sinks would eventually come completely loose and fail. The lights had to be replaced, gels were cut and carefully stored. Speakers were tested and re-coned if blown (many usually were). Speaker cabinets had to be sanded and repainted flat black. The wear and tear of nightly loading and unloading would cause huge splinters that could rip up your hand if allowed to go unchecked. In most cases you wore work gloves anyway to try to minimize soft tissue damage to your hand when the splinters got you. Road cases had to be loaded after being checked for completeness. Where possible, duplicates of critical items were packed. We couldn't take a spare mixing board but we took extra mics, EQs, and crossovers. In the event of, say, a mixing board going down (That didn't happen to me even once), the contingency plan was to use the monitor board in the house, and mix the monitors off the same board from there. Being on the road was kind of like a NASA launch (only working out of a truck).

The final event before you left was "the load". Loading a sound and light truck (or trailer) is an art form. Road cases range in size from briefcase size to the size of a large refrigerator. Most of the big cases and the big speaker cabinets had wheels. That still didn't help if once in the nose of the trailer it had to be hoisted to the top level or up-ended. The key to not getting hurt was trust in your partner. He knew how to lift, when to lift, and when to let go. Failure to do it right could end up in hernias, broken toes, or worse. Most roadies have had at least one road case dropped on their foot, so many of us wore steel-toed boots. Even with that protection I had to have foot surgery in 1993 to correct problems caused long ago by a road case landing on my foot while loading a truck.

Then the roadie packs his personal things. Most of us had an Anvil briefcase to carry the essentials like an extra T-shirt, an electric razor, a toothbrush, toothpaste, a bar of soap (more on showers later), microphone diagrams, drugs (carefully hidden), a VOM, a couple of screwdrivers (the tool kind, not the drink), a good pair of dykes (diagonal wire cutters, you all have such dirty minds), letters from home, etc. Actually, most of us carried an Anvil briefcase because it just looked cool (I know that's why I did). The typical Anvil briefcase (made by a company in California named Anvil Cases) was made the same way as all the Anvil road cases. It is typically made of plywood covered in a skin of colored plastic called Kydex. It has metal corners and edges for protection. It was usually emblazoned with back stage passes to show everyone who you have worked with, and hence how experienced you are. Road Managers however rarely had Anvil cases; they liked the metal Halliburton briefcases, usually silver. A good roadie would also need several other items to complete his "gear". A good knife, either a "Buck" or a "Case" with a leather belt case to hold it at the ready. I know what you are thinking, but this knife was rarely a weapon, mostly a tool for stripping wires or cutting through old gaffer's tape. Then you needed a roadie wallet, which was really just a biker or trucker wallet with a chain attaching it to your belt. The theory here was pickpocket protection. (Really, just like the Anvil case it just looked cool at the time). Then throw about a dozen skin tight t-shirts and 3 pairs of jeans, some underwear and socks, and maybe a coat into an old suitcase or duffel bag and you're ready to go "on the road".

Shocking Experience

◆

By the way, since we are on the subject of shop maintenance, a tour came back from Florida that I hadn't been on, but I had sure heard about it. The other crew had done a series of shows with the Patti Smith Group, and Tom Petty and the Heatbreakers opened. The infamous gig was outdoors and Tom got knocked unconscious from an electrical shock while singing into a vocal mic. The headline in Rolling Stone that week read, "Tom Petty almost killed in freak lightning strike at outdoor show in Florida". Well, there were storms that day, and he could have been the victim of a strike, but I have a different theory. When we were going through the testing of the equipment before sending it out again I found a loose wire (actually it was disconnected). Not just any wire, but the main ground wire for the electrical grid supplying power to the PA. Any stray voltage (a common occurrence outdoors) instead of being routed harmlessly down the ground wire would potentially build up and find another path to ground (like through Tom's lips?). Just a theory, and who am I to argue with Rolling Stone anyway?

Get Down Tonight

◆

Once in a while a cakewalk gig would pop up. I got one of these in the summer of 1976. It would be a huge disco show in Washington, D.C. at the Capital Center. The show would include K.C. and the Sunshine Band, Rufus, featuring Chaka Khan, Heatwave, The Robot Band, and Trammps. A Dallas company called Showco was doing the sound and lights. When they had an unusually large venue (like the Capital Center rigged for maximum capacity), they would contract for "supplemental sound". Basically another company (me in this case) would truck in PA equipment and stack it on top of the existing gear. Mics and boards weren't needed, just extra PA. In fact only one roadie was needed so I was solo tonight. Drive to DC, unload, hook up to Showco, load, drive home, easy money. Also during the show I had nothing to do so I actually got to go trolling in the audience for young ladies that wanted a lasting relationship (as long as it only lasted about two hours). Everything went perfectly. It was a union house (with forklifts) so I lifted nothing. My speakers went on top of theirs to create a monstrous stack of power. Once I confirmed that my system was on line and in sync with Showco, I took the rest of the day off. I got to meet KC (a very unassuming guy) during their sound check. I also got to sit at the main board during the Rufus sound check and give my two cents worth to Chaka's soundman who had struck up a friendship with me. Chaka came out to the soundboard and based on the conversation he wasn't just her soundman, if you catch my drift. All the other bands had their time to check sound, and after a gourmet meal in the green room (I told you this was one of the best jobs I had ever been on didn't I?) they opened the house. K.C. was hot, it was the height of Disco, and every female under the age of 40 within a three state area was at this show. I walked around the front edge of the crowd sporting my all access back-stage pass. Then she came up to me. Her name was Stacy or Leslie or something like that. She was probably 16, give or take a year, but she looked every bit of 21. She was decked out in full groupie costume, heavy make-up, short tight dress, high heels, you get the picture. She wasted no time in asking me the two key questions. "Are you with the band? And "Can you get me backstage to meet K.C.?" Yes and Yes. I exaggerated and said K.C. was a personal friend of mine (well I had met him earlier in the day). She said she would do ANYTHING to go back-stage with me (she really emphasized that word ANYTHING). Ok think fast, I would need a pass and a quiet place where we wouldn't be dis-turbed. First things first, the pass. "Wait right here, don't move." I pleaded, as I headed for the backstage area to find a pass. Tactical error, I should have already picked up a spare, I always carry a spare. Oh well, no sense in crying over spilt milk, there is the Road Manager for K.C. I approached him and said "Hey I just ran into an old college friend that wants to meet K.C., I need a pass, OK?" He said. "She's not old enough to be in college." Damn! He had seen me talking to her from the stage. "No really, it's the sister of an old roommate of mine she's like family to me." My desperation was beginning to show. "I'm going to do you a favor (At last! A back stage pass!) I'm going to keep you from going to jail. She can't be a day over 15 years old, they'll throw away the key." I was about to start arguing that she was at least 16, but I realized that it would be a losing battle. I went back out to the audience found Leslie/Stacy and told her they were all out of passes right now, but could I sit with her and watch the show? She just turned and walked away. The

last thing I heard was her sweet little voice saying, "Too bad you could-
n't get me back there, I'm REAL good."

I cursed that Road Manager for years after that night, but today I
realize he was absolutely right. Karl's Roadie Rule #9 "Everything happens for a reason". By the way, the entire show was fantastic, but it was a
bitter consolation prize.

Attempted Murder

◆

I mentioned Patti Smith earlier, and although she wasn't one of my regulars, I did have occasion to work with her on several memorable gigs. For those of you not up on 70's Punk Rock, Patti was probably the second most successful graduate of CBGB's club in New York City (behind Talking Heads). She had her first hit in 1975 with "G.L.O.R.I.A.", the remake of the song written by Van Morrison and later covered by The Shadows of Knight. Of course being sung by a female gave it a whole new (at the time not so politically correct) flavor. She gained a reputation as being out of control on stage as parodied by Gilda Radner on the original Saturday Night Live "Candi Slice" bits. Gilda would stagger around the stage and sing unintelligible lyrics obviously drunk or stoned. Patti at times would become a tragic caricature of "Candi" in a twisted self-fulfilling prophecy. At the time I was first doing shows with Patti, the "Easter" album was released and Patti finally had a mainstream hit with "Because the Night" written by her friend Bruce Springsteen. Once again I found myself on monitors, and once again trying to keep up with a very LOUD band. Let me take a moment and try to describe what I mean by LOUD. As I have mentioned previously, the monitor man has a speaker right next to him that he listens to the same thing the band does, at the same volumes. PSG (Patti Smith Group) had a basic request, turn it up as LOUD as it can go without feeding back or blowing up. To demonstrate how LOUD that is, imagine this. Every time JD (the drummer) would hit his snare drum, you blink involuntarily. This would be similar to the blinking that you would have done if someone fired a high caliber pistol near your head. Even though you knew it was coming, the sound of the report coming from the handgun would cause you to flinch and blink without really wanting to. So, even though you knew JD was going to hit the snare at a precise moment, your body would still react by blinking. When he stepped on the pedal of the kick drum sending the padded end of the stick into the membrane of the bass drum, the low frequency vibration would actually move your intestines slightly in sympathetic vibration, you would feel it in your gut. When he smashed his drumstick down onto the high hat cymbal, the sizzling high frequency would penetrate your ears and be clearly heard by you for hours after the show was over. Please be clear on this, it was LOUD on that stage. With that in mind, let me tell you about the show that I tried to kill her. It was Detroit (maybe Chicago), and I had picked up some shows with Patti during a hiatus from Jean-Luc Ponty. My partner from JLP, Louie, was with me as well, doing the lights. The load in and set-up were uneventful other than Louie was as sick as a dog. He was a big Italian and never admitted to being sick, but today he was very sick. We started the sound check on time, and things were going well. The monitors were loud enough, mostly because we were in a traditional theater with lots of drapes to absorb the stray sound waves. Acoustically it was a very good hall. With the monitors pretty much set, I just watched as the band fooled around on stage. Louie was near me at my board when I heard him say; "Oh shit!" "What's wrong?" I screamed (remember it was LOUD right now). "Par lamp out! One of the spots!". What he was saying was that a bulb had burned out, and it was one that would have to be replaced because it spot lighted something specific during the show. Some lights wouldn't be noticed, this one would. The problem was that after the lights are aimed, the band places their equipment on the stage and there is no practical way to get an "A frame" ladder up to change the bulb this late in the game. "I'll go up!" Louie shouted. "No, I'll go!" I volunteered. I knew what had to be done, and I knew Louie wasn't well enough to do it. He didn't argue.

What was needed right now was a human monkey. I abandoned the board (things were going OK, and it was LOUD enough) and took a new par bulb and put in down the front of my T-shirt (the bulb is roughly the size of a large car headlamp). I shimmied up the Genie Lifter with that bulb safely tucked between my stomach and my tight shirt. The genie lifter was about twenty feet up, but the trick was to getting over the edge and up onto the top of the truss. Now remember that there isn't much light up where I'm at (it's all pointing down at the stage), and I am being blasted with Patti's voice singing "Set me Free" as every monitor on stage was aimed right at me up on my temporary perch. I worked my way above the band and over to the defective par bulb. I carefully removed the connector (Louie had killed the power to it) and I connected the new bulb. I signaled Louie and he faded it up to verify the viability of the replacement. It worked. Now to get down safely. Logic dictated that it would be silly to risk carrying a defective bulb down with me the same way I carried the new one up, so the thing to do was a controlled drop. I moved to a spot a good fifteen feet or so from where the band was, and Louie waited below me. I hand signaled 1,2,3 {drop}. Louie made the catch without fanfare. Mission accomplished, time to climb down. At the exact moment I dropped the bulb, we must have caught Patti's eye because she stopped the band mid cord, and then broke the silence with "What the F*** are you doing?" "Are you trying to F***ing kill me?" "G** damn it you dropped that thing, and could have hit me." (Remember she has a microphone and a very LOUD monitor system). All I could do was try to look non-threatening, twenty feet in the air, trying to keep my balance. She continued, "Don't you know that if I was killed I'd be just like Jimmy Hendrix, or f***ing Janis Joplin? I ain't ready to f***ing die yet! Is that what you want for me to be f***ing dead martyr like f***ing Jim Morrison?" "Somebody get that little f***er down from there." "He's trying to kill me!" "He's trying to kill me!" Believe me when I say, I wanted nothing more in this world at that moment than to be down. By now Patti's Brother Todd (also her stage manager) had reached her, and had taken the mic from her. I slowly climbed back down the lifter, and awaited my fate. Todd had control of the situation, and had already started to calm her down. He turned to me and said something like "get lost for a while", so I left through the stage door to the street. Louie followed me out and said, "That was uncalled for, that bitch is crazy". "No big deal," I said, as I tried to shake off the adrenaline pumping through my system.

Later, near to show time, Todd came to me and said, "don't worry about it, just lay low for a while." Lay Low? How was I supposed to mix monitors eighteen feet away from Patti and not have her notice? "It'll be alright," Todd said.

Todd was right, Patti didn't say a word to me about the attempt on her life that night, or ever again. She just plain forgot all about it. "Long live Candi Slice!"

Garden Party

———————— ◆ ————————

A pleasant surprise musically was the six shows I did sound for Rick Nelson. I remember being the one "stuck" with doing the shows at a dinner theater in Rochester. "Rick Nelson? Are Ozzie and Harriet going to be there too?" I quipped. Little would I know how far away from Ozzie and Harriet the shows would turn out to be.

Rick was a formidable presence on stage. He was exactly as I pictured him, perfect smile, perfect hair, and perfect manners. His band was a nice mix of professional and playful, and included a guitar player from Elvis Presley's band. The Road Manager "Clark" was great to work with, and was careful to warn me before I met Rick not to call him "Ricky" (He hated to be called Ricky). Rick didn't have his own soundman, so I got the honors. We did two shows each night for three nights, and since I was about 15 miles from home, I got to sleep in my own bed each night. I was expecting to hear "Garden Party", "Traveling Man", and "Hello, Mary Lou" which I did. What I didn't expect was great rock and roll tunes like "My Bucket's Got a Hole In It", and many pop country songs that would be the forerunners of the style of songs sung today by country artists like Garth Brooks.

The second night I remember seeing a beautiful young girl getting the royal treatment during sound check. She looked to be about sixteen, although it was very hard to tell. She was dressed up in a very expensive dinner dress, and had enough make-up applied that she could have just as easily been over twenty. I forget her name today, but Clark introduced me to her that night out at the soundboard, prior to the second show. "She's a big fan of Rick's", I remember him saying. I didn't give it a second thought, as she watched the entire show sitting next to me at the board. The show went perfect, as she disappeared backstage at the conclusion of the encore. About twenty minutes later as I was securing the board and was about to head home, Clark came out to the board and invited me to the dressing room. "Why?" I asked, since roadies usually aren't given special invitations to the green room post-show. We're having a "scene", he said smiling. "You want in on it?" My god, the girl. I thought for a second trying to rationalize it by telling myself that she must be at least eighteen. I didn't want my manhood questioned so I blurted out, "If I go back there theoretically, what number would I be?" "Well, let's see, Rick, the band, the crew, probably 11th or 12th". "No thanks" I said, his answer having made my decision for me. I did not sleep well that night. The third and final night the young girl was not in attendance. A much older lady (probably pushing 30) had replaced her. However, like the girl, she was gorgeous and was wearing a very expensive evening dress. I was told later that she was a "pro". There would be no sharing tonight.

"Good night Ozzie"…"Good night Harriet".

On the last day of 1985, Rick, his fiancé, five members of the Stone Canyon Band, and their pilot were all killed in a fiery plane crash. "Good night Rick…sleep well."

Luck of the Irish

◆

Here's a quick story that demonstrates three of Karl's Roadie Rules. In 1977 I did a one nighter with a group from Ireland named "Horselips". Now before you say you never heard of them, remember back and try to recall their big hits off the "Aliens" album, "Speed the Plough", and "Sure the Boy Was Green". It may sound silly now but back then this group was predicted to be the next trendsetter in rock and roll. This brings me to Karl's Roadie Rule #13 "Never try to predict which artists will be stars, you will be wrong well over half the time." (It turns out the only trend they had right was the name of their album. In two years the first of the "Alien" movies would be released). Anyway, hindsight is always 20/20 so lets play along for a minute and pretend that we don't know that they do not become big stars. Once again I was on the monitor board, but this show was surprisingly different. I assumed they wanted as much volume as possible so I equalized the stage for LOUD. The band was amazed. They had no idea that monitors could get that LOUD. One of the band members commented that it was the first time since the beginning of the tour that he had actually heard the other singer that he was harmonizing with. It turns out that they had been using very primitive equipment in the UK, and the roadies they brought with them were good band roadies, but they weren't very "state of the art" when it came to things like monitors or parametric equalizers.

They were so grateful that every member of the band thanked me personally at the end of the show. Then…an unexpected twist.

The Road Manager approached me and invited me to go on tour with them that night! The record company was paying all the bills, and the band decided that I would be a valuable addition to the crew, enhancing the band's performance. I had to choose right then, they were leaving in about an hour. Enter Karl's Roadie Rule #2 "Never work directly for a band". I had seen enough Band Roadies out of work, which is why I chose to always work with a sound and light company. Besides, I had a pending tour with Jean-Luc Ponty soon (working with the sound company of course). I went with the sure thing. I politely declined the band's generous offer.

Finally, there is Karl's Roadie Rule #9 "Everything happens for a reason." I got word a month or two later that one of the Horselips band roadies apparently fell asleep at the wheel and drove their truck into a bridge abutment somewhere in the Midwest.

No Checks Please

◆

On the road, transactions were almost always handled in cash. This was the case for everything from a drug transaction to a sound company getting paid by the promoter for the services your company provided that night. This is partially dictated because in many cases the promoter didn't have all of the money needed to pay the band, sound company, light company, union crew, and the venue, until shortly before showtime. Every so often, a promoter wouldn't have enough money to pay everyone, or just wouldn't pay anyone; hence paranoia by anyone owed money on the road.

There was to be a show in Bridgeport, Connecticut in a hockey rink. We were doing sound and lights for what was supposed to be a monster funk show. The load in was smooth, union crew, forklifts, very cool. We brought everything we had for the PA (we needed it). The stage was at one end of "the ice" with open seating on the remaining floor (of course the ice was covered with plywood), and the normal arena seating was available as well. The venue was probably capable of holding over 15,000 fans. The show seemed well organized and nothing seemed unusual. There were six or seven bands including "Willie Alexander and the Boom Boom Band", "The Jimmy Castor Bunch", "BT Express", "The Manhattans", and "Bobby Blue Bland". There was plenty of promoter representation, plenty of food, plenty of security, nothing really out of the norm. Sound check was long and tedious, which was normal for that many bands. Everything was status quo. About a half an hour before the show I went looking for the promoter to get paid the $5,000 that we were owed for providing sound and lights. I had heard ticket sales were good (something that a paranoid roadie starts looking into as early as when the truck door is cracked at load in). Strange, I couldn't find the promoter, only his hired help. Nobody knew where he was. I started to alert the various band Road Managers. We also alerted the stage union and security (really off duty cops, good to have them on your side if things got hairy). They had already opened the doors and ticket sales were indeed good. It wasn't a sell-out, but it would be a very full house. The start time came and went and no promoter. We all began to come to grips that he had skipped with the gate. Not a bad scam, collect all the ticket money, don't pay anyone, and take off before the show starts. A consortium consisting of representatives of several of the bigger bands, the sound and light company, the union, and security convened to decide what to do. The bands were split, some wanted to play others wanted to get paid or pack up. The union didn't care because it turns out they get paid in advance. It was the same with the arena. Well I had to go with Road Rule #10 "Get the money before the show", and I didn't dare come back to Rochester without the cash AND trying to explain why we did the show anyway. Once the sound and lights were pulling out, the show was pretty much extinct. We left the PA on long enough for the police to announce that due to "circumstances beyond our control" the show was canceled. They assured everyone that they could go to the place they purchased their tickets for a full refund, even though that eventuality was in doubt at the moment. We struck the gear with a hand full of uniformed police between the crowd and us. This was a very unsettling experience. I even considered going ahead with the show at one point, but the bands were pulling their gear so there was no turning back now. We closed the doors and didn't stop until we got into New York State.

Now it's a year or so later, and we are doing a show in Cleveland. This show is much smaller than Bridgeport (and is in the same theatre that I did that show with Blue Öyster Cult back on my first road trip). The show on this night is to star "Cameo", "Bottom & Company", and "Maze." Like Bridgeport everything went well, good crew, good food, good promoter. Tonight though I wasn't going to wait until 30 minutes until curtain to get paid, I had learned my lesson. I confronted the promoter during sound check and presented him with our invoice for $5,000, the agreed upon price. "Hey no problem, you guys are great," he replied, "come with me". He led me to a stage office he had commandeered for the evening and produced a briefcase. Out of the briefcase he handed me a business check carefully made out for $5,000. A check! Did this guy think I was new? "I'm sorry, I can't take a check unless it's certified," I asserted. He looked like I had just insulted his mother. "It's good, you can call the bank," he offered. "Not on a Saturday night", I pointed out. "Let's call your boss", he countered. So we called the owner of the sound company at home back in Rochester, luckily he was there. I presented the problem and he gave me the answer I knew he would give, "cash only, no checks". Myself and the other sound and two light roadies went across the street and had a nice Chinese dinner while the promoter tried to gather up $5,000 in cash on a Saturday night. Bear in mind that this was years before ATM machines. We returned to the Agora about an hour before the show completely prepared to strike the show. There was the promoter, notably irritated, waiting for me. "Come into my office" he said closing the door behind me. "Here it is, "please count it". He had pulled it off; he had produced $5,000 in cash. I started counting the large stack of bills and realized where it came from. It was all in denominations of fives, tens and twenties. He had cashed his own check at the box office. I had the money and that's all that mattered. The count was right; the show was a go. After I had stashed the cash in my Anvil briefcase (without anyone seeing) I left the office and went to my place at the monitor board.

Usually show cash is kept in your billfold or hidden in your pants if it's a lot. With all the small bills it pretty much filled my entire briefcase, not leaving me any options. I locked the case and then hid it inside a larger road case, which I sat on for the entire show. The show went smoothly. I'm sorry but I don't remember the performance, but you'll understand why shortly. At the conclusion of the show things happen very fast. The same paranoia that forces cash transactions also mandates a mad dash to the stage to retrieve and account for all the microphones. Failure to do that could cause one or two of the most expensive mics to accidentally end up in a band roadie's back pocket, and then spirited away (e.g. "I didn't see any microphone"). The show ended, and I had a dilemma. Guard the cash, or get the mics. Remember Roadie Rule #3 "Never turn your back on anything of value on the road." Well that didn't help since I had to favor one valuable thing or another. I thought about leaving the briefcase hidden and gathering the mics. No good, that case would be opened in a matter of seconds, and if a stagehand found my briefcase hidden there he'd figure out it was valuable. Then I got it! I had been hanging out with a security guard all night stage left. I removed my case from its hideout, handed it to the guard and asked him if he'd watch it for a minute or two. I hit the stage worried because precious seconds had expired with my valuable mics exposed. I grabbed the four most expensive ones and headed back to the mic case next to the guard who was watching my briefcase. I looked up and he was gone.

I couldn't have been gone more than 30 seconds, long enough for him to turn tail and run with the $5,000. I also lost my first Anvil Briefcase that night, including dozens of backstage passes that proved I was now an experienced roadie. Ironically the Blue Öyster Cult back-stage pass from that very spot in that very theatre from that first road trip two years ago was now gone forever as well. The trip home that night was long and hard. I wondered if I'd have a job on Monday morning. I called Duffy at home Sunday and gave him the bad news. At first I think he suspected that I had pocketed the cash, but I must have been convincing because he allowed me to come to work Monday. However he wasn't at all happy about losing the money.

There are two things that haunt me about that night. The first is that I have no doubt now the promoter's check was good and that if I had accepted it, everything would have been fine. Second, this would not be the last time the city of Cleveland would be horribly cruel to me.

Gimme Three Steps

◆

Once again I found myself doing work in conjunction with Showco. This time it was three shows that they sub-contracted to us due to logistics. This 1977 tour was Lynyrd Skynyrd and we were to provide sound and lights for three shows starting in Detroit. The tour had picked up these three shows after it had started, and they were "out of order". You see most tours are logical, for example Chicago, then Detroit, Cleveland, and Pittsburgh. The routing of the tour generally makes sense since it costs money to move trucks, equipment and personnel long distances profitably. When a tour "picks up" some dates late, they rarely fit into this logical routing. Showco's trucks and equipment were on the wrong side of the country to make it to these three shows and then resume the original tour. That's were we came in, the substitute sound and light system.

The first show was at Pine Knob, an outdoor venue near Detroit. It's semi covered, and is a clone of various other successful open air halls around the country such as Wolftrap and Tanglewood. Virtually every type of music was played at Pine Knob from Classical to Hard Rock. Tonight it would be Lynyrd Skynyrd, The Atlanta Rhythm Section, and Mahogany Rush.

I was as excited about doing sound for Skynyrd as I had been for any show up to that point. They were probably at or near their all time peak popularity, and they were (up until that night) one of my favorites.

Along with my euphoria also came a sense of confidence. Actually in retrospect it was a severe case of over confidence. I had been a roadie for almost a year, and had not been on more than three one nighters in a row. I had yet to actually do a tour, but I thought I knew everything there was to know about sound, and specifically mixing monitors. At Pine Knob I would learn two things, one…that I didn't know everything, and two…humility. The load in was heaven. Back the trucks up to the stage and have the union crew (at this point in my life I loved union crews) unload everything. It was a semi-strict house, which meant you weren't supposed to touch anything, but they let you as long as you didn't abuse the privilege. In strict "hands off" houses it can be a complete drag as you literally have to get a union sound man to move a mic cord three inches, or adjust a microphone a little closer to the drum head. The weather was nice for a Detroit summer day, and load in was on schedule. I confidently prepared for the show with every trick I knew to get the stage monitors LOUD. I had actually gotten quite good at it in the relatively short time I had been mixing solo, but I still had lots to learn. There were two big cross stage stacks (mini PAs on either side of the stage pointed at the band to supplement the floor monitors) and a third stack behind the drummer. I felt I was ready for anything. Led Zeppelin and Pink Floyd could both be on stage having a "battle of the bands" and I'd be able to satisfy their insatiable stage monitor needs. Wrong.

Load in and set-up took about four hours, then the band showed up about 4 PM for sound check. They were just as I pictured them (from album covers of course) Ronnie Van Zant was being fawned over in his classic round flat top hat (I'm not sure exactly what to call it but in virtually every picture of Ronnie he is wearing it). The band got right to business with what seemed like a small army of band roadies. I did my usual glad handing, "Hey, how are you boys doing? My name's Karl and I'm on monitors tonight, you need anything you just let me know." "Where's Showco?" one of them asked a band roadie like I didn't exist.

"Not coming tonight, still on the West Coast." Well, I now figured I would have my work cut out for me, but it wasn't unusual that they would be attached to their regular sound company, so I didn't give it too much thought. After all we were only doing three shows, then they'd get their precious Showco back. There was talk that if we did a good job, we would be hired to do some more pick-up dates for the tour later in the year. I was determined to blow them away with my mix that night.

Now this may sound like I'm making an excuse but outdoor gigs can have as many problems acoustically as a bad indoor hall, there is just no way to predict until you set up. The variables include the design of the hall, the size of the audience, the barometric pressure, the temperature, relative humidity, exact placement of the stacks (Hey maybe Gordon Lightfoot was on to something after all) number and placement of microphones, and a thousand other details. Some of these details are in the sound crew's control, most are not. I set the stage monitors up the way I had done dozens of times before with great success, and we started the sound check. JT was my partner that trip, and was not my usual partner (and not particularly happy I was along). I replaced his partner (Bobby) at the last minute but I don't recall why, it may have been something as simple as the owner being mad at him, or a suspended drivers license. The sound check did not go well. From the first song Ronnie motioned for more volume. More? I had started with everything full open; I didn't have anything left to give. I learned much later that an experienced monitor man would have started out absurdly low, and then inched the volume up little by little each time they asked for more. This plays a trick on your ears and since you hear it getting incrementally louder it satisfies the need for LOUD volume. So I went to "Plan B" and just like the Sly Stone show I "tweaked" the sound. I tweaked and tweaked and tweaked some more. I used graphic equalizers in tandem with parametric equalizers until I had over equalized (another rookie mistake from the roadie who didn't consider himself a rookie. JT was doing fine in the house. Skynyrd had a soundman, so JT only had to baby-sit, answering questions, and preventing any damage from happening to our system due to any over zealousness on the sound guy's part. The further into sound check the more disgruntled Ronnie became. The other band members didn't seem to have an opinion, except when Ronnie asked them if it was LOUD enough, then they would say something like, "It could stand to be louder". I was frantically trying to get more dBs out of the system, and the more I screwed with it the worse it got. At some point Ronnie came over and said to me something along the lines of, "Does your system suck? or do you just not know what you're doing?" I'm not sure exactly what I replied but I know it wouldn't have won any Nobel Peace Prizes. I've told this part of story over the years that Ronnie and I got into a fistfight. Upon further review, that did not happen, although we did trade some heated words. The Road Manager for the band finally got between us, and declared the sound check over. Good, I thought we have two more bands to check anyway, and I can get this fixed before the show.

If I was to do this day over, and I have hundreds of times in my head over the years, I would have been a politician instead of an indignant fool. If I had turned on the charm and stroked Ronnie's ego instead of challenging him, this might have been a happier ending. Also I should have admitted right there, right then that I was in over my head. I should have gone to JT, offered to baby-sit the mains and let him take a crack at the stage. My pride got in the way.

Oh yeah, I forgot a very important additional factor. I was also trying to impress one of the back up singers. Early in the sound check, I struck up a conversation with Leslie, who in a matter of less than fifteen minutes I had developed a huge crush on. She actually seemed rather ambivalent to me, but I tried my best to dazzle her with my wit and experience as a professional soundman. After several pregnant pauses in our lame one-sided conversation, I found myself talking to one of the other singers, Cassie Gaines. She was one of the most genuinely nice performers I had ever met on the road. She told me her brother Steve had recently joined the band, and talked about what a great opportunity this tour was. Like an idiot I kept trying to talk to Leslie, who was more petite than Cassie with a younger face. She also was starting to get annoyed by my persistence. So now the real truth. I was in over my head, was being publicly called an incompetent, and this was happening in front of Leslie who I was having delusional fantasies about. So I did what any testosterone filled roadie would do, I snapped.

The rest of the sound check went OK, but not great, Atlanta Rhythm Section was also at a popularity peak. The album (remember CDs hadn't been invented yet) "Rock and Roll Alternative" had recently been released and "So Into You" was a top 40 hit. Mahogany Rush featuring Frank Mario was just plain LOUD, and I don't recall much about their performance.

The sun finally set, the temperature cooled off and they let the partying hoards in. I stayed on stage forgoing food to continue tweaking the stage system, getting deeper and deeper into making the problem worse. (Probably the second best thing I could have done at that very moment, besides giving the mix to JT, would have been to set every single control back to zero and start over) As I tweaked the acoustics were still changing due to the drop in temperature and the additional dampening created by the soft fleshy crowd.

The concert went, in my not so humble opinion, fantastic. The crowd went wild from the first power chord of Frank Mario until the final encore. Things were not completely kosher on stage though, as most everyone was asking for more gain, and I couldn't give it to them. Musicians make do and LOUD monitors or not all three bands performed (to the audience) like there was nothing wrong. As mad as I was at Ronnie for our earlier "run in" I was mesmerized during the show. To see him less than twenty feet away singing "Gimme three steps", "Saturday Night Special", "Gimme Back My Bullets", and "That Smell" was awe-inspiring. I was unfortunately on the wrong side of the stage to continue my fruitless flirtation with Leslie (I was stage left, the

Honkette's were on stage right). The band continued as the fan's participation in the show reached a fever pitch. "Sweet Home Alabama" and of course a very long version of "Freebird" to cap the night. It was over, I had survived the evening, and we had two more nights left for me to hit on Leslie Hawkins.

The crowd wasn't even gone yet, and I had barely gathered the precious mics when the Road Manager approached me and said, "We won't need you boys tomorrow night, we've made other arrangements." My blood turned to ice and a chill went down my spine, as my legs turned to warm soupy Jell-O. "Other arrangements?" we'd just been fired. No, I'd just been fired. The gigs were paying $7,500 a night. I had just cost my company $15,000 because of my arrogance.

I had many long rides home from the road, as you have read or will be reading soon. This was perhaps the longest. To make things worse, I never got a chance to say goodbye to Leslie or Cassie.

We spent the night at a hotel since none of us had the energy (or ambition) to "dead head" home. I probably blamed everything and everybody but myself when we got to the shop. Duffy must've bought my story or he was too close to sending me out on the first Jean-Luc Ponty Tour (coming up in a few chapters) because the Skynyrd incident never came up again.

In October 1977, during the Ponty Tour, I was pulling an all nighter driving the motorhome in Northern Florida. The sun was just coming up, and I was listening to the news on the AM radio. What I heard that morning made me pull over to the side of the road and cry. A plane carrying the Lynyrd Skynyrd band had crashed about 600 miles away in McComb Mississippi. Four members of the band were dead. Ronnie Van Zant, Cassie Gaines, her brother Steve Gaines, and Dean Kilpatrick (the Road Manager). Seriously injured were the remaining artists including Leslie Hawkins who eventually required plastic surgery to rebuild her shattered face.

Now, over twenty years later...

To Ronnie, I can now only say, "I'm sorry, please forgive me."

To Cassie, I can only finally say the "goodbye" that I didn't get to say.

Heartless

◆

Many tours were just never meant to be. Our sound company would bid on them and for one reason or another, we either wouldn't be the low bid, or we would win the bid, and the tour would cancel just prior to launching.

One tour we didn't get was a planned tour of Steely Dan in 1978. Steely Dan was primarily a studio band and was widely known to be averse to touring because they didn't feel the quality of the current sound reinforcement systems was a high enough quality to reproduce that "Steely Dan Sound". It was said that they would plan a tour and then cancel it after the rehearsals because either Donald Fagen or Walter Becker couldn't accept the quality of the PA. We bid on this alleged tour only to be told that upon review of our proposal our sound system wasn't adequate. They never did do that tour; in fact it wasn't until the early nineties that a portion of the original "Dan" did a live tour.

During the summer of 1977 I was slated to do 27 shows in 26 days (one show was an afternoon gig) with Jeff Beck, Jan Hammer and Narada Michael Walden. The power rock trio was at the peak of their popularity and this tour was going to be big venues. I was going to mix monitors (which with no vocals would be a piece of cake). We literally had the trucks packed and were ready to go when we got the call. The tour had been canceled, no reason given. The story we heard was that Jeff had broken up with his girlfriend and flown to Paris to find her.

Later we also heard something about a nervous breakdown. All I know for sure is there was no tour. Other roadies in my sound company had worked with Jeff Beck Group previously, but I never did get to see him play live.

Another "near miss" was a four month tour with Bob Marley and the Wailers. We had won the bid and although the trucks weren't packed we had started on the tour prep. Again I was assigned monitors (although I don't know why after Skynyrd). The other roadies were kidding me that to be accepted by a reggae band, I had to smoke ganja until I was coughing up blood. I had smoked some pot in college, but actually had quit about the same time as becoming a full time roadie. I found it very hard to work professionally and smoke pot, so I didn't do it. They all had me convinced that if I didn't show solidarity with the band and crew by smoking with them they would never trust me. My apprehension about this issue faded when we got the dreaded call. The tour had been canceled, this time because Bob had suffered a football (soccer) injury to his foot. It wasn't until years later that the true reason came out. Bob had been diagnosed with cancer and needed to have a toe amputated. He refused the procedure due to his Rastafarian religion. Bob died in May of 1981 the result of cancer migrating to his brain, lungs, and stomach.

Then there is the tour that might have changed my life. A competing sound company that actually had its shop in the same industrial park as ours was the regular PA company for "Heart". On rare occasions I worked with Ray's company with the permission of my boss, when things were slow for us. One time when I was doing a show with Ray he asked me if I would consider switching to his company. He had a Heart tour coming up and wanted me to mix the stage. My heart stopped. You see Heart was my favorite band in college just a year or two earlier. I always had a fantasy about meeting Nancy Wilson. I always rationalized in my head that if I could just meet her; she would fall hopelessly in love with me. Now don't get me wrong I'm not talking about stalking her or anything, I just had the hots for her. Now I could have my chance. I had heard that Nancy was dating Heart's soundman at that time so I figured I would have a shot at winning her affection too. I told Ray I'd think about it. It was a hard decision but Heart was about the only thing that small sound company had going at the time, and to take that job I would never be able to go back to my present company, so once again (like the earlier "Horselips" offer) I stayed with the sure thing, and turned the Heart tour down.

Karl's Roadie rule #9 "Everything happens for a reason".

I always rationalize the choice I made that day by telling myself that things could never have worked between Nancy and I, after all she is so much older than I am (by 2 years and five months).

Class Acts

◆

Believe it or not, some of the shows I worked didn't have any high drama. There was no shouting, no fighting, no bad sound; nothing really noteworthy for this book, except many top notch excellent shows by performers with tons of class.

I frequently drove a truck to Buffalo to provide sound at a symphony hall named "Kleinhan's". On several occasions I had the privilege to provide that sound for Ray Charles. My contact with Ray was always brief, but pleasant. He didn't have a traveling sound man, and he would always remind me to make sure it wasn't too loud (apparently he had had bad experiences with local sound guys getting a little out of hand from a volume perspective). Quite an entourage always surrounded him. I also specifically remember a young black man that was always within an arms length of Ray every second. He was a very personable young man, but I got the impression that if anyone ever made any kind of unwanted or threatening move towards Ray he would hurt them without hesitation or remorse. Ray's show was always the same, predictable and great. He usually did two shows, and they were so consistent that if camcorders existed back then and if I had permission to record both shows I doubt most human beings could have discerned any difference between them. Even his "adlibs" were identical between songs each show. Even today when I see Ray perform on TV he sounds the same, looks the same, and appears to have not aged a bit. He is the epitome of consistency, and that is a good thing.

Another performer that I worked with at Kleinhan's at least twice was B.B. King. Like Ray he didn't have a road soundman, so I got the nod. Also like Ray, he was a man of few words. I remember him as being all business, put on a show and make it a good one. He would sweat from his forehead by the end of the third or fourth song, possibly due to the lights, probably due to his intensity. And of course his leading lady Lucille always gave her usual stunning performance (Lucille is, of course, his famous electric guitar).

Still another class act I got to mix sound for in 1979 was Joan Baez. It was at Tanglewood outdoor theatre near Boston. This hall is almost an exact duplicate of Pine Knob, but the results on this night would be much different. The opening act was Liv Taylor, an old friend (remember the hurricane?). It was a marvelous show. Joan was a joy to work with, very easy going. The crowd was great, appreciative and responsive. Liv and Joan both put on superior shows. It was pure and simply the way all shows should have gone. If every show went that well I'd probably still be mixing sound today (well, not really, but I'm not ready to tell you the true reason I left the road yet)

Hello Dolly

◆

When I met Dolly Parton on stage I was immediately taken by two things. No, not those…(although her breasts were very large, and her reputation preceded her). At sound check when I introduced myself, and asked her what she wanted in the stage mix, I couldn't believe how short she was and how sweet she was. This was probably in 1977, and she was starring in her own variety show named "Dolly", but her true acting debut in the movie "9 to 5" was still several years away. If her "down home country style" that defines her today is a put on then she's been pulling off a great acting performance for a long time. That afternoon, she spoke in that decidedly Tennessee drawl that is her trademark. That night she put on a show like I'm sure she had performed at the Grand Old Opry on many occasions. Her new hit was "There you go again", and of course she sang her classic renditions of "Jolene" and "Coat of Many Colors". A very nice show, a very nice lady.

It turns out that among all the rock stars I worked with, the two stars that turned out to be the biggest international superstars had nothing to do with Rock & Roll, they were Dolly Parton and Bill Cosby.

My First Tour

◆

Little would I know when I signed on for the 1977 Jean-Luc Ponty tour, that I would eventually do sound with him more than 200 times over the next 3 years. I didn't even know who Jean-Luc was. Since you also may not be familiar with his work, here's a quick review.

Jean-Luc Ponty (pronounced: John-Luke Pon Tee) was born in the Normandy region of France. He had began his training on classical violin by age 5, and entered the Paris Conservatory of Music at age 15. By 1968 he was on the cutting edge of a new genre of music called jazz-rock. He came to the United States from France in 1969, and worked with the George Duke Trio and Frank Zappa. His electric violin and unique style won him many accolades at the very beginning of jazz-rock-fusion. About this time he also did session work on Elton John's "Honky Chateau". Back in the US again he recorded albums with Frank Zappa and the Mother's of Invention, and then moved on to join John McLaughlin and the Mahavishnu Orchestra. In 1975 Jean-Luc went solo and recorded the first of his many ground breaking albums. He single-handedly brought the violin out of the 19th century and into the 20th.

Within all that background I said the same thing most of you just did. Jean-Luc Who?

Sure I had heard of Frank Zappa, and certainly Elton John, I had even heard of the Mahavishnu Orchestra, but not Jean-Luc Ponty. It turns out though, that I had worked with many bands with a similar style. Billy Cobham, Return to Forever, and George Duke were all shows I had worked on in my tenure as a roadie up to that point. That first show was more than a pleasant surprise.

The tour was to take three months and it was to start in Ann Arbor Michigan on September 17, 1977. I flew into Detroit with my partner for the next two years, Louie. The equipment on this tour would be moved by tractor trailer and an air ride trailer. The driver was Fred, he worked for our sound company, Louie was the number two light guy, and I was on stage mix. Jean-Luc had a soundman named "Trout", and a light man named Russell. There were also two band roadies, Larry and Joe. The band consisted of the following artists (for some of you these names will be familiar from bands they worked with after Ponty, but I'll expand on that later). Jean-Luc played electric violin; Ralphe Armstrong was on bass, Allan Zavod on keyboards, Steve Smith on drums, Daryl Stuermer and Jamie Glaser shared guitar duty. Jamie had just replaced Alan Holdsworth, who had played guitar on the current album, for the tour. The current album was "Enigmatic Ocean", which was the fourth solo album from Jean-Luc following up "Upon the Wings Of Music", "Aurora", and "Imaginary Voyage". The tour manager's name was Pat. That night after load out, the six members of the crew would pile into a motorhome for the next twelve weeks. The band and the manager would, of course, travel by air. Now on with the show.

That first show was unknown territory for me. I was unfamiliar with Ponty, his band, and his music. Louie and I had never been on a real "tour" before, only disjointed runs of two and three shows strung together from different bands. We had never lived in a motorhome with 5 other grown men, and had never been out on our own for more than a few days. Louie didn't know how it would be to work with (but really work for) Russell, and likewise for me and Eric (Trout). By the way I never asked Eric how he got the nickname "Trout", but we all assumed it was due to one of his eyes that kind of bugged out and looked off in a different direction. We all also assumed that it was due to some kind of childhood accident, but again nobody ever asked him that I am aware of. I do know one of the main reasons he got the gig was that he spoke perfect French. Jean-Luc was comfortable with that I think. Now Trout was a very good soundman, but everything else being equal it didn't hurt that he spoke Jean-Luc's native tongue. Russell was a different matter. He didn't get along with anyone right from the start, which is not good if you plan on spending the next twelve weeks or so driving around this great country of ours in a 28 foot motorhome with 5 other adults. Right from day one he became the outcast, and he became the object of ridicule from Joe, the band roadie who at that point had the most seniority with Ponty and hence "ran the show". Joe was a large man that reminded me of George Thorogood, probably a jock in high school, and was very loud and boisterous. He had been with Ponty for a year or two dating back to his early club days. There was no doubt who had Ponty's ear and who ran the crew. Joe was the only person Jean-Luc trusted enough to touch his precious electric violins and his prized bow. Later I learned that the bow alone was worth many thousands of dollars. Joe also serviced the guitars. Larry was Joe's faithful sidekick, a country boy in the big city. Larry took care of the drums (no small task) and Zavod's keyboards. One thing was certain; they were both incredibly devoted to Ponty and would have walked on hot coals if he had asked them to do that.

And then there was Fred, our truck driver. I'll come back to the show in a minute but I think it's time you met Fred. Fred worked for our Sound and Light Company, and he had one job, to get the equipment to the next gig on time. This was different from his mission in life, which was to have sex with as many women as possible. He never failed in either his job or his mission.

Back in Rochester Fred actually lived with the owner of the company, Duffy. Duffy had a nice house out by Lake Ontario, and since Fred was gone most of the time, he paid rent to Duffy and stayed there when he was in town. I would guess Fred was about 45 back then but it's hard to tell since he had lost most of his hair and he was trying hard to cover up the bald spot with what was left. In other ways he was an average man, average height, average weight and build, very average looks. He had those truck driver teeth that kind of protruded out like they were just a tad to big for his mouth, and they may have in fact been dentures. One thing for certain about Fred, he never met a woman he didn't like. He would find women at the Laundromat, in truck stops, backstage at shows, anywhere. His batting average was close to a thousand, and his secret? Easy, he only dated plain, homely or downright ugly women. And he actually preferred them married. He treated them like a queen (at least until he had finished with them) and they responded by giving themselves to him freely. It was so bad when he was in town that Duffy actually had T-shirts printed up that in bold block letters said "I'M NOT FRED". The theory was that if Duffy was out mowing the lawn and a jilted husband came looking for Fred they wouldn't accidentally kill Duffy before they realized they had the wrong guy. Now Duffy was no angel either, but he preferred the younger (and much better looking) ladies. Duffy was probably in his late 30's then, but father time had not been kind to Duffy. His long gray hair and rough complexion would give you the impression that he was older than Fred was. The best way I can describe Duffy would be to image a Grateful Dead Fan that had been following the band around going to shows for twenty years and was still partying with (and dating) college girls.

A hobby shared by Fred and Duffy was their Harleys. They both had bikes way too powerful for their age, and a great cause for concern for all of us that they would kill themselves any day. Fred even figured out a way to take the bike on the road with him. He welded a little platform on the back of the tractor trailer cab, and then using the truck's ramp (and a little roadie power) he unloaded it every noon during load-in, and we re-loaded it back on and strapped it down every night before pulling out. Since Fred had no real duties during the day, this gave him incredible flexibility to cruise around town, looking for Harley Davidson shops (he collected T-shirts from every city) to looking for unhappy (and rather plain looking) house wives. Fred was one of my true heroes.

So here we are at the beautiful Hill auditorium in Ann Arbor Michigan. Louie and I have flown in, Fred is at the dock with the sound and lights, and Joe and Larry have driven the motorhome in from California. The band, the road manager (Pat), and the band's equipment have arrived via Boeing 737.

The first gig of any tour is a shakeout, everyone is figuring out what is expected of him or her, and where exactly he or she fit into the pecking order. Pat was the road manager but he definitely wasn't the one in charge. In a quiet and very soft-spoken way Jean-Luc was clearly the final authority on any matter that came up. Since Joe knew him the best (what he liked or didn't like, etc.) he also commanded a lot of authority on that first day. Pat was probably third just because technically he was in charge of everything from the band to the crew to the money. I just was as accommodating and pleasant as possible (having learned what the opposite will get you ala Skynyrd). I paid strict attention to each band member during sound check with lots of "That level OK for you Daryl?" and "Do you need more kick drum in your mix Jean-Luc?" It was an unremarkable first sound check, nobody yelled or made demands I couldn't fulfill. I could tell this was going to be a great tour. If only their music doesn't put me to sleep!

After sound check we set up the opening act, two guitarists named Pat Martino and Booby Rose. Four mics, very simple. Then we had about three hours until the show, so we all relaxed back in the green room and waited for dinner.

This will be a good time to talk about promoters and contracts and the infamous riders in the contracts. Now a promoter is the person who stands the most to gain (or lose) at a specific show. If he does his or her job and sells enough tickets while balancing the expenses, a profit is made. If ticket sales stink, or he "comps" half the town, or he spends too much money on the catering, he stands to lose his shirt. Sometimes at the last minute costs are cut to avoid too bad of a blood bath. That's where the contract comes in. The contract and the riders built into the contract are for the protection of the band and crew. If the terms and conditions of the contract are not met, the band has the option to not play. Since we have already been paid (in most cases) the only losers in that case are of course the promoter and the fans. It is very rare to cancel a show because the meal was bad but the threat of show stoppage is used when needed. Now I'm sure you've all heard the ridiculous demands written into some band's contracts, as they have become part of rock folklore. The most famous one is the rider for Van Halen that states that a certain number (I think it was 3) pounds of plain M&M's will be provided backstage for the band and crew and that there shall be no brown M&Ms! As ludicrous as this sounds I'm sure it was something built into the contract to test the promoter to see if he or she had even read it and were willing to live up to it. I'm also sure that many a college intern working for the promoter sat backstage and meticulously sorted M&Ms all afternoon to comply with the request. I always wondered where the discarded brown ones went.

Our contract wasn't quite so unreasonable. We were to be provided six cases of Perrier, six cases of Heineken (both adequately chilled), six cases of name brand soft drinks (we preferred Coke and Dr. Pepper), French wine with dinner, and no fast food. Chicken dishes were acceptable with prior approval (well you don't want chicken every night do you?) but steaks, prime rib, Lasagna, or seafood was the best. Now understand that the crew almost never drank beer during the day (the band would from time to time) and we rarely finished all the Perrier or soft drinks. What I would come to find out is that one of the ways to make "mo' money" on the road was to store up supplies like a pack rat. Every night we would strip the dressing room of anything left over that was eatable, and certainly anything in bottles or cans. They would be stored in the motorhome and used as needed during days off, etc. This brings me to Karl's Roadie Rule # 7 "Have your salary sent home, live off your per diem." You don't need much money on the road (unless you have a drug habit more on that next tour) so like many of my road-mates I never saw a paycheck on tour, they were sent to my bank and deposited. We all lived off our "per-diem". Per Diem is Latin for per day. The IRS allows you to receive a certain amount each day for food and incidental expenses since you are traveling. You don't have to report it as income (since you theoretically spend it every day) and the company gets to deduct it since it's a true expense to them. The reality was that since most of your food was taken care of, the per diem money was extra tax-free income and was figured in as part of your pay from the time you signed on. At the time I started this tour I believe the IRS per diem rate was $20 per day. That meant I had $140 a week in pocket money, if I could find my meals in the dressing rooms, or in the refrigerator of the motorhome.

I almost forgot, we've got a show to do.

The Ann Arbor kick off show started right on time (as most Ponty shows did). The opening act was good, but did nothing to curtail my apprehension about the potential excitement level that a jazz-rock band led by a violinist could attain. After a short break The Jean-Luc Ponty band took the stage.

The stage was black as I helped the band to their spots. My Kel-light at the ready, illuminating the safe passage through the maze of cables and connectors. Unlike that Blue Öyster Cult show so long ago, there was no fog machine, no roadie with a flashing red lights on his head, there wasn't even a single flash pot. There was however, excitement.

Jean-Luc hit the first cord as the band joined in simultaneously. I was expecting soft jazz, fall asleep jazz, jazz your parent's love jazz. What I got was what I would later hear Jean-Luc refer to as "Classical Jazz Rock". It was powerful, it was compelling, and it was really quite loud. I knew that sound check had not been anywhere near this loud, so I compensated with more gain before anyone could ask. Even so I immediately scanned the stage for the band's body language, or any hand signals that would indicate if the monitors were acceptable. Everyone seemed OK, so I watched and waited. At the end of the first song Daryl (who was stage left nearest to me) came over and asked for just a little more violin. By the second song Stevie motioned for me to come over. When I got to the kit he also asked for just a little more violin. My only other request that night was later on when Jean-Luc asked me to turn the drums down a little in his monitor, and add just a little more violin. I was learning my first lesson with the Jean-Luc Ponty band, "Keep the violin on top". What that means is that with every instrument being equal, the violin needed to be just a little more equal or "on top" of the mix so there was never any doubt as to who's band it was. It is similar to a singer's voice being "on top" of a pop song. The drums, guitars, and keyboards are as important, but the vocals are the most prominent. Since we didn't have any vocals, the violin was the most prominent.

The show consisted of virtually the entire "Enigmatic Ocean" album, and selected cuts from the previous albums. The music was powerful and deep, I don't know how else to describe it. It's like the difference between a stream and the ocean, they both consist of moving water, but one's deep and the other isn't. This music told tales without words. Consider the suite "The Struggle of the Turtle to the Sea". There are three parts (totaling over 13 minutes) that is better at describing the agony of the hatching turtles from their eggs, the mad dash across the sand to avoid being eaten by the awaiting predators, and finally the satisfaction of the survivors reaching the relative safety of the Ocean.

The way the band complemented each other was amazing. Jamie's guitar and Jean-Luc's Barcus Berry violin are almost indistinguishable on the opening songs "Overture and "Trans-Love Express". Daryl's first solo during "Trans-Love" proved on a nightly basis that he could be a great rock guitarist if he chose that route. During the entire song the backbeat was maintained by Ralphe on the bass and Stevie on the drums. Flawless.

Then there were songs like Mirage, which (instead of putting you to sleep) would take you to an incredibly calm place. I never measured it but I'm sure everyone's blood pressure dropped during that song.

Then there were the solos. Every song had one or two built in, and Jean-Luc graciously shared the spot light for a minute or two with every other band member. It became clear to me that not only Jean-Luc, but also his band had big followings. As each member would take a solo the crowd would erupt with appreciation, especially for Ralphe.

Ralphe Armstrong was one of the youngest members of the tour, and had been with Jean-Luc for years. He was a very large black man that reminded me of "Rerun" on the Cosby kids, instead of possibly the best electric bass player I had ever heard. One of Ralphe's gimmicks was to transform his Gibson bass guitar into world war three by use of an effect pedal. During his solo in "Struggle", he would step on that pedal completely change the sound to something that resembled a dying elephant screaming out in pain, and at the same time boost the volume to several times louder than it had been a split second earlier. This caught me off guard once, this first and only time. Everything on my board overloaded, and I thought for sure I had witnessed a complete destruction of the monitor system. Karl's Roadie rule #11 "Never under estimate the value of dumb luck." The system survived, and I never again missed that cue (now that I knew about it) when Ralphe stepped on that pedal.

Jean-Luc had some effects too; none as thermonuclear as Ralphe's pedal but just as attention grabbing. He used a device called an echoplex, which allowed him to replicate his notes and make it sound like there was two or three violinists playing simultaneously. This was especially impactive on Jean Luc's solo song entitled "No Strings attached". By the time he was at the finale crescendo it sounded like there was a complete orchestra instead of just one Frenchman. There were drawbacks to the echoplex though. It was state of the art when he started using it but by this tour it was not the latest thing available. The echoplex was really just a tape loop, that repeated over and over so you could record a few notes and they would playback, the tape would loop around, the notes would play again, voilá, a delay. The problem was that the quality of the tape was always in question. If it degraded it didn't sound live, it sounded like a bad tape recording. The heads of the unit had to be cleaned and demagnetized constantly. I made a mental note to talk to Jean-Luc about a new invention when I got the chance. A manufacturer named MXR had started using computer chips to temporarily store the electrical impulses digitally, causing a delay without any tape. As soon as I had some credibility with him, I would suggest he try one.

The crowd at this first show started slow at the beginning of the show and built intensity song by song and was finally whipped up into frenzy by the first encore. Although I had no way to know there that night in Ann Arbor, I was to see this fanatic devotion to Jean-Luc and his genre of music over 200 more times during the next two years.

After his trademark encore of "New Country", (Ponty's closest thing to a mainstream hit although it sounded more "country" than jazz, hence the name) and a long standing ovation, we loaded the truck. This was no small task since this configuration of gear had never been together before tonight. I became the truck loading specialist. I guess I volunteered, but I don't specifically remember doing that. Fred loaded his bike (with our help) and he headed for the second show. We all piled into the "Tarantula" (the motorhome) and headed there too. It seemed like it would take forever to get to Las Vegas, which was to be the last show on this tour. One member of the crew wouldn't make it to Las Vegas; he didn't even make it to Nebraska.

In hindsight I should have bought Russell (the light guy) a copy of Dale Carnegie's book, "How to make friends and influence people", because he lacked both of those skills. One person that Russell got on the bad side of quickly was Joe, the band roadie with seniority. I don't want to say Joe was a hot head, but today when I hear about someone in California killing another driver on the freeway because he got cut off in traffic, I always wonder if that might be Joe. With that said Russell had a chip the size of a grand piano on his shoulder, and Joe was just the guy to knock it off. Louie wasn't real fond of Russell either, but working with butt-heads sometimes came with the job. Louie was pretty easy going but Russell could get under his skin. Russell had his opinion about the lights and that opinion should be good enough for everyone else too. The fact of the matter was that besides interpersonal difficulties, it turns out Russell wasn't a very good light man. His Waterloo however, was not helping with Tarantula. He wouldn't drive or clean up the motorhome. Since he wouldn't drive, that meant more drive time for the remaining five of us, not a good way to endear you to others. Joe got into it with him several times about little meaningless things, and the lights didn't get better. During the first break (a few weeks into the tour), Russell didn't return, he had been replaced. It turns out Joe had told Ponty that if Russell was back he would quit. Joe was still at the top of the crew food chain (and importance) so Ponty had Pat fire Russell. The replacement was way worse. Steve was an overweight "lighting designer" from New York. His lights were better than Russell's was but this guy was just weird. He would lay in his bunk and chant "mantras" (I wish I were kidding). He also wouldn't drive Tarantula, and we really didn't want him to. He didn't last very long at all. We dropped him off in New York City between gigs in Raleigh North Carolina and one in Connecticut. Then a wonderful thing happened, they gave Louie his shot.

I guess they were out of choices but Pat told him that if he did well the next few shows he could finish the tour as "Lighting Guy". Now Louie was no slacker, he had been paying attention to what the first two did. He watched what they did right and what they did wrong. He listened to the daily input from Jean-Luc, Pat and of course Joe, and mentally absorbed it all. When he was given his chance, he was ready.

He already had a lighting design planned using the available tools. He also now knew all the songs. On that first night in Connecticut he executed flawlessly. He won the job for the remainder of the tour. We still needed another warm body, and we added a friend of Joe's that helped Louie set up the lights, and guess what else? He drove the motorhome!

Rosie

◆

What I didn't know in October of 1977 as we were doing shows in Florida, was that Jackson Browne had released the definitive "Road" album. "Running on Empty" was a monster hit with road oriented songs such as "Stay", "The Load-Out", "The Road" and what would become and still is my favorite "road" song…"Rosie". If you have this album (or CD) please put the book down right now and listen to "Rosie". Now with the lyrics in mind here's my true story. I will insert the lyrics during the story, so that you can identify any similarities. Remember that although the song was recorded in September, I didn't hear this song until after my first JLP tour was finished in mid-December.

At a show in Florida (I think it was in Gainesville), we got to the load-in and there was a beautiful dark haired girl hanging out near the stage door. Julie was a student from the school that was sponsoring the show that night, and she was extremely friendly. After some interesting small talk, and her patiently waiting for me to unload the truck, I asked her if she was going to the show. She didn't have a ticket but she'd like to go. I offered her a backstage pass and a seat next to me on stage for the show. She gratefully accepted.

She was standing at the load-in when the trucks rolled up.
She was sniffing all around like a half-grown female pup.
She wasn't hard to talk to, looked like she had nowhere to go.
So I gave her a pass so she could get in to see the show.

She hung on my every word that afternoon, watching my every move. She wanted to know everything about my job, how the monitors worked, everything. We were really hitting it off, she was attractive, intelligent, and she really seemed to like me! The show started and she sat very close to me for the whole show. I got her one of our 144 available Heinekens, which she gratefully accepted. I expertly mixed the monitors that night; half showing off for Julie, half hoping the band would notice this babe sitting at the board with me.

Well I sat her down right next to me while I got her a beer.
While I mixed that sound on the stage so the band could hear.

At the end of the show she was asking questions like, "What are you doing after the show?" and "Where are you guys staying tonight?" I figured I was "in". About then the show ended and the band was filing past us, headed to the dressing room. She nudged me and asked for an introduction to Steve Smith, the drummer. "Sure, hey Stevie, I'd like you to meet my friend Julie." "Hi Julie", Steve replied, "want to party with the band?" "Sure, Let's go", her words struck deep into my heart like a serrated dagger. I never saw her again.

The more I watched her watch them play, the less I could think of to say.
And when they walked off stage, the drummer swept that girl away.

Well I guess I might have known from the start, she'd come for a star.
Might have told my imagination not to run so far.
Of all the times that I've been burned, by now you'd think I'd have learned.
That it's who you look like, not who you are.

But Rosie you're alright—you wear my ring, when I hold you tight—
Rosie that's my thing

When you turn off the light—I've got to hand it to me
Looks like it's me and you again tonight, Rosie.

So we went back to the hotel, just me and Rosie.

As humiliating as the whole incident was, the final insult came the next day at sound check. Steve (who was having a contest with Jamie to see which one of them could attain the highest "body count" during the tour), came up to me and said, "Hey Karl, I want to thank you for Julie last night." "With all the girls I've been with, she was THE BEST I'VE EVER HAD." "She was wild, hell, she was into things I can't even describe in the English language." "Thanks again buddy."

I didn't eat any dinner that night, for some reason I had no appetite.

By the way the Jackson Browne "Running On Empty" album was a great tribute to "The Road" and his road crew. We heard after the tour he decided to take a hiatus, and laid off the entire crew. So always remember, Karl's Road Rule #2 "Never work directly for a band."

A Day in the Life

◆

Ever wonder what a typical day in the life of a Roadie is like? Well, actually that's a trick question since there is no such thing as a typical day for a Roadie; there are, however, average daily events. Let's start your roadie day about midnight in Cincinnati. The doors to the trailer are shut and locked, and everything has been stripped from the Taft Theatre's dressing room. A final check of the stage to verify nothing of value has been overlooked, you say goodbye to the union stage crew, and everyone piles into the motorhome. The system for determining who drives is an inexact science that combines shrewd negotiation, assessment of each roadie's current fatigue, and in some cases blatant bribery. Sometimes it was as easy as someone volunteering.

You feel good so you volunteer to take the first shift. No one argues. You are now leaving the deserted downtown streets of Cincinnati and you need to travel 622 miles to be at the stage door of The Morris Stage in Morristown New Jersey by noon (a mere 12 hours from now). A few minutes earlier you had asked the Union Electrician what the easiest route out of town was so you head towards his landmarks. The lights are all blinking yellow in unison for as far as you can see and there is a fine mist coming down to force the use of the windshield wipers. Just enough moisture to obscure your view but not enough to irrigate the grime in the path of the blades, you respond by treating the glass to

some windshield Visine. You find Highway 71 and head North for
Columbus.

A Co-Pilot is not a luxury that can be allowed. Sleep for everyone not
in the driver's chair is mandatory. You have two Dr. Peppers in the cup
holders within your reach, and the CB radio is turned down very low
with the squelch set very high, so that you won't accidentally wake up
your mobile roommates. Aerosmith plays softly, as well, but it's hard to
hear due to the static. The beat of the wipers eventually matches the
beat of "Dream On" and then continues past it to go out of sync. You
settle in for a long drive. Luckily you are alert but you know that's not
likely to last. If everyone drives his share it would equal about two hours
each. That's not very likely either. It's just like that scene in "Platoon"
where Charlie Sheen finishes his watch and tries to wake up the next
guy. If you can't get the next guy up, you stay on watch (or in this case
you keep driving). If there aren't any headwinds you can get about 500
miles without a refueling stop. You end up driving for four hours before
you finally pull over.

In the rest stop one of the band roadies comes up and relieves you of
the keys. You buy a Baby Ruth bar from the machine and inhale it with
three bites. You'd really like a Butterfinger too, but you don't have
enough change (the machines back then didn't take dollar bills). You
quickly get back on board since you are always paranoid about being
accidentally left behind at a rest stop. Every roadie has heard the stories
of a crewmember left behind, and not discovered until hours later.
Safely inside you remove your T-shirt in preparation for slumber, and
for the first time tonight you catch a whiff of how bad you really smell.
You really need to find a shower tomorrow. You think The Morris Stage
has one in the dressing room, but you can't really remember. The
shower in the motorhome is of course out of the question. Potable
water is too precious to use in mass quantities like that, and besides
there are seven cases of Heineken stacked up in there right now. As the
Motorhome lurches forward being dragged by the headlights, you

scientifically checkout the condition of the driver. "You OK?"…"Yup".
Now that you have satisfied yourself that he isn't going to nod off at the
wheel, you crawl into your bunk. A split second later you wake up in
New Jersey. You wonder if we had acquired a warp engine during the
night. No warp engine, but somehow the Motorhome had successfully
found its way through Columbus and Pittsburgh and finally to
Morristown. You had garnered about six hours of sleep; it seemed like
six minutes. You ask the light guy, "what time is it?" "11:45, (15 minutes
to load-in)". You grab a semi-clean T-shirt, put your steel toes back on,
and head for the stage door with your toothbrush in hand. Finding a
sink, you scrub your teeth and consider yourself lucky since you
remember the times you had to use warm Perrier to rinse the foam
from your mouth. You grab a half a turkey sandwich off the deli tray
and woof it down. You pop a Coke and head for the dock.

Time to go to work.

You get to the stage door in time to see Fred backing the rig. He
almost always got it backed on the first try; it was sort of a pride thing
with him. It takes him twice today; he must be in bad shape after that
eleven and a half-hour drive. You unlock the doors, fold them back and
lock them to the box. Fred backs up the final ten feet. As the stage crew
gets their final swigs of coffee and finish the last bites of donuts, you
assess the stage. Loading dock, good local crew, and no surprises on
stage (you've played this hall at least twice before that you remember). It
will be your job to go in the box and direct the unload, you ask a familiar face from your last visit if they have a shower. "Yeah, there's one in
the dressing room" comes the welcome answer. You start to move the
first of over 100 various sized road cases that need to disembark. The
cases almost all have oversized castors, but many are very dense and
heavy and they do not move without a struggle. The stage crew inte-
grates with the roadies as the cases flow out towards the four corners of
the stage. Orders are barked out in shorthand "down stage left", "upstage
center", or "stage right stack." The local crew is fluent in this form of

communication, as the cases take their appropriate locations. The stage begins to resemble a large zig saw puzzle just after the pieces are removed from the box. The entire truck is off loaded in about 30 minutes, and then the fun starts.

The locals pair off with the sound, light, or band roadies as the orchestrated chaos begins. The PA stacks are one of the first things to go up so that they will clear the stage for the light rig assembly. You build the base of the PA carefully checking the stability of each cabinet, applying a strategic nail where needed. As the pile gets bigger you climb on top to pull the horns up to the top. The speaker cables around your neck are connected one at a time to each speaker as the other end hits the stage to be connected later on solid ground. As the stage right stack takes shape you are thrown large two by fours (spray painted flat black) one at a time, so you can prop up the front edges of the horns, aiming them at the various nooks and crannies of the balcony. Gravity is the primary tool used to hold the stack together, since any nails used will cause delays later when the stack is disassembled. After you are satisfied that the stack is aimed correctly (and stable), you repeat the process stage left. As soon as your speaker cabinets aren't in the way the light guys start to build the grid. Two large aluminum trusses are bolted together with quick release pins. The Genie towers are positioned at the Four Corners of the grid and the trusses are attached to the towers. Large electrical cables are connected; par lights that had been carefully housed in the protective confines of the square truss are lowered out of their perch so they are free to be aimed later. The two trusses are connected together with aluminum beams forming a large square structure. Once everything is ready four men simultaneously crank the four towers lifting the structure to a height of about twenty feet. While the PA and lights are going up another small group of crew has moved the sound and light boards out to the house. Each of these pieces of equipment weighs about 500 pounds, is very fragile, and can be worth up to $25,000. A spot in the audience has been chosen by the promoter (per your contract) to be roped off for use by the two engineers. Frequently they have not blocked out enough seats or the spot is totally unacceptable. Since you have final say on this matter, you change the location and let the promoter's rep know that he will have to move 24 ticketed fans come show time. He protests, but it's not your problem. Several small cases holding equalizers and effects are placed next to the boards, and the "snake" is unwound off its large reel on stage making it's way up the aisle to connect the mix with the stage. Within a few minutes a race between the roadies that are on stage wiring the sound and connecting the lights ends up in a dead heat with the roadies in the house connecting the boards. It will soon be time to fire up the PA, and start checking lights. One of them is on the very top rung of an "A" frame ladder, the other one at the board bringing the faders up one by one. Another roadie starts marking the stage with black gaffer's tape, performing the role of stand-in, so the lights can be directed at the imaginary band members. Hand signals are used to aim the lights and prompt the movement to the next fader control. Shouting doesn't usually work because the PA is about to awaken. You pop your cassette (you always use the same one) into the portable deck. You slowly turn up the bass cabinets first and the muffled sounds of rock and roll (at least the parts below 800 cycles) shakes the room. Everything sounds OK so far, so you bring up the mids, now the hall fills with Mick Jagger singing your favorite test song "Shattered" "Look at me! I'm in tatters....shattered." Now the highs, the music crystallizes and takes form, "Go ahead bite the big apple, don't mind the maggots!" Now that the copper coils deep inside the magnetic housings have begun to warm up you can safely bring up the gain. You need to check for acoustic problems in the room so you open it up and walk the hall. As quickly as possible you run to the back corners, walk the width and breath of the hall to check the evenness of the mids and highs. You rush to the balcony (time counts here because taking too long could piss off the stage crew). You check the angles of all the mid range and high frequency horns visually, but mostly with your ears. A second song replaces the Stones; it's Jeff Beck's "Blue Wind", no vocals, but music closer to the type being played tonight. You finish your walk before Jeff can finish, satisfied that the PA is ready for action. By this time your partner who is on the stage has fired up the monitors. No music here, he's airing them out, looking for feedback. "Check one, two, Tesssssssssst three four, sssssssheck one two, tessssssssssssssst, three four." "Sssssssssssssssssssssssssss, tesssssst, sh sh sh scheck, one two." {There is actually a point to all this inane chatter, he is looking for any problem frequencies that could trigger feedback during the show, and an "sss" or "ch" sound can commonly cause them} As he finds offending hot spots on the audible frequency spectrum, they are quieted using equalizers and parametrics. By now the lights are done and the band roadies take over. Now that the stage has some breathing room, the band gear is brought out from the wings where pre-assembly had taken place. Everything is placed on its mark (the black gaffer's tape) so that the lights will find their targets during the show. Concurrently the monitor guy starts micing the gear, hooking mic cables to small snakes on the stage that are connected to the main snake running out to the house. By sound check every mic will be connected to the control board in the house, so that you can control the level and characteristics off every single mic on stage. The stage mix has a split of all the mics so he can control them separately on stage as well. By now the nine foot Baldwin needs to be put up (did I forget to mention that we carried a nine-foot Baldwin Grand Piano with us?) After removing its Anvil case protecting its black lacquer finish, it ends up on its spine, perpendicular to the stage. Two of the three legs are attached (one front and the rear one), and we prepare for more of your volunteer work. You can't remember how you got this task, it probably just happened because nobody else would do it. After a detailed briefing with the stage crew, and only with a roadie or two that you trust mixed in, six to eight men tip the Grand Piano forward towards the audience. They catch it when it gets nearly

level, resting on the two legs. You now get on your back, with the third
and final leg in your hand, and with a corner of a Grand Piano
(weighing as much as a small car) hovering above you, you calmly
attach the leg. When you finish, you scamper out of the way and they
set the last corner down gently on its new support. The pedals are then
attached (which is much lower drama). You call out to see if the piano
tuner is there. {An interesting side note is that many of the piano tuners
we ran across were blind. I actually preferred them since they were very
fast and very accurate, so I requested a blind tuner whenever possible)
Sound check is about 15 minutes away as the notes are adjusted one by
one, while you pet the guide dog. The band roadies are tuning the
guitars using oscilloscopes and pignose amps. The band gets there a few
minutes early and wanders around getting in the way. The Road
Manager rounds them up and takes them to the dressing room so your
crew can finish.

Your thoughts are on just one thing, a shower. It will have to wait at
least another hour.

The tuner is finished for now (he will be back just before showtime
to re-tune it) so is your new friend "Mozart" the Belgium Shepherd. The
band roadies are done and the band starts filtering out to the stage.
What follows is about 15 minutes of complete confusion as the musicians that haven't touched their precious instruments in over 16 hours
get reacquainted. The drummer beats, then adjusts, and then beats his
drums again. The guitarists play scales, and the keyboardist tunes and
programs synthesizers. Eventually the organized sound check gets
started.

You sit in the best seat in the house, mic in hand (it's wired to the
stage mix, so everyone on stage cannot only hear you, they can hear you
breathe). The drummer's check comes first, so you say "Right Kick" in
your mic. The drummer steps on the pedal of the bass drum about once
a second. You bring up that mic (you prefer Sennheisers 451 mics for
the kicks) and adjust the tone of it to get the most out of the acoustics of

the hall. Since the kick drum is the foundation for most of the music, a lot of time is spent getting it right. You repeat the process for the Left Kick (Yes, in case you were wondering he has a bass drum for each foot). You move on to the snare, another critical piece of the mix. Next you ask for the hat (high hat symbols) and then for the kick, snare hat combo. Now you are starting to build a mix based on the levels of the mics relative to each other. The process continues until you have the whole kit. On this tour that means 12 separate mics, all deliberately positioned with booms and goosenecks to be in the optimum position to give you the best sound without interfering with the drummer's field of battle. Next the bass guitar, only two channels here. All the electric instruments have a direct input (electronically pure sound, the same as what is being sent to the amplifier on stage) and a mic on the amplifier itself. This mic picks up the altered sound caused by the amplifier and speaker's interpretation of the electronic signal being sent from the pick-ups in the guitar. These two sources can be very different, and can vary in quality. An example is that sometimes for no apparent reason the direct signal may have a bad hum, or the mic may be feeding back. When both are working perfectly you find that a mixture of the two is the most pleasing to the ear. That is what you work on now, mixing the two channels in proportion to each other, and adjusting their characteristics to get that "Ralphe" sound. After Ralphe lets loose with his effect pedal (you only allow him to do it once during check so you can gauge a safe level) you ask Stevie and Ralphe to play together. This is critical. You have to get this sound right since it's the foundation for everything else that happens on stage. You repeat the process with both guitars and the keyboards, meticulously equalizing the level of each individual instrument to be heard without overpowering any other instrument. The last piece before the violins is the grand piano. The nine foot Baldwin is a challenge to accurately mic. You need precision and a degree of volume. You have found that a small condenser mic wrapped in acoustic foam placed in the largest of the holes on the sounding board does a good job of capturing the lower frequencies. The highs are collected by a mic suspended over the short strings on a boom mic. It takes some tinkering to get it right every night, but you are very familiar with the big black monster, and you get the right sound in less than ten minutes. Jean-Luc takes center stage (he's been out in the house next to you offering suggestions up until that moment). He puts each of four different colored violins through their paces. He plays several snippets from the songs that will certainly be played during the up coming show. His final chore is to check the effects rack, using the echoplex to multiply the apparent number of instruments to several dozen. He barks at the band roadie that the sound is "dull", and Joe grabs a bottle of denatured alcohol and proceeds to clean the heads. "That's better", he says, as he calls for the whole band. The whole band plays one song ("Trans-Love") and then retires to the green room.

No time to eat yet, there's an opening act tonight, and it's a big one. Ambrosia (remember them from Buffalo?) has been booked to open the next three shows. Unlike some opening acts that have two or three mics, this band will require moving and readjusting all 24 channels. Also this band has vocal mics and will undoubtedly need some monitor gain. You take out your pocket notepad and deliberately note the setting of every knob on the ADM board. Each channel has 6 different controls and there are 24 of them, then there are the main EQ controls, grand total approximately 175 numbers to be recorded and reproduced during that change-over between bands. Your partner is striking the mics while the band roadies move the JLP gear out of the way. Ambrosia's roadies set up in front, and the negotiation starts. "Can you move the grand off stage?" "No, it'll go outta tune, how about you set up in front of it?" A compromise is soon struck where the Grand is rolled back far enough to allow the opener's keyboard stack to be assembled in front of it without sacrificing the delicate tuning. Mics are moved; a new soundman takes his spot where you usually sit (you feel strangely like your territory has been violated) as he starts the same process you completed only 15 minutes ago. The check goes much quicker than yours, mostly because they are told up front they have 30 minutes to complete it period. They don't quite finish but are shooed off the stage by the promoter at 7.

Now you have to choose. You have one hour to eat or shower. You pick the shower since you've been grazing all day off the deli trays. The band will be sitting down to a nice home-cooked (catered) meal, so you can use the dressing room shower. You really hope there is hot water as you find a towel and a bar of soap. As the water warms you rinse off the bar of soap several times "just in case" since you never know who used it last. It takes several agonizing minutes, but the shower finally starts coughing up its warmest water. The soap, water, and body grime combine together forming a foamy dark liquid that spins down the drain. You start with your hair, since you aren't sure how long the hot water will hold out and that area of your body needs cleaning the worst. No shampoo, you ran out last week and haven't gotten around to re-supplying so you use the bar soap as a substitute. You hurry for several reasons. One if you are quick you may get some food. Two, there is a show to do in a few minutes and if they open the house the "cattle" will want to hear walk-in music. Three, and the most serious, you are highly vulnerable for road pranks in that shower. Butt naked and soaking wet, you could lose your towel and clothes, have cold water thrown in on you, or have some other humiliating thing happen that somebody just made up. You finish the blessed event without incident, dry off, get dressed, brush your hair, and head for the board.

The doors are about to open so in goes the Steely Dan tape. Not too loud, but loud enough to make the hall not seem too quiet. "Daddy don't live in that New York City no more", finds its way from the magnetic coding on the cassette, down the snake, to the amplifiers, all the way to the transducers in the speakers, which vibrate some air that moves into your ears vibrating little bones that cause your brain to recognize them as sounds.

You now get your first (and only) break of the day. It lasts about 45 minutes. You use the time to repair a bad mic cord that you identified yesterday (I know you thought you were on break, well this is as close to a break as you get). The soldering iron attains the magic temperature, and you apply a mil-spec {military specification} solder connection. After reassembling the XLR connector you test the repair with your VOM. The operation was a success. You flip the tape over. The house is now mostly full, as you notice it's about five minutes to eight.

You pick up the intercom headset and push the amber call light several times. The monitor guy picks up the other end and lets you know we're on schedule. The soundman for Ambrosia makes his way out to invade your turf. You yield your throne (but only temporarily) as you assume baby-sitting duties. You must ensure that the equipment is not jeopardized, and that Ambrosia doesn't use all the volume available (that's reserved for your band).

Now the first pay-off of the night, the house lights drop, the crowd cheers and as the stage lights come up to reveal Ambrosia, the sound of their first note reaches your ear just as your adrenal gland releases a miniscule amount of fluid into your system, causing a "chill" to go up your spine. Just like the shows you did with them less than a year ago, the band accurately reproduces eight of their popular recordings. The fans reward the artists with enough applause to warrant an encore. At the conclusion of the encore the stage fades into blackness and is replaced by the house lights coming up.

You regain your rightful place at the controls, pop a tape in, and begin painstakingly restoring the settings you had discovered earlier during sound check. You know that these are only the starting points, and that the attributes of the hall have changed in the last few hours. You complete the resetting of the board in about five minutes. A security guard takes your place as you head to the stage to see what's left to do. Ambrosia's gear is off stage left, they're going to go ahead and load out. That's OK with you, plenty of crew and it's not too cold out, so the door can stay open for a few minutes. Your partner has already set up most of the mics, as the band roadies move everything back to the designated locations. You adjust a mic or two on the kit and then toy with the high piano mic. Time to test each mic. One by one you either say "test" or "check" or tap on the mics in succession. The monitor guy raises his hand each time you successfully test the next mic. When you get to the 24th one, you head back to your board.

Now for the next fifteen minutes or so, you get to sit at the board and mentally prep for the show. Actually you are scoping the crowd, looking for bootleggers, checking out the babes, and trying to look cool. Sometimes people come up and talk to you. "How did you become a roadie?" (I should have told them to read my book someday), "Is Gene-Luck a nice guy?" (Actually it's Jean-Luc), "What's Jamie like?" (I need to remember that one, until I can check and see if Jamie's available tonight). You look down and your call light is flashing. You pick up the headsets and hear the road manager say "end of the next song". You mentally estimate that Donald Fagen has about 30 seconds left. He sings, "…don't take me alive" and the music fades. The house lights gasp, and go black; the crowd erupts in the blackness. A few barely distinguishable points of light flit around the stage as the roadie's flashlights maneuver the band to their lairs. The applause is broken as the voice of the road manager permeates the darkness from off stage. "Ladies and Gentleman, Jean-Luc Ponty!"

20,000 watts of colored light floods the stage as first notes find their way to the fans. This is your busiest few minutes of the day. You have to make changes quickly with no hesitation. You first raise the main volume, compensating for the cheering crowd. Then you make sure Jean-Luc's red violin in on top. It is. Add a little bottom to it and move to the drums. Plenty of kick, add a little snare, on to the bass. A little muddy, add some top, lower the gain just a tad, balance the guitars, where's the Arp?, add more keyboard, a little more, there it is. Back to the violin, still on top, tweak the mid range just a smidge. There! Perfect!!

You stay vigilant for the entire show. As the audience's ears get accustomed to one volume level you take advantage of the human bodies uncanny ability to sense an almost imperceptibly small volume change slowly and subtly increasing that volume during the course of the evening. It gives the effect of each song being just a little more powerful than the preceding one. You have every note of every song memorized and if anything is not right it registers immediately and you make the needed adjustment. It's a good show, the crowd is appreciative and you take a moment to smile to yourself, satisfied. The last song comes to an end, and Jean-Luc says, "Thank you for coming to our show, good night!!" and the band exits the stage. The house stays dark and the stage lights glow deep amber, barely on. The crowd continues to applaud, as the band regroups. About three minutes later (that seem like 30) the lights come back up as the band predictably returns. They react to Jean-Luc's head nod by breaking into "New Country", the recognizable hit off the album "Imaginary Voyage." The crowd claps to the distinctive country-jazz beat. The song comes to its conclusion too soon, and again he tells the crowd, "Goodnight". Again the lights dim but the house lights do not automatically come up. Here the fans have their own destiny in their own hands. If they respond with loud enough applause for the next minute or so, they will be treated to a second encore, but they have to earn it. Louie is under strict orders not to taunt the crowd using the stage lights, if they are to get the second encore they'd have to get it the old fashioned way. You look down and see your call light flashing, it's the road manager, "What do you think? do they deserve one more?" You look around the hall and see a young man with his shirt off standing on his seat working the crowd with his arms, urging them to not give up. "Sure, one more." You smile as the band takes the stage and does a song off the "Aurora: album. Now the show is truly over, you've only seen a third encore once, and that was at the Palladium in New York, the house lights bring everyone back to reality and "the cattle" file out of the exits.

You remain at the board, softly playing the Taj Mahal exit music, while watching the crowd disperse. The girl who asked about Jamie earlier comes up to you wanting to meet him. You found out he already had a "date", so you tell her to try again next time we're in town. Disappointed, she leaves without comment. (You and the crew have a long drive tonight, so trying to convert yourself to being her second choice has no value). The band equipment is already being put back into their corresponding road cases. The microphones have already been tucked in to bed for the night, and cables are being collected. As soon as a majority of the crowd is gone you kill the sound and tell the stagehands it's OK to kill the power. You secure the EQ rack, and with the help of the union steward you replace the lid on the main board and twist the latches shut. You leap up onto the stage and assess the progress. The PA starts to come down, so you grab your gloves, tag the biggest union guy to join you, and prepare to take residence in the nose of the truck (When exactly, did you volunteer for that duty anyway?). The last item off the truck eleven hours earlier becomes the first one back on. You build a wall of bass cabinets, and top it off with some cable bins. The union guy is considerably larger than you, and seems to enjoy seeing if you can keep up with him as you jointly throw the cases into place. After the "dance floor" is full (the raised area in the front of the box) the lighting trusses roll in. The cases are getting bigger now so the box fills up quickly now. Your partner is sending the cases in the right order, the wrong case in the wrong order would be a time consuming irritation that does not happen tonight. By the time the last case is loaded your new shower is pretty much spoiled. Fred nudges the truck forward about ten feet and you swing the doors shut. Padlock in place, you now need to help Fred put his bike back. With that done it's time to walk the stage and dressing rooms. Not much left tonight, more Heineken that we don't need. Why couldn't there be some bottled water for a change without any carbonation? You say goodnight to the Morristown crew and head to the motorhome. "Who's driving first?" the drum roadie asks. You stay quiet knowing that you drove at least twice as far as anyone else last night. Louie breaks the silence by saying, "I will". No one argues. You hit your bunk, and hope the warp drive is still in good repair. Midnight arrives to find you unconscious; the day is now officially over. Another one now begins.

Ode to Mary Jo

———————— ◆ ————————

Be careful what you ask for, sometimes you get it.

It was immediately after a show in Norman Oklahoma. I had left the stage and was out in the house boxing up the main board when Mary Jo came up to me and stood there like an orphan cat. She was tall, about my age, with long straight dirty blonde hair. A very good looking girl with a kind of country innocence. "Hi, that was a really great show." Her words were soft with a faint Oklahoma drawl. "Glad you enjoyed it" I replied, expecting the next words coming from her mouth to be, "What's Jamie like?" or "Can you introduce me to Steve?" but she said instead, "How's it like traveling with a band?" I was stunned. "Pretty cool, you outta try it," (I figured what the hell let's see where this goes). "I'd love to go on the road, how would a girl get to do that?" OK, this has got to be a sorority gag. "Well, (I was trying really hard not to laugh), if you really want to go you can be my guest". "Just go home and pack a bag, we'll be leaving for Dallas in about an hour." "Really?" she asked. "Absolutely". "OK, I'll be back." She ran out the front door.

Well I figured that was that, I went about the business of load-out. As we closed the doors to the trailer I turned around and there she was. She had changed into jeans and a T-shirt, and unbelievably she had an old bulging suitcase. "I'm ready to go." "What is that?" Joe asked angrily. "This is, uh…what's your name again honey?" "Mary Jo" "Oh yeah, this is Mary Jo, she's going to come with us tonight." I had just ventured into uncharted waters. We had never had this situation come up before, there was no precedent. Joe spoke, "It's OK if she comes but here's the deal, she sleeps in your bunk, (logical, there weren't any spares, and I really didn't mind), she keeps the motorhome clean at all times, and she finds her own way home, whenever that time comes." (Maybe I'm safe here, she'll never agree to this) "OK" she said as she boarded the Southwind RV. A few minutes later she asked which bunk was "ours", "this one" I pointed.

Now it would seem on the surface that I have wrangled a pretty sweet deal, a housekeeping sex slave for the remaining month of the tour, right? Not exactly. The bunks are all open and four grown men sleep within a few feet of each other, one sleeps on the floor and one drives, not really an amorous setting. Somebody else drove so I got into bed leaving my pants on (well the lights were all still on, give me a break) Mary Jo crawled in (fully dressed as well), and we fell asleep sandwiched together in that small bunk. By the next day Mary Jo was making friends with the other roadies. She especially took a shine to Louie. For someone so aggressive when she was booking passage, she was very discreet. To this day I'm not sure which roadies she slept with, (if any) but I do know that she never had sex with me. By day two she had already "adopted" me as her little brother, the kiss of death for a horny 21-year-old male. "I could never make love to you, you're too good of a friend." She must not have wanted to be friends with the band however, since she started spending a majority of her time with them. She would still return to the motorhome most nights for the drive to the next town (nobody in the band was fond enough of her to buy her plane tickets). She kept up her end of the bargain by keeping the motorhome clean, she even got the shower cleaned out and working. "Louie claimed that she took a shower with him in there to christen it, but I can't see how they both fit (although it's fun to try to imagine). Mary Jo even met my parents, she was with us when we laid over in Houston for two days and had Thanksgiving dinner at my parent's house (more in a later chapter). My parents never asked anything about Mary Jo, I don't think they really wanted to know. As we worked our way up the West coast Mary Jo made her move. It was Jamie. Roadie Rule #12 Always trust your first instincts. You see my first impression was correct; she had come for a star. What she had under estimated was Jamie's love of the chase.

The ironic thing was we were all getting pretty attached to Mary Jo; even Joe was warming up to her. The motorhome had never been cleaner. It was in Medford Oregon, at a show in a National Guard Armory. Jamie pulled me aside just before the show, and gave me the word. It would be up to me; after all I was the one that recruited her (although by accident). I was to ditch her tonight in Medford. I don't remember the show, but it probably wasn't too good since an armory isn't a state of the art venue, also I was a bit distracted. I knew what had to be done, the deal we had made with Mary Jo a mere two weeks earlier had to be enforced. I found her after the show, and told her the tour was over for her. She didn't argue, staring back at me. It was raining, and I set her suitcase out on the asphalt, and we drove away. I still remember her silhouette, back lit from the lights in the building, standing in the rain, motionless.

Surprising, this is not the end of the Mary Jo story. About a week later we were in Las Vegas staying at the Aladdin. We had just played the final gig of this tour in the Aladdin Theater. I was wandering around the casino lobby, looking forward to going home the next morning when I saw her. "Mary Jo, what are you doing here?" "I need to see Jamie," came the desperate answer. "He doesn't want to see you," I said trying (and failing) to sound compassionate. I just need to see him, he'll change his mind, please Karl, let me see him." That did it, Jamie would kill me but I would take her to him. As we walked towards Jamie's secret room number, I made small talk. "So how'd you get here?" "The promoter gave me a ride." The promoter? From Medford Oregon? That's a 900 mile drive! I started to ask her what she did to get a man to drive her 900 miles, and where exactly she had been for the last week, when I realized I had just answered my own questions. I mumbled something inane like "Oh, that was nice of him." We arrived at Jamie's room; you could see the excitement in her eyes. She must have really had it bad for him. I knocked on the door lightly, maybe he wouldn't hear me, and she would give up. Fat chance. After a long minute, the door swings open. Jamie is standing there in boxers. I start to explain that she forced me to violate his trust in me when I realized there was additional movement in the shadows. As they came into the light two completely naked girls came up on either side of Jamie. One of them kissed his ear and asked, "who's your friends?" Jamie said, "This is Karl, and this is Mary Jo, you guys want to come in? We're having a party." I shook my head no, and turned to walk away. Out of the corner of my eye I saw Mary Jo shrug her shoulders as she entered the room to join their party. The door closed, and I went back to my room.

I never saw Mary Jo again, but she sent me a letter or two after the tour. She had quit school and was working as a spot light operator at a local Norman club. She was hoping to become a roadie soon. Her unanswered letters eventually stopped, so I never found out if she lived out her dream by becoming a real roadie.

Bonnie Raitt's shower

—————————— ◆ ——————————

We did three shows with Bonnie Raitt on this tour. The shows were in Austin, Dallas, and Houston. Bonnie was big in Texas, probably bigger than we were. The management companies of both bands had previously worked out "an arrangement." Jean-Luc would headline the show in Houston, Bonnie would headline the Dallas and Austin shows and we would "open" those shows. Bonnie and her band were great to work with. The first night I noticed that the first case off their truck was a tiny anvil case. It was a cube about 10 inches on each side. I asked a band roadie, "What the hell is in the baby case?" "Cookies!" came the surprise answer as he opened it up and handed me an Oreo. The "cookie" case was always on the tail of the truck and they stocked it with various cookies that were always available for the crew and band. A very nice touch.

Bonnie was 28 when I met her, but she looked much older. She had that swatch of gray hair that gave her that "road hardened" (yet dignified) look. This was already her seventh year of touring, and she had recently released the "Sweet Forgiveness" album. The Del Shannon remake of "Runaway" was a big hit, and remains one of her flagship songs today. A good portion of her show was Rhythm & Blues. She had a small apothecary jar that she wore on one of her fingers, which allowed her to play "slide" guitar. Her big haired bass player, "Freebo," didn't seen to take anything seriously, except the music. He also doubled as the band's tuba player on certain songs. The shows with Bonnie were phenomenal. Half the crowd was there to see her, the other half to see Jean-Luc. Everyone at those shows got more than they paid for. I believe to this day that many of the R&B fans that came to see Bonnie, became JLP fans. I know that a lot of the hard core jazz rock fans that came to see us became Bonnie Raitt listeners. The other memorable thing for me was that for the first time (there would be others) my family got to see the show. The show in Houston was special for me. I was still living in Rochester and I hadn't seen my parents or younger brother in about a year. They came during the afternoon to the Houston Music Hall to hear the sound check. My brother was an aspiring drummer (still in high school at the time) and he was invited by Steve Smith to play his drums. Keith sat down and gave that drum set a workout. I don't think he mastered the double bass drums but he adapted to the amplified sound and the LOUD monitors behind him. Ralphe and Jamie joined him for a brief impromptu jam before Jean-Luc came out, and the real sound check started. I also regret not having enough snap to pop a tape into the cassette deck, to record Keith's moment in time.

The shows with Bonnie went by too quickly, but it's an encounter I had with her the day after the Austin show that I want to recount. After the day off in Houston for Thanksgiving, we traveled the three hours to Austin for the final show of this leg. We played the Paramount Theatre that was in the process of being restored. Because we had just had a day off, we didn't have rooms in Austin. The bands were both leaving the next morning, so we parked the RV in the hotel parking lot for the night. There was no big rush to leave town so we found ourselves relaxing at the hotel pool with most of the members of both bands. I struck up a conversation with a man I had seen with Bonnie for the last few days. I asked him what he did, thinking he was probably a record guy, production manager, or something. His answer caught me off guard. "I'm Bonnie's old man" "I don't do much of anything." "Oh," I shrugged. Nice work if you can get it, I was thinking to myself. About that time Bonnie came over and laid on a lounge chair wearing a tasteful swimsuit. We talked for what seemed like a long time, but it may have only been five or ten minutes. Typical road small talk. "Where are you headed next", "Who have you worked with lately", "How do you think the show went last night?"

Then with no warning, she threw me a curve ball.

"Did you boys have rooms here last night?" she smiled. "No Miss Bonnie, it wasn't in the budget." We've got rooms waiting for us tomorrow night in Tucson." I assured her. "Well, no offense but you boys are a bit ripe, would you like a shower?" Would I? Road Rule number 14 states, "Whenever given an opportunity to take a shower, do it." I wasn't quite sure what she had in mind, but I was able to compose myself long enough to say "Yes Ma'am."

She reached over and picked up a phone that I hadn't noticed up until that moment. It was on the wrought iron table next to her. She dialed the front desk and said, "This is Bonnie Raitt in room 162, please bring twelve bath towels, and several bars of soap to my room as soon as possible please." She then handed me her room key without any hesitation and said we could take as long as we needed for every one of us to take a shower. I quickly organized the crew (including our housekeeper Mary Jo) and cycled them through her shower one by one. I went last, and was amazed at the trust this woman had placed in people she had only known for a few days, and would likely never see again. Her jewelry and cash were laying out on the dresser; expensive clothes and instruments littered the room. I finished my shower and savored the extra thick hotel towel against my skin as I dried off. I took one last look around her deserted room, and returned her key to her at the pool.

"Thank you Miss Bonnie, that was very nice, the guys really appreciated it." "I hope we get to work with you again someday." "You're welcome, and I'm sure we will cross paths again sometime, the road's a pretty small place."

It may seem like a small thing to you, but in the more than 40 years I've been alive, that single act of kindness ranks as one of the nicest things anyone's ever done for me.

Bonnie however, was wrong about one thing, I never did see her again.

We headed for the next gig in Tucson.

There's no place like home

◆

I mentioned that we had a day off after the Houston show due to the Thanksgiving holiday. I knew my parents wouldn't mind, so I invited everyone to dinner at my parent's house. I'm sure it was quite a sight that day in the suburban Houston neighborhood when a 28 foot motorhome pulled up to the Kuenning house, and six roadies and a girl piled out of the side door. The first order of business was showers, number two was laundry. Between these two strains on the capabilities of the homestead, the water heater was warming water non-stop for at least 36 hours. My mother must have felt like a Frat Mom, but I'm sure she loved every minute of it. As she prepared the traditional turkey dinner with all the fixin's, the boys played basketball outside in the driveway. Joe was showing us how to "dunk" a ball (a relatively new development in the NBA that had been brought over from the recently disbanded ABA earlier that year). My brother's backboard was mounted on the front of the garage roof, and had just been repainted a pristine white by my Dad. The first time Joe went up to dunk, he shattered the backboard by accidentally grabbing the rim.

There were no other incidents at my parent's home that I can remember. I don't think they asked why Mary Jo was with us, but I'm sure they figured it out. Mary Jo was on her best behavior, and was in full "perfect little southern lady" mode. She helped my mother prepare and serve dinner, which I know was appreciated. Eventually all the food was consumed, all the clothes were washed, and everyone had taken at least two showers. It was time to leave. I said goodbye to my parents knowing it could be another year before I saw them again.

My parents still live in that same house, and my wife and I now live in the house next door. They no longer have to wait a year to have dinner with me; it's usually every Sunday.

Cultural Exchange

$\blacklozenge$

I forgot to tell you that we had exchanged motorhomes for this leg of the tour for a slightly larger one. "Tarantula" had been returned, and the new one was a 28 foot Southwind that we rented from a broker in California. It had served us well so far and now it was headed back towards its home across the desert. Besides Mary Jo we had an additional passenger. Steve Smith decided to travel by ground for a few days, the remainder of the band had flown to Tucson about the same time we were all taking showers in Bonnie's room. We had Steve all geared up to go across the El Paso border to Juarez. He wanted to see the "donkey show," which is Juarez lingo for visiting the red light district. Steve was just one of the guys during this part of the trip. He was not only a great drummer; to me he was also a great friend. We had a grand old time driving to El Paso. When we got near the border, we parked the RV and five of us walked across to another country. Mary Jo and several adventure adverse guys stayed behind.

Stevie, Louie, Joe, Larry, and I got into a cab and before we could say "sexually transmitted disease", he offered, "You wanna see donkey show?" "I take you best donkey show Mexico" "Young girls, big donkeys, you see, good show" "Yeah, we want to see the donkey show", I exclaimed confidently. The car was almost as old as I was. The upholstery was frayed, torn and completely gone in several spots (like where you sat). The smell was somewhere between week-old tequila and month-old air freshener. There was no fare meter—like everything in Old Mexico, the fare was negotiable. We pulled up to an old decrepit building that had no signage, no hint of a retail establishment: just a large heavy wooden door. We paid the driver (probably at least twice as much as we should) and opened the door to the "donkey show." Now we all knew was there weren't actually donkeys; we didn't want to see any donkeys anyway. We wanted some senioritas. We were greeted by a matronly old woman who took our drink order. "You want drink?" "Cervesa, tequila?" Steve started to order an ice water when I interrupted, "Cervesa fria, por favor" "in bottles" (I didn't know how to say bottles in Spanish, but I knew enough not to drink anything not in an unopened bottle). The beer eventually showed up (pre-opened and not so "fria"), they pretended not to understand about the unopened part. Oh well, maybe there's enough alcohol to kill anything that's in the water they used to dilute the beer. Anyway if things work out, the water would be the least of our public health concerns tonight. Along with the delivery of the beer came several ladies. Each one of them singled out their targets. Steve got a very good looking bottle blonde in hot pants and a pink halter top. I got a woman that was somewhere between two to three times my age. They all asked for us to buy them drinks, and then we could see the donkey show. I had warned the boys in the taxi that we would be subject to a non-stop monetary extraction tonight, but I figured this was a required step, so I held up one finger and said "uno." They all ordered mixed drinks that could have been iced teas just as easily as a whiskey and waters. After about ten minutes of uncomfortable silence, the one that spoke the most English said, "Time to see the donkey." Each girl (or older woman in my case) took their partner's hand and headed off for the hallway leading to the rooms. I tried to let mine down easy. "Look I don't want to go with you, you're too old. I want a younger girl, OK?" She pretended not to understand, and pulled my hand again. "Hey, no, not going, want girl, OK?" She said, "OK, I get young girl, very pretty, she be in room, you wait, OK?" Now we were getting somewhere. I went into the small room with no furniture except a small bed, no wall color, little light, and an unidentifiable, unpleasant smell. I sat there for quite a while waiting for the beauty queen I had been promised. A tall, skinny man with a skinny moustache showed up instead. "Inspectione!" he demanded. Oh, I get it, another reason to get my wallet out, "quando?" "Cinco Dollars" "Dos," I countered. "Cinco!" He was pissed now, so I gave him the five and dropped my drawers, he gave my prized possession a very quick glance to validate my healthiness (obviously a highly trained medical professional), and he left the room. The door finally opened, and a hand reached in and turned off what little light was left. She quickly came over to me and said in relatively good English "Twenty dollars," which I produced. As I sat on the edge of the bed, she went to work, and as my eyes finally adjusted to the light, I realized it was the same old woman from the sitting room. I can't believe I fell for the old "bait and switch, without the switch." Nothing left to do but finish as quickly as I could and get out of there before anyone saw who I was with. The good news was that the donkey show our cab driver had brought us to apparently was an "oral sex only" house. I closed my eyes and used all my powers of concentration and imagination to bring an end to this humiliation. A few minutes later she fled the room, having earned her money. As I was pulling up my pants, I realized she had covertly put a condom on me prior to the act. It made me mad at the time, but to this day I am grateful to her for that ploy. Now let's get out of here while we still had a shred of dignity left. About then I heard Steve shouting, "Hey come back here." This is not good, we are in a foreign country, at a whorehouse that we don't even know the address of, and Steve is picking a fight with a hooker. I entered the hall to see Steve, barely dressed, trying to convince the blonde girl to come back into the room with him. The inspection guy was now between the two of them, and suddenly seemed to speak and understand English pretty well. "You all leave now, or we call Police" "But I want to make love to her, she's so beautiful," pleaded Steve. The look on the face of the

young blonde girl with the black roots was a combination of indigna-
tion and a little fear. Steve looked at me and explained, "She just wanted
to give me head, I want her to screw me, hell, I'll pay her extra." Larry
and I grabbed him, and we all regrouped on the street outside. Into a
cab, and back to the border. The U.S. border guard asked, "anything to
declare?" For a moment I felt like saying, "yes, we all just did a stupid
and awful thing, and I want you to arrest all of us," but I contained
myself. The adventure was now over. None of us ever chose to talk
about that night again; it was supposed to be an exciting boy's night
out, a testosterone outing. If we were going to degrade a couple of
women, that would be OK, after all, we paid for the services rendered,
right? What really ended up happening that night was that we were the
one's that were degraded.

Back to the desert crossing.

Oil's well that ends well

———————◆———————

After the Mexican crossing we played shows in Tucson and then Phoenix. It was a short time after that I found myself taking the wheel of the RV. Now when we had enough gas, and we had foodstuffs and beverage, we would go into "cruise mode" as we headed to California. This is how "cruise mode" worked. On a long straight section of the road, the current driver would engage the cruise control (usually going about 70). Then he would move the seat back as far as possible. Now comes the tricky part. The "new driver" would slide in on top of the old driver almost sitting in his lap. The old driver would fall out of the seat to the floor, evacuating the chair for the new driver. Oh yeah, while this happened a third roadie (standing behind the drivers chair) was holding the wheel and watching the road. The entire event took a total of about three seconds after the roadie controlling the steering wheel said, "go!" The amount of time we saved by doing this maneuver instead of pulling over was probably a grand total of ten minutes a day. As careful as we always tried to be, this was very dangerous.

Kids, like many of the other things in this book, please, "don't try this at home"; it was an incredibly stupid thing for us to do.

Anyway, I now had the wheel, and we were streaking for the West coast. The road was flat and the weather was hot. Everyone was further back in the RV relaxing on this travel day. I noticed a noise coming from the motor. It was subtle at first but I could tell from my truck driving duties that what was probably going on was that we were a little low on oil and the valves were knocking. We probably should have stopped and checked the oil at that point, but an RV that couldn't stop for a driver change wasn't about to stop to check the oil if it wasn't mandatory.

I kept driving, after all this was a rental, it would be OK, and I'd give it a quart when we needed gas.

As you may have guessed we never made it to a gas station. It sounded like several firecrackers went off in succession under the motorhome, as the forward momentum died. About that time a piece of metal came up through the housing releasing heavy black smoke into the cabin. I urged the wounded hulk to the shoulder as we assessed the damage. The piece of metal that protruded from the hump between the two seats was a rod or a lifter or something that should still be safely inside the engine block bathed in oil. The engine was (to use a highly technical term) "blown." Joe was livid. Of course according to Joe, this blown engine was my fault, and I made that assertion worse when I mentioned that I had heard the engine complaining earlier and had chosen to ignore it.

We removed our belongings and left the Southwind RV on the side of that desert road. We rented a car and five of us crammed into it. The others were dropped off at an airport and got to fly to California to acquire a new mobile home. I was nominated to be in the rental car, partly because of my size (small) and my participation in our dilemma (large). We all got to the next gig without further incident. I think when we got back to California someone called the RV broker that had rented us the Southwind, and gave them its approximate location.

Important motoring tip: "Always check the oil."

Just for Openers

———————— ◆ ————————

On this first JLP tour we had the opportunity to work with many other fine artists besides just Bonnie Raitt and Ambrosia.

The Little River Band opened for us during several shows. They were promoting the "Diamantina Cocktail" album that included many of their now classic hits like "Happy Anniversary", "Help is on its way", and "Home on Monday." The Australian band must have been home sick since out of 9 songs on the album; three were about being away from home. In addition to "Home on a Monday, there was also, "Days on the road," and "Take me home." The Little River Band was a nice complement to Ponty, and they were received well by the jazz oriented crowd.

There was however, one very strange quirk about one of their guitar players. During the sound check of the first show we worked with them, I was confronted by that guitar player. In a heavy Australian accent he said, "How the hell do you expect me to perform with a black monitor?" "Excuse me?" I said, wondering if he was kidding. "All stage monitors are black, aren't they?" By now a crowd of roadies and artists had gathered stage left. I couldn't have guessed what was coming next if I had been born a clairvoyant. "If the monitor is black, the devil can jump out of it during the show and get me," came the stunning response. "I refuse to play tonight if I have to use this cursed monitor." After a short pause to compose myself I spoke. "What would it take to make this monitor OK to use tonight, should we paint it white?" I was biting my tongue so

129

hard I was afraid it would start bleeding. "That would be acceptable," came the unbelievable answer.

So there I was trying to conduct a sound check, and now I had to magically turn a flat black stage monitor with a black grill cloth into a pure white monitor with a white grill cloth. Luckily the local stagehands were able to help me out. They found some white enamel paint (it was going to take at least two coats), a brush, some turpentine, and they even found me some white fabric that seemed to be a loose enough weave that I could re-cover the speaker grill. It took all the available time leading up to the show, and the newly whitened speaker was still drying during the performance, but we got him his white speaker.

I am happy to report that to the best of my knowledge, the devil didn't get him that night either.

Another regular opening act on the tour was Larry Coryell. He played guitar, mostly acoustic, but sometimes electric. Larry had a Latin flavor to his guitar style, and is generally considered one of the top jazz guitarists in the world to this day. I never understood why Larry didn't get more notoriety; I guess it's just the nature of jazz musicians to go unnoticed by the masses. Along with being a great artist I always considered Larry to be a friend. I had many long talks about "nothing in particular" with him and I always circled the dates he was opening for us on my itinerary. He remains a force in jazz music today, as do his two sons Julian and Murali (whom I never had the pleasure of meeting, since they weren't born yet when I was a roadie).

In late 1977 there were on-going rumors that the 60's group "The Byrds" were going to get back together. Part of the fuel for that fire was the shows that were done by founding members Roger McQuinn and Gene Clark. In Portland and then again in Seattle, they opened for us, and it was a special treat. I was on stage mixing monitors as they did acoustic versions of "Feel a whole lot better," and "Tambourine Man." Roger even played his electric famous 12-string Rickenbacker for renditions of "Eight miles high," and "So you wanna be a rock and roll star."

The Byrds never did get back together again, largely due to David Crosby rejoining Crosby, Stills, and Nash and touring early in 1978. (I was lucky enough to see one of those CSN shows in Buffalo, although I didn't get to work it) What I didn't know when I was working with Roger and Gene, was that Gene was having an ongoing battle with alcohol abuse. Gene Clark died of apparent alcohol related health problems in May 1991.

How Much Wood Can A Woodchopper Chop?

$\blacklozenge$

I mentioned earlier that Steve was trying to add to his "body count" (during the "Rosie" incident). During that first tour, I learned of a common road game played mostly by band members (I suppose on big "mega-tours" the roadies played too, but I never saw it). Anyway, it was called "chopping wood", or "getting the wood", and both were code for "scoring with chicks". The way it worked was that points were awarded for having sex with any new girl. If the player had ever had sex with her previously (like on last year's tour) it didn't count. I don't think oral sex counted either, which was why Stevie was so upset down in Juarez. To keep up with your rivals, at least one conquest a day was almost a necessity. To overtake a front-runner a player had to employ twosomes or creative scheduling (one in the morning, one in the afternoon, and of course, one after the show.) Now let me also clarify that not every member of Jean Luc's band played, it varied from tour to tour. Jean-Luc himself did not participate, in over 170 shows, I never once saw him succumb to the desires of the road, a testament to his long and happy marriage to Claudia. On this tour the trophy (there was no actual trophy) would clearly go to either Steve or Jamie, the only two real participants. Zavod had pretty much dropped out, while (just like Jean-Luc) I don't think Ralphe or Daryl played at all.

Now there is a popular story that some rock bands (who shall go nameless, but they are the ones that demanded that there be no brown M&Ms in the dressing room) actually had colors and codes painted on the crowd control walls. After the show they would allegedly make contact with their favorites by telling the roadies to go give a pass to the brunette at "Blue 6" or the blonde at "Red 4." I do not doubt this happened, but we had a more subtle way of "selection." Directly after the show, the players who hadn't already found "the wood" (or stolen it from the monitor guy) would gather backstage near the monitor board, just as the crowd was dispersing. Then using the intercom system, hidden by the curtains, select from the small group of willing "lumber" that invariably gathered near the sound board. The sound man would then escort the "lucky winner" or "winners" backstage for their introduction to the band, and their subsequent addition to the wood pile.

I'm sure that to this day there is a housewife out there that 20 years ago had her special night with Jamie, or Stevie, or one of the thousands of road musicians, and remembers how she was "different" or "special" in some way. It reminds me of that sad Karen Carpenter song…

"Don't you remember, you told me you loved me baby?"
"You said you'd be coming back this way again, maybe."

About the worse thing the "wood choppers" had to worry about back in the late 70's was getting a dose of "the clap." "Safe sex" back then, if it was practiced at all, was employed to avoid any unwanted pregnancies. Today, faced with the reality of diseases like AIDS, HIV, HPV, Hepatitis B & C, and more, this kind of irresponsible behavior cannot be conducted by anyone, at any time, anymore, including famous musicians, or not so famous music fans.

California Dreaming

◆

So we crossed into California (my first time of many) and started to work the coast. LA was the adopted home of Jean-Luc, as it was for most of the other band members as well. Ralphe was from Detroit, Daryl from Wisconsin, Stevie from Boston, Jamie from Long Island, and I think Allan was from Mars or somewhere equally as strange. Everyone either lived in LA, or San Francisco, or spent a majority of their time here. Joe and Larry were from here as well, and this road was a familiar place to them. We played the Santa Monica Civic Center (a great venue). Prior to that show, we had a blessed day off, and were able to see one of the other crews (from my company) do a show with Janis Ian, at that same hall. We even had time to stop in Malibu, and I had my first ride at a new kind of "go-kart" track called "Malibu Grand Prix." I remember thinking how cool it would be if the concept caught on and we could get a fun place like this in Rochester. Next it was up to The Community Center Theatre in Sacramento, then a short drive to The Paramount in Oakland. There are Paramount Theatres all over the country, and they are all wonderful. If you are fortunate enough to have one in your town, and it's still open (or better yet if it's been restored), appreciate what you have, and treat them with the respect they deserve. They are vignettes frozen in time, most are very much like they were during the vaudeville days, and some have been declared historic landmarks. From Oakland we went all the way down to San Diego and did a show at the Civic Theatre. With a day off to travel we then drove the 1000 miles to Eugene Oregon. This was a college gig at the EMU ballroom (U of Oregon). Another Paramount was next in Portland (this is the first of the three shows Roger McGuinn and Gene Clark opened). It rained the whole time, per the town's reputation (sorry Oregon travel bureau). We then headed to Vancouver, British Columbia. Since we would have to clear customs we had to hurry since we didn't know how long the border would take. That next morning I was driving trying to make time, when someone woke up, and said they wanted to stop for breakfast. "We don't have time for breakfast, we're too tight on time!" Joe then woke up, and echoed the need for food, "pull in there" he demanded, pointing at a McDonald's. I was a little testy due to being awake the last few hours, so as I slowed to make the turn I decided to make a point. I would show everyone how displeased I was with this unwise stop. I didn't bring the motorhome to a slow enough speed to comfortably take the turn into the golden arches. The plan was to jostle everyone just a bit, as I turned too sharp. The best laid plans of mice and men go astray, and this morning was no exception. The entrance to the restaurant was not properly graded to easily accommodate a 28 foot motorhome traveling at an optimum speed. I hit it going about 15 mph. My point was made! The back end of the vehicle left gravity's grip, and most everything in the motorhome became airborne. As we landed, a horrible sound scraped the underbelly. Anyone not yet awake was now. We listed left, and then listed right, and settled down as our momentum waned. Joe got within an inch of my face and screamed obscenities at me…I guess I deserved it. No harm done, we didn't tip over, right? A blue trail in the parking lot answered that question. I had ripped a hole in the motorhome's sewage system. Again, no problem, we don't really use the john anyway and it's a rental, right? No such luck this time, Joe wanted it fixed.

We cleared customs and got to the gig on time. The load in at the Queen Elizabeth Theatre went better than could be expected. For the first time in a week we had about two hours to kill, time for a shower! Joe stood at the door to the motorhome and advised me that if I didn't fix the motorhome I'd be walking to Seattle. I became Mr. Goodwrench.

I assessed the damage that really wasn't too bad considering the violent impact. The offending hole was only about an inch square located in a 4" PVC pipe. I asked a stagehand if there was a plumbing store anywhere near the gig. There were no Handy Dan's or Home Depots back then but I did find a neighborhood hardware store about 3 blocks away. I figured if I bought a new piece of PVC pipe I could glue it into place replacing the old one. As I was looking at the sizes of pipe available a brainstorm came to me. I bought a one foot piece of pipe one size too big (4½") and a bottle of all weather cement. Then I talked the store into cutting the piece in half lengthwise. I then glued the half pipe over the top of the broken and slightly smaller pipe, using a liberal amount of glue. It worked! and it only cost me a few bucks. I was out of the "dog house" (or is that the "motor-dog house"?). Anyway we were on to Seattle, toilet in tact. For those of you in Seattle can you guess the name of the Theatre? That's right, another Paramount. I had an hour or so before the show and had a long talk with Roger McGuinn over dinner prior to the show. Like the conversation a week or so earlier with Bonnie, it was about nothing specific or important. We did the show, which I generally remember to be one of the best of the tour, and headed to Medford. It was soon to be "D-day" for Mary Jo. Jamie was becoming bored, and was losing the contest to Steve, due to Mary Jo's clinging. As covered in a previous chapter, we left the Armory, and left Mary Jo behind. We headed to the Civic Auditorium in Redding. Northern California is breath-taking, someday I may move there. After that show we had a five hour drive to Santa Cruz and a day off. We played the Delmar Theatre. Tom Petty had played here recently and a local artist had painted the Heartbreakers logo (off their debut album cover) on the wall near the load in door. The tour was almost over, and I was ready to go home. We had this show and one in Las Vegas, then home. I had a girlfriend waiting for me (I thought) back in Rochester, and I had made it through the entire tour without doing any drugs. Now drugs were not completely unknown to me, I had smoked some pot and hashish while in college, but I had always resisted coke and harder drugs. I guess I knew in my heart that if I tried cocaine just once, I would like it too much. This first big hurdle had been cleared. We left California, and headed to "Lost Wages".

Viva Las Vegas

———————◆———————

We negotiated the twelve hour drive to the land of a million slot machines and settled in for a day and a half off. The first order of business was laundry, our rooms at the Aladdin wouldn't be ready for several hours so we headed to downtown Las Vegas (away from the strip) and found a Laundromat. There was an adult bookstore next door, and slot machines beside the washers. I spent money on all three choices. We were ready to check into the Aladdin.

The hotel was magnificent by 1977 standards. The one armed bandits were all mechanical, and video poker hadn't been invented yet. The drinks were free if you were gambling (and who wasn't). Then we got the best news a roadie at the end of a tour could get. There was a concert tonight at the Aladdin Performing Arts Center, we were invited (as VIPs), and the artist was going to be "Queen". We kept our eyes peeled for signs of the band all day. Finally that afternoon I saw Brian May and Roger Taylor in the lobby. They walked right by me, Roger slowed up to read my T-shirt (It was a JLP shirt of course) Once he realized I was with Jean Luc I was sure Brian and him would stop and engage me in a stirring conversation about road life or groupies or something. He looked rather disappointed by my shirt and kept walking. I thought about saying something like, "I've got passes for your show tonight, I'll see you blokes later!" Fortunately, my roadie etiquette kicked in and my mouth stayed shut. I spent the rest of the day and about a hundred dollars of my "per diem" on slots.

Some of the band went backstage but Louie and I found our seats in the house. Queen hit the stage and I saw one of the most memorable shows I have ever seen. It was the beginning of the "Jazz" tour. This was new material for Queen, including "Fat bottomed girls," and "Bicycle Races." Of course they were still exploiting the success of the "News of the World" album and I joined thousands of fans stomping and clapping to "We will rock you." Freddie had lost the long hair of Bohemian Rhapsody days, sporting an ultra short hair style. He worn skintight hot pants and no shirt which didn't do anything for me, but I'm sure it was a big hit with the female fans. It was a great show, by a great band, in a great theatre, the perfect way to end a tour. Instead of going back to my room I went to the casino lobby. I had already lost about a hundred bucks (a lot of money for a $25 a day roadie) so I walked around and watched the seasoned citizens feed the machines. After an hour or so (it was about 2 AM now) I noticed that the crowd had thinned out, but the slots were starting to pay out more often. A woman that looked a lot like Mrs. Robinson in the Graduate that had one too many Rob Roys told me it was because the casino loosened up the slots during the off hours to encourage the customers to stay up all night. It sounded good to me so I started playing the dollar slot (three dollars each pull!) Believe it or not, I hit three jackpots within about a five minute period. I now had recovered my originally lost "C" note, and had built up about $300 in profit, almost instantly. Happy ending you ask? No such luck. Now I had consumed several complimentary rum & cokes, so greed set in. I continued to play those slots for hours and as the sun was coming up I broke even. Actually I was just broke. Maybe Mrs. Robinson was right; I had capitalized on the late night/early morning easy slots, and then, just like Cinderella, had over stayed my welcome. I found Louie, and he loaned me five bucks, so I could buy one of those $3.99 Las Vegas breakfasts. After a few hours of sleep and a marvelous shower (I hope I have impressed upon you how precious showers are by now), we prepared for the show. I didn't know it then but it was to be the last show for many of the regulars on this tour. Joe had screwed up earlier on the tour by losing Jean Luc's prize bow. We thought it was stolen in Baltimore, but later in the tour a radio station DJ in Atlanta called Pat and told him the missing bow had been found in the grand piano of the club in Atlanta we had played. That night we had used the house piano due to space limitations, and during load out Joe laid the bow down inside the open grand piano. Someone must have closed it about that time and Joe never missed it. Jean-Luc had given up finding it and two nights later in Morristown PA, bought the best bow he could find (about $800), but his bow was worth several times that figure. The money, however, wasn't the object since the new "cheap" bow didn't feel or sound right. When the bow showed up (a minor miracle in itself) nothing was said to Joe, but everyone knew he was in deep dung. When we reconvened in April for the next JLP tour, Joe had been replaced. We also lost two members of the band. Steve Smith went on to work for Ronnie Montrose {more on that tour later} and eventually became the drummer for the pop group "Journey". Daryl Stuermer became the long time touring guitarist for "Genesis". Jamie wouldn't be back for the next tour either, but would return to JLP later in 1978. I never did hear who the official winner of the wood chopping contest was, so let's call it a tie. We finished the show and said our good byes. I flew back to Rochester with less than a dollar in my pocket.

On April 27, 1998, the Aladdin Hotel & Casino was imploded to make room for a new Aladdin complex to be started soon (the Performing Arts Center was thankfully spared, and was to be restored). The Aladdin was ten years younger than I am, too young to die such a violent death. I know it's just a building but I teared up when I saw the footage of the destruction.

In 1991 Freddie Mercury died of complications caused by AIDS. Like the Aladdin, he was also too young to die. Queen was arguably the most consistently popular British rock band since the Beatles. One of my many regrets about my first tour was that I didn't break roadie decorum and use my pass to get backstage to meet Freddie Mercury, and maybe ask him for an autograph (blasphemy).

When I got home I called Karen, my casual girlfriend for the last year. She said she was too tired to see me, and that she had class tomorrow early. I knew something was wrong, it was only about 9 PM on a Sunday night. I hadn't even seen her new apartment (she had moved into it while I was on the left coast. Not being someone that takes no for an answer, I drove over to her new address, and knocked on the door. She answered in a robe, not at all excited to see me. (Does anyone else besides me NOT see this coming?) Karl, I couldn't stand you being gone so long, I've made some changes. "Oh?" what kind of changes. About that time a feminine looking guy (I'm sorry, that's how I remember him) walked up and asked Karen if anything was wrong. She looked at me in the eye one last time and said, "I'm sorry." The door shut.

I went to my car first angry, then sad, then back to angry when I realized how much unchopped timber I had left on the table in the last few weeks, then sad again, as I cried for about five minutes hitting the steering wheel with my fist. I went home and one of my roommates Royd, said "let's go over to the "Cellar" at school and get drunk. So I borrowed five dollars and we went. I met his new girlfriend, and she suggested that I might like her roommate Patty. I was open to suggestions, so she went up to their dorm room, and talked her into coming down for a beer. We all ended up back at our townhouse at two AM when the bar closed, and Patty ended up spending the night.

About a year and a half later, I married her.

We were divorced four years later.

Truck Driver's Daughters

◆

After spending almost a non-stop week with Patty, it was time for her to go home to Cleveland for Christmas (there's that damned city again!). We said our good-byes, and I settled in for an uneventful Christmas in the frozen tundra of Rochester, New York. The day Patty left I followed Duffy, Fred, and Ronnie (the other driver for our company) to a local pool hall dive. Ronnie looked a lot like a tall Willie Nelson, and had a Harley just like Duffy and Fred. They brought me along since they were worried that I was already spending too much time with this new girl, what was her name Pam? no Patty. They were glad I had finally ditched Karen (I guess I left out the part about her dumping me when I told it), but didn't want me "tied down" again so quickly. They insisted that I come with them because; unbeknownst to me Ronnie's two daughters were up from Texas for the holidays and would be at the pool hall. I guess if I were tempted I would forget about Patty, good guess. The older buxom daughter (I forget her name) was probably about 20, and she took a shine to me right off. We shot pool and she told me about what a two-timing loser her boyfriend back in Texas was. The younger slender daughter "Dee Dee" claimed to be 18 (the legal drinking age in New York at that time) but later I learned she was barely 17. She didn't seem to like me at all. We all played pool, and drank beer, talking about Texas, and rock concerts, and sexual innuendo. Later the "bikers" decided to take off for an early evening ride. Ronnie turned around, almost as if it was an after thought, "Karl, do you mine giving my girls a ride home?" "No problem," I said, with the surprise showing on my face. Eventually we all piled into my 1971 Toyota Celica, and we headed to where they were staying. When we got there, I expected an awkward moment. How would the older one and I get rid of the kid sister, and still maintain everyone's dignity? I got my answer as the two sisters both got out, whispered between themselves, and Dee Dee got back in and closed the door. The older sister waved good night and said something like, "You two kids have fun." And then she was gone. I looked at Dee Dee, and said "OK, now what?" "I guess you better take me to your place, since I don't have a place here."

We went back to the townhouse, and spent that night and the next several nights together. I even spent Christmas and New Years with her over at Ronnie's house. Is this a great country or what? Then a couple of days after New Years, Patty came back to town. I briefly considered juggling the two, but opted for Patty fulltime. I didn't return any of Dee Dee's calls, and a week or so later I heard that her and the buxom sister had made their way back to Texas.

I worked with Ronnie on two more tours, and he never mentioned her to me again, except once. About three months after the Christmas pairing, we were all in the shop, prepping for the upcoming April JLP tour. In front of everyone he said, "Hey Karl, I got a phone call from Dee Dee last night." "Oh," I acted disinterested. "Yeah, she called me to let me know I'm going to be a Grandfather."

My heart stopped.

Well that settles that. I have to go tell Patty goodbye, quit my job, move to Midland, Texas, marry Dee Dee, and raise my child. The rest of my life had just been arranged for me. After a long pause, and thankfully before I could say anything, Ronnie added, "Yup, I'm gonna be a Grand Daddy and Dee Dee's gonna be an Aunt, cause her big sister's pregnant." Everyone was rolling on the concrete floor in hysterics by

then, except me. I was suddenly very sick, and I didn't dare throw up.
Instead of vomiting, I loaded the truck.

Road Etiquette

◆

There is an unwritten set of rules for all non-famous people that work with famous people. For our industry, I call it "Road Etiquette. This set of rules is a bitter pill that has to be taken, or you wake up from your wonderful dream. You are unlike the fans that can ask for their autographs, take their pictures, and say stupid things to their favorite artists like "I have ALL your albums," or "My sister is SO in love with you." Also fans can overtly show their excitement saying things out loud like "I can't believe I actually touched him, I'll never wash my hand."

Roadies have no such luxury. You must remain professional at all times. Definition of professional: no emotion, especially when it comes to being in the presence of a famous person. It means you talk to Bill Cosby or Dolly Parton in the same tone of voice, and the same eye contact that you would use with the union electrician. Photos are frowned upon unless you have earned the right to "hang" with the inner circle of the band. The inner circle usually includes the band members, their families (if present), the road manager, and sometimes long time band roadies. Even if you were an "insider," and you took some pictures they should be casual pix, not a tourist shot. ("Can you use my camera and take a picture of me and Carole King?" and then you put your arm around her, and say "cheese") The shots taken should be "action" shots, or "gottcha" shots. Generally pictures just aren't taken. Roadies just do not ask for autographs EVER. Most stars really hate the whole autograph thing. You hear them talk about how they hate it, but are forced to do it so they don't get a reputation as the jerk that won't sign autographs. With that knowledge, if you asked for an autograph you would appear to be a hypocrite.

The other part of road etiquette involves guests. If you are inner circle you can pretty much get as many backstage passes, as you want. Usually, however, these are "restricted access" passes, which just means your guest can't go certain places (like the dressing rooms) without an escort. If you are not inner circle you may, or may not, get passes, depending on the confidence level the manager has put in you. The reason for the stinginess is that with those passes comes responsibility. Anytime your guest does something wrong, it's your fault, end of discussion. You have to police your people, or it's your head. Nobody can get too drunk, get too high, eat the band's food, be too loud, trip over any vital cables, take any souvenirs, ask for any autographs (yes that rule extends to your guests as well), or touch any equipment (unless it happens to be equipment that is attached to a musician, and the touching is invited). Introductions are generally acceptable if done at the appropriate times. Just after sound check, is generally the best time to introduce your girlfriend, brother, cousin, college roommate, or parents, to the band. If you are a band favorite, you'll be the beneficiary of comments like "I don't know what we would do without our man Karl, he's such an important part of this show." or "We're so lucky to have Karl, we'd be lost without him."

Another part of Road etiquette is being invisible. During the show you are to stay as unobtrusive as humanly possible. I used to wear blue jeans and black T-shirts to enhance my stealth look. You have to stay out of the light and in the shadows, during the show. If a trip has to be made to the stage it is made quickly, and with a straight line. Whenever possible reaching over or through the amp line to fix something is preferable to entering the stage. The same rules go for the sound and light men out front. Potentially, they could be a huge distraction because they are bathed in colored light, unlike the stage roadies. When I was out at the board I always tried to keep my movement to a minimum, and I moved rather slow, so I wouldn't attract much attention.

The final unwritten rule involves bootleg recordings. It would be very easy for me to pop a tape in the deck and press the record button, producing a flawless live tape of the show, which potentially could be mass produced later and sold. This just wasn't done. If tapes were made they were done with the knowledge and permission of the artist. Usually they were made for them to critique their own performance (like the George Carlin show). All it would take would be for you to make an unauthorized bootleg once, and get caught, and you would probably never work in this business again. Your company would be forced to fire you or they would never work again either. A very high price that none of us were ever willing to risk.

Besides certain things "just weren't done" on the road.

Quickies

◆

As I have previously mentioned, between tours I would do a lot of "one night stands." Here are some "quickies" (stories about one night stands) I did with various artists, in no particular order.

Taj Mahal: I always enjoyed shows with Taj. His style of blues is timeless. The show I remember the clearest was a very cold outdoor show at University of Pennsylvania (probably in 1978). It was in the "quad", for those of you that know the school, and based on the number of fans in attendance, my guess it was put on by the school for free. My favorite Taj Mahal song was always his rendition of "She caught the Katy" (and left me a mule to ride). I was pleased when in 1980 it was used as the opening song in the "Blues Brothers" movie. I also looked up an old high school friend that night, Lee, that was attending the school to become a lawyer. We actually hooked up just prior to the show, but I was so busy showing off, (trying to disprove my high school moniker of "geek") that I'm sure I made a fool of myself. I was also in the beginning of my drug abuse phase (which I will detail in an upcoming chapter), and I think I was actually stupid enough to partake of the white devil powder in front of Lee. I never saw, or heard from Lee ever again, I hope he became a lawyer, and I hope he reads this book (I'm really OK now, my old friend). The show was great, except the temperature dropped unexpectedly, and I hadn't brought a jacket. I froze my ass off. Quite a change from the Outlaws show in the "arena like an oven" gig.

Dave Mason: 3/2/78, in Detroit at Cobo Hall. This was a monster show. I was doing supplemental sound for my buddies at Showco (ala the K.C. gig). Just like the show in DC this was union house with fork-lifts, a dream gig. Again I was solo, since there wasn't much to do after a quick set up. I have to tell you about Cobo hall. I don't think there is a bad seat in there. It's like a giant teacup, with the stage at the bottom of the cup, and the seats all layered up the sides of the cup. The acoustics were very good for an arena. I supervised the PA equipment being stacked on top of the massive pile started by Showco. I hooked up their signal to my amps and I had the next six hours or so off. The opening act that night was Bob Welch, formally with Fleetwood Mac. The show was either sold out or close. I remember waiting in line to get paid, each of the vendors being ushered into a secure office one at a time. When it was my turn I entered the room and was amazed to see huge piles of currency on one table, matching piles of bundled ticket stubs on another. Armed guards watch my every move, as I was inches away from over a hundred thousand dollars in small unmarked bills. Someone was at the other table counting ticket bundles (many bands are paid based on actual ticket sales and want the real ticket stubs counted to ensure proper payment). I presented my invoice (I think it was $3,000) and he started counting out hundreds, and fifties until he reached the right total. I wrote paid on the invoice and handed it to him. He reminded me of King Midas in his room full of gold, except this was a room of green. He said "next" and I was ushered back out.

The show was one for the ages. I was a big "Traffic" fan when I was about 13, and I really wanted to see Dave. I also wanted to see Bob Welch since he had a great album out back then, named "French Kiss." I was behind the stage left stack for most of the show, as he sang his hits, "Sentimental Lady", and "Ebony Eyes". From my vantage point on stage I could look around (actually up) and see virtually every fan. There didn't seem to be any obstructed view seats anywhere, except a few directly beside the stage on either side, which were blocked by the immense speaker stacks. After an excruciatingly long change over, Dave Mason came out to play. Like Bob, he had a recent album and a big hit with the song "We just disagree". The show was flawless. Dave must have played every song he had ever done, including some old Traffic stuff. I remember the crowd didn't want the show to end and I didn't think it ever would. There had to be at least three or four encores. Eventually I got to load-out and drive home. An interesting bit of trivia I discovered as I was researching this book. Dave Mason started out as a roadie in the early 60's. He worked for The Spencer Davis Group, who had among others, Stevie Winwood in the band. Of course you Traffic fans know that Steve, Dave, and several other famous artists eventually became the group "Traffic". You see, not all of the band roadies are frustrated musicians, some actually become great musicians. Lastly, I should again mention Karl's Roadie Rule #5: All headliners started out as opening acts, in most cases, they will be opening acts again someday. I bring this up because I recently saw Dave Mason again live, playing the "Sugar Festival" in Sugarland Texas (opening act).

Gene Roddenbury: While still a student working on the Tech Crew, I provided sound for a lecture by Gene Roddenbury, the creator of Star Trek. It was in 1975 and Star Trek had been off the air for about five years. There was a small following of Trekkies, mostly from the engineering school I would guess, but the overall attendance was disappointing. Like my engineer brethren I too was a big Star Trek fan, although at that point I doubt I could be considered a Trekkie. I had seen every episode several times, and was still disgusted at NBC for canceling the show after three seasons. I did not ever expect the series to be revived however. It was a thrill to shake Gene's hand and introduce myself as a fan (I know that was against roadie etiquette, but I wasn't technically a roadie yet). He spoke not only of the past, but he also spoke of the future. He answered repeated questions about why the show was canceled (bad Nielson ratings), and he answered questions about the future of Star Trek. He explained that even though the series was dead and probably would never be a viable option for TV again, he spoke of a movie deal that was early in negotiation. A Movie? About Kirk and Bones, Klingons and Mr. Spock, Tribbles and the Enterprise? Not in this lifetime I thought. I had violated Roadie rule # 13, Never try to predict which artists (or in this case movies) will be stars, you will be wrong well over half the time {well actually I hadn't written the rule yet}. As you Trekkies know Star Trek the Motion Picture (they now call it Star Trek One) was a big hit for Paramount several years later, and has spawned seven Star Trek sequels, and three successful TV spin-offs to date.

Rick Derringer: The shows I worked with Rick Derringer were all college shows, and were always a lot of fun. He is a rather short man (taller than Dolly Parton I would guess, but not by much). I suppose that is why the musicians he chose for his band were even shorter than he was. The only exception was Myron, the drummer, who was a bit taller, but that fact was concealed by the fact he sat down the whole show. Rick had this great gag he did on stage that was made possible by his use of wireless guitars (a radical innovation for the late 70's). He would be playing a riff on the guitar, as would the rhythm guitarist, when they would both throw their guitars in the air at each other. They would then catch the other's guitar, and continue playing without missing a note. It took a lot of timing and practice, but it was a very cool effect. Rick had made his fame as a key member of the Edgar Winter Group, and as a solo did several songs associated with that band. Of course "Rock & Roll Hoochie Coo," was always his song, and remained his anthem as a solo. The last time I saw him was directly after a show, back at the hotel. Myron, Rick and me were "partying" in my room. Actually, it wasn't much of a party, but I had just scored some "primo blow", and was feeling generous. Instant party. Then the three of us stayed up (like sleep was an option at that point) and talked about nothing for quite a while. Like so many of the artists I worked with, I never saw Myron, or Rick ever again. Myron got a new gig a few years later as Pat Benatar's drummer. He was her drummer during her highly successful period in the eighties. Rick also took a change in direction, and among other projects has been the producer of several Weird Al Yankovich's CDs and his Children's television show.

The Spinners: I did one show with The Spinners; it was the only time I can remember a contract rider biting me in the ass, instead of an unsuspecting promoter. It was a pretty simple show. There was no opening act; the set up for the band was pretty standard stuff. Really the only thing going in that was different was that the venue was a Jai Lai court. I think the gig was in Connecticut, or some other state where wagering on Jai Lai was legal. Anyway the Spinners were to perform between the afternoon games and the evening games to boost the attendance of both sessions. Load in was a little strange but nothing too difficult (the stage was an odd size and configuration, since it really wasn't a stage at all). I prepared for an uneventful sound check, which of course ensured that it would be far from that. When the band arrived, one of the vocalists called me over and said, "We can't use these tripod mic stands, where are the round bottoms?" He was referring to the AKG mic stands that we used (as did virtually every other sound company in the country) that have a fold out tripod base. He wanted the old mic stands with the round heavy cast iron bottoms. Those older stands had two problems, weight and durability. The weight is obvious; the bases were very heavy so the stand wouldn't fall over. Multiply a heavy base times 24 or 32 copies, and you have a lot of dead weight to load and unload every night. The tripods folded open, and were light relative to the old fashion ones. The main problem though was that every time you used the old one you had to screw the tube into the base since if you tried to transport them assembled they would break off. The threads were very delicate, and tended to cross thread, or strip. They were just a hassle, so we left most of them home. This turned out to be a bad idea on this trip. The Spinners show it turned out was as much choreography as music. The tripod legs interfered with their footwork, and they had several times where they would throw the mic stand forward (without knocking it over) just enough that the weight in the base of the stand would recover and pull itself back upright. The tripod stands would just fall over when pushed. I apologized for the problem, and suggested that they just not do that thing where they push over the stands. Their road manager then produced a copy of the agreement my boss had signed for today's show. Damn, there it was in black and white, "you shall provide no less than five chrome plated, round based mic stands, of appropriate height to support microphones (model Shure SM-58 or equivalent) for vocals. I ended up going to a local music store that afternoon and buying four stands for the retail price (about $80 each). We could have bought them wholesale back home for about $20 each. The show did happen, and we did get paid (although the profitability of the trip was diluted a little). One of the singers did push a little too hard one time during the show, and his stand smashed to the ground (and damaging the mic) despite being provided with a brand new chrome plated, round bottom mic stand per our contractual agreement.

REO Speedwagon: Our company did several shows with REO early in my roadie career. The encounter I want to talk about here I was not working, I was a back stage guest. A friend of mine that used to work for our company was on tour with a band named "Starz", that was a Kiss knock-off. They were the opening act for REO, on an extended tour, and they stopped in Rochester while I was on break. I showed up at the Rochester Auditorium to see my old friend. The show was well done. Starz had lots of pyro-technics, which I found very interesting. REO put on one of its no bull rock and roll shows. Lots of good music, by some guys that have been doing this for a long time. I went backstage immediately after the show, being careful to not interfere with the load out process. I talked to Wylan while he worked, packing up his gear so the show could be reproduced in the next city. About that time, the lead singer for REO, Kevin Cronin, wandered out on to the stage towards us. Kevin came right up to Wylan and me, and said, ""Hi Wylan, how's it going?" "Just fine, hey I'd like you to meet a good friend of mine that I used to work with, Karl." "Karl this is…"

"I know who this is, I interrupted."

Then inexplicably I said something I couldn't believe was coming from my own mouth. In that instant in time that the data received by my ears (Wylan's attempt at an introduction) was processed by my brain, a decision was made to make an attempt at humor. Kevin had very long hair, like many other lead singers of popular bands, and with that in mind here comes the attempted joke.

"I know who this is, I interrupted." Who wouldn't know who this is (Kevin is still smiling at this point as I took has hand and shook it aggressively) I'm a big fan, I can't believe I'm really meeting…. Geddy Lee!

Nobody laughed. Kevin looked at me like I was an idiot (a safe assumption). He said nothing and walked off the stage. My friend said something to the effect of "Nice move, a**h***."

As of this writing, both Rush (the real Geddy Lee's band) and REO Speedwagon, are both continuing to play music, and I still to this day, wish I hadn't tried that feeble joke.

The Politics of Opening Acts and Load outs

◆

When you are in the audience of a live concert, what you don't realize is that there were a lot of pre-show negotiations that have taken place. A lot of these political power plays revolve around the opening act or sometimes load outs. I have several opening act and load out stories that I'm going to tell now; most are really about control, power, and egos.

Sometimes the opening act is a group or an artist that feels for whatever reason that they shouldn't really be the opening act. The promoter, or their agent, or their manager, or somebody, has made a terrible mistake. But, since they have to open, they test everyone involved by making questionable or even unreasonable demands. They may want more stage space (which usually requires moving something like the drum kit or the grand piano), they may want more time to play, put up a large sign, or ask for more microphones. The headliner can respond by saying no, or compromising on a specific issue (we can't give you eight more mic channels, but we can swing four). Once in a while someone gets unreasonable and bad stuff happens. One such occurrence happened when Michael Franks (Popsicle Toes) was opening for us. The manager for Michael was very demanding. He was impatient during our sound check and then nobody moved fast enough. I think he was used to being the headliner, and didn't like the loss of control being number two. Our road manager had already left with our band, when the fireworks started. Fred was our driver that tour and for some reason he hadn't taken the Harley out, choosing instead to stay and "supervise" the sound check. None of us really minded, since Fred rarely interfered with us while he was pretending to be in charge. Tonight was different. In retrospect I would guess that Fred was tired (probably a long drive the night before) and of course the opening act manager had been testy all day. The manager came up to me and announced that the set-up for his performer was inadequate, and that we would have to move some of our equipment to allow them more space (this was one of those power plays I was talking about for those of you paying attention). I had politely said no and the manager was walking away from me (apparently to file a protest with the promoter) when out of the blue, Fred decks the guy. All I saw was the guy hitting the stage floor, hard. Fred had connected and gotten everything. He was holding his hand, which was apparently damaged. The roadies for the band came to get their fallen warrior, as we corralled Fred. It kind of reminded me of a cold war stand-off. Neither side wanted to escalate the action or use their nuclear arsenal, so an uneasy (and unspoken) truce was enacted. We kept Fred on ice (away from the stage) all night, and there were no further repercussions. Fred never did give any of us a plausible excuse for cold cocking that manager.

A similar story happened at a big show featuring The Charlie Daniels Band, Dickie Betts and Great Southern, and my old friends The Winter Brothers Band. I was actually running a spot light that night with Dick (the guy that I did that first BÖC show with). At the end of the show we wanted to get out before the semi's started backing up. We knew the stage crew and they gladly obliged us. About the time we were wheeling the trouper road cases towards the side door, a CDB roadie grabbed me and told me to help him pack some cases. He had assumed I was one of the college crew and that I was helping the spot light company instead of helping him. I said, "I'm not stage crew, I'm a spot guy." He then turned and grabbed Dick and said, "Hey, how about you, does anybody do any f***ing work around here?" Dick just walked away not even giving him an answer. The band roadie grabbed Dick again, spun him around and punched him in the face. Like Fred's shot, he got all of it. Blood erupted from Dick's face, the nose apparently broken. Now if you remember, Dick was a large guy, but this roadie was a corn feed country boy as well. Dick walked away (another cold war scenario, since we knew the stage crew we would have had plenty of backup, had a full scale rumble broken out). Dick never entered the launch codes and we cancelled Def-Con 5. We did however load out our two spot lights prior to the band. It may have been my imagination, but I also remember that the student stage crew was moving a little crisper during the remainder of the load out than normal.

Two other minor incidents both involved my delivery of a rented Hammond B-3 organ. Many rock bands used B-3s but some didn't carry them on tour for various reasons including the fact that the vacuum tubes that were used in its amplifier were very fragile. Now a Hammond B-3 is that classic rock and roll organ with the distinctive "warble" sound. The high frequency horn actually spun in the cabinet and depending on the speed of the spin (which was controlled with a foot pedal) different effects could be achieved.

Sometimes I would have to deliver a B-3 to a show on a one night rental basis (not exactly a glamorous job, but it was very easy). One show I delivered and set up the B-3 for was The Allman Brothers Band and The Marhall Tucker Band. Greg Allman was playing the organ, and I adjusted the pedals for him during the sound check. I don't think he completed a sentence, mumbling a word here or there until he was happy with the adjustments. The show was pretty good as I remember, but the load out was the main thing that I remember about that night. As the show ended, I quickly packed my two cases, rolled them to the stage door, and headed for my truck. A band roadie (they're all trouble makers aren't they?) stopped me and said, "you aren't loading out before us, you'll have to wait." "It'll only take five minutes, you guys aren't ready to load yet anyway," I pleaded. "No, you have to wait," as he called for his 18 wheeler to back up to the dock. One of the union stage crew managers quieted walked up to me and said, "side door." I knew what that meant. It was a pain to load out the stage entrance and down the flight of stairs but I was like family to the Rochester IATSE and they were about to make a point. I backed the truck up to the stairs and six union hands stopped what they were doing (packing up the band) and focused their attention on my B-3 and me. Everything stopped on that stage except my priority load out. It would have only taken one stage-hand to roll the Hammond off the dock into the six-wheeler. It now was going to take six of them a good fifteen minutes to carefully ease the cases down the stairs and then up a ramp to my waiting truck. The band roadies couldn't do a damn thing at that point because they knew better than to agitate the union any further than they already did. I closed the door, and drove off, smiling to myself.

By the way…I made no Cher sighting that night.

My final load-out saga was a similar tale of a Hammond B-3 delivery. This was to a SUNY college gig starring Robert Palmer. Bear in mind that "Addicted to Love" was a good eight or nine years away from being recorded and his only real hit was "Sneakin' Sally through the Alley." Now for some reason, I remember him as being a real jerk that day, but I don't remember the details. I delivered the B-3 and set it up, then sat around and watched the sound check and eventually the show. As unpleasant as the afternoon was (similar to the Elvis Costello show, lots of yelling and rudeness) the show actually kicked butt. I remember thinking to myself that this guy should be a big star someday if he ever stops being an a**hole. At the shows conclusion I went for the quick load out again. This time I had it "sussed" {figured out}(a little British lingo since we are dealing with UK roadies in this story). I went for the truck first and backed it up to the stage door. A student crew member boxed up the gear and was going to meet me at the door. As I jumped up onto the dock an English roadie said "Just what the f*** do you think you're doing mate?" "Loading the B-3 and then getting out of your way." "Says you," his eyes were glassy; he was "pissed" {drunk}(more British lingo). "You better move that piece of shit truck now!" We now had what's known in the westerns as a "Mexican Standoff." My truck was blocking the dock and his crew had control of the stage (and my B-3). I was willing to see how far he would take this game of Poker, when one of the students came over to me and told me the school didn't want any trouble. "Could you please move your truck?" I knew when to fold, and I reluctantly yielded to the Brits. Of course, I sat in a very conspicuous spot where the band and crew could see me watching them for the 45 minutes or so it took to finish loading out the sound, lights, and band gear. I never got any eye contact from any of the band roadies, and I carefully never said a word. After they were gone the stage crew apologized for the delay, and thanked me again for not causing trouble. We loaded my two cases onto "Red". They all let me know that I was in the right, and I had been the bigger man as well. I felt pretty good on that drive home, and I hoped that the Brits would experience good old American hangovers in the morning.

Sometimes it's just better to just walk away.

Rarely Tour the Earth

◆

Another tour with high hopes, and low outcomes was the 1978 Rare Earth tour. It was supposed to be about 40 shows over a six week period, but things looked bad from the start. As you may know Rare Earth had been a monster group prior to Woodstock and into the early seventies. By 1978 they were going to start the "comeback tour" that would endear them to a new generation. Good plan, poor execution.

We were to start in Savanna, Georgia at an outdoor gig put on for free by a local radio station. I wasn't thrilled about the shakeout show being outside, especially since the lead singer was also the drummer (very difficult to mic and extremely difficult to do monitors). You guessed it, I was on monitors. We heard that the tour was in financial trouble from day one, but the production company had paid us quite a bit of cash up front (sort of a retainer), so we headed to Dixie. We arrived at the "stage" which was a semi-flat area of antique stone and brick surrounded by brick walls. OK, I have now seen audio hell, and this is it. The show was to be at lunchtime so here we are loading in at about 6 AM, by moonlight. Actually the moist sea air, the warm smell of moss, and the historical setting surrounding us were all kind of nice in looking back. Savannah is certainly a beautiful town. We did the show with no real hitches believe it or not. The band was as good as I remembered them from my old cassette tapes, and their appearances on Don Kirshner's "In Concert" TV show (that I never missed on Friday nights as a young teenager.). They played perfect renditions of "Hey Big Brother," "I'm Losing You (I know)," "Get Ready," and of course, "I Just Want to Celebrate." After the show there wasn't much celebrating, just apprehension about the tour. Several shows had already been canceled due to low ticket sales. The next show scheduled (that hadn't been pulled) was Seattle. The light guys left to drive the sound and light equipment across this great nation while my partner and I got to fly home. We were going to fly out to Seattle in a few days to really start the tour, when we got the call. Tour canceled due to lack of interest. The light guys drove home and we licked our wounds. We actually did OK with the up front money; it was just a big disappointment since I really did enjoy this group and their music.

Besides, it's times like this when you count your blessings. At least you weren't a Rare Earth band roadie.

Hay, you must be Buck Owens

◆

Before you accuse me of not being able to spell, let me explain. I found myself somewhere in New England (I think it was New Hampshire) at an auto racetrack. We were to do a show with Buck Owens and his band (of Hee Haw fame). When we got to the track I couldn't believe my eyes when I saw the "stage". We were to set up on a large "hay wagon," then it would be pulled (by a tractor of course) to the front of the grandstand. Karl's roadie rule #4 "When confronted with an insurmountable odds, improvise." We borrowed some rope from the stage crew (or maybe it was the pit crew); anyway we tied the stacks down to the wooden wagon. We used several rolls of gaffer's tape as well securing everything that we could to survive the "pull" to the destination.

I'm happy to report that the show went fine (go figure). Buck was very pleasant, nobody punched anybody, nobody's dog got ran over, the music was fun, and the crowd loved the show. The only things missing were Roy Clark, Minnie Pearl, and Junior Samples, and we could have shot an episode of Hee Haw.

By the way, we were still finding straw in the equipment a month later.

Carole King

During a two week break during a Ponty tour in November of 1978, I had what I consider one of the greatest strokes of luck in my road career. I couldn't believe my ears when I was told that I would be trading my two week vacation for a quickie tour with Carole King. Most roadies would be angry, but I was elated. In the days before CDs I had literally worn out my vinyl copy of "Tapestry." There was another twist to this gig as well. Since Carole had minimum PA requirements, a light opening act (her own group called "Navarro"), and she was playing halls we knew had great stage crews, I did this mini tour solo. I had no partner, no monitor guy. The house mix was to be done by me, the monitors were mixed from out at the main board (by me), and the truck was driven by me. The only thing I didn't have to do was sell any T-shirts. The shows were at some of my favorite venues. The Tower Theatre near Philadelphia in Upper Darby, where the gear had to be loaded in through the audience. The cases came down the truck ramp, into the foyer, down the center aisle, up another truck ramp on to the stage. It was a scary load in, but the crew made it easy. The load out was even worse since it was uphill, and you were tired by then. We also played the Orpheum Theatre in Boston, the Palladium in New York City, the Capital Theatre in Passaic, New Jersey, and Constitution Hall in Washington D.C. A collection of the some of the finest halls on the Eastern Seaboard.

The shows were a blend of Navarro opening the show, Carole playing with Navarro, and Carole playing solo on the grand piano. The fans were mostly older than me (22 at the time) with probably an average age over 30. They were attentive and appreciative, and Carole exceeded their expectations. She also easily exceeded mine. I was very nervous at the first sound check, since I had never worked a show this big by myself. Would I let Carole down? Would the shows go OK? If something on stage went wrong, who would fix it? I couldn't very well leave the main board, run backstage, fix the problem and run back to the main, could I? Carole melted all my apprehensions within a few minutes. She had a casual calmness about her that was contagious. Nothing seemed to bother her, and since she had that attitude nothing bad happened to bother her. I firmly believe that we all have some self fulfilling prophecy in us. What I mean by that is that bad things happen to people who expect everything bad to happen to them, and good things happen to those people that only expect good things to happen. Carole was one of those second people. Anyway, despite the fact that I was working as hard as I ever did on a tour (due to my being solo), I wasn't my usual frantic self. She was very personable, and talked to me like I was as important as the promoter, her manager, her band, or even as important as her. She didn't have that "star" attitude, which most artists with the top selling LP album of all time would be. The mix each night went very well. This was due to the acoustics of the aforementioned halls, Carole's great musical ability, and the absence of any need to attain significant volume levels. A high light of the Passaic show, was Carole bringing one of the original "Shirelles" out on stage to sing with her near the end of the show. My personal high light was at the final show of this tour in DC. To set this up…I was exhausted. I had been running on fumes for several days, and this was the last night. I had a long drive to Rochester and a flight to restart the Ponty tour on the West coast to look forward to the next day. I remember thanking Carole prior to the show for the chance to work with her, mix her sound, and hear the songs I truly loved all performed live. She turned it around and thanked me for my help making this tour a success. I took my place at the board, and prepared for the final show. The show started, and everything was going fine, after seven shows I didn't really need to make many adjustments during the show, just sit back and relax. Relax. Relax. Relax…

I woke up with a start. Carole was receiving a standing ovation, the show was over.

My God! I had slept through the entire show.

I looked around to see who had noticed. Nobody was paying any attention to me; they were all paying homage to Carole. She was thanking the crowd, explaining that this tour was now over but that it had been such a success that another one would be in the not to distant future. I checked the volumes, had it gotten too loud? Was it too soft? Did it feedback during the show while I was asleep? No, I assured myself that would have certainly awakened me if that had occurred. All I could do was stand there and act like I had been mixing the board for the entire show.

Nobody from security, the stage crew or Carole's entourage ever said a word to me about my unscheduled nap, so I just loaded my equipment. I had said my goodbye to CK prior to the show, and since she was now consumed backstage by the music media, record company types, and some fans, I left without comment.

Long live the King.

Let there be light

◆

Sometimes even with good intentions, mistakes are made. One universal mistake that is made by millions of well meaning people on every continent every day is "assuming." As a rookie roadie I learned the hard way never to assume.

It was a double show with Commander Cody and the Lost Planet Airmen opening for the New Riders of the Purple Sage. There was an early show and a late show at the Auditorium Theatre in Rochester. I was in my usual spot stage left on monitors. This becomes important later since I was positioned directly next to the Auditorium's lighting control panel, and my friends from the IATSE stage crew.

I've never been to a Grateful Dead show, but from what I know of them, this show was a first cousin. The crowd was very dead-head like, and there was a lot of pot being smoked. It was like every member of the audience knew every word of every song from both bands. I got the feeling that they had all seen these bands before many times, and I was probably right. In fact besides the stage crew I probably knew less about these bands and their music than virtually anyone in that audience. Commander Cody played a mixture of styles that could be generalized as "RockaBilly." Their big hit from their first album (popular while I was in the tenth grade) was "Hot Rod Lincoln." As is usually the case during a double show, time was critical. The first show had a finite number of minutes before the fans had to be herded out the doors, a new set of replacements seated, and a duplicate show performed. Also from a roadie's perspective, it was like having three opening acts. Set up the headliner, do a sound check, set up the opener, do another check, do the opening show, set up the headliner and do that show, then set up the opener AGAIN, do that show AGAIN, and so on. Any delays would cause a domino effect that would last until the grand finale at load-out. Commander Cody played for the designated number of songs and left the stage. With the stage black, and the crowd knowing what to expect, they were summoned back to the re-luminated stage for an encore. At the conclusion of that song they headed for the dressing room. After the changeover NRPS took the stage and had the audience on their collective feet. I remember that the lights were particularly effective that night due to all the smoke that poured onto the stage from the audience (and it wasn't coming from a fog machine). The audience sang along with every song, it was like the world's largest Karoke. Eventually the songs ended and the band exited the stage. I sat at my board awaiting the inevitable encore, which came shortly after. They returned to play "Panama Red," as the crowd yelled the lyrics along with the band. At the end of that song, the band exited again. The stage was still black but I ASSUMED that they were done, after all there was still another show to go and they had played the obvious encore song. I was looking at the union light man (like many of the local crew he was in his sixties and had ear plugs in) when he asked me, "House Lights?" I nodded, "House up!" The lights in the audience went up and a huge moan like a dying whale went up from the crowd. What I didn't know about NRPS (that the crowd apparently knew) was that they always played at least two encores, sometimes more. With the house lights up, the crowd reluctantly complied and streamed to the exits. The road manager for the band came over to the geriatric electrician and started yelling at him, "Who the hell told you to bring up the lights?" He sheepishly pointed at me. All I could think to say was, "I'm sorry, I thought they were done."

"No, they weren't done you idiot!" He stormed off towards the dressing room to explain the "faux pas" to the confused band.

Needless to say I didn't call for any lights during the second show.

Roadie Rule #15 Never Assume.

My Fall during the Spring Tour

It is now April of 1978, and the Jean-Luc Ponty Tour Spring Tour begins. As I mentioned in the Las Vegas story, Steve Smith, Daryl Stuermer, and Jamie Glaser have not returned. Steve was replaced on drums by Casey Scheuerell who had been playing with Gino Vanelli, while the new guitarists were now Peter Maunu and Joaquin Lievano. The tour was a month long without any breaks.

It was to be a turning point in my young life, and not a good one.

I had been seeing Patty for almost four months. She spent most of her time at my apartment, and rarely went to class. She was becoming disillusioned with Graphic Arts School (Printing) and would eventually quit at the end of that school year. I was getting ready to go away for four weeks, and I needed to have a "serious" talk with Patty. "I think we should be adult about this," I started, "We should be free to see other people while I'm gone, and see how we feel when we get back." She was not at all happy about that arrangement, but reluctantly agreed.

This was the first of many mistakes I would make during this tour.

The other mistake involved drugs. I haven't really talked much about drug usage up until this point in the book because at first I refused to get involved with them. Based on what I heard about coke, I knew that with my "hyperactive" nature, I would probably like it. I avoided it (although it was openly available at most shows), by convincing myself that it was a path I didn't want to go down.

I was actually quite proud of myself prior to this tour, even my girl-friend Patty had an affinity for various drugs, and I didn't succumb to any of them. With this background now disclosed, let's get in the motorhome and drive.

We had a new addition to the crew. Pat (the road manager) had hired a friend of his to drive the motorhome. He wasn't paid very much, and had never been on the road before. A few days into the tour, he became a liability. He would hang around during sound check and the show and then would be sleepy when he should be driving to the next gig. We asked him nicely once, then we told him not so nicely several times to sleep during the day. He just never got the hang of "day sleeping". Louie or I would stay up with him because we didn't trust him driving alone. We all feared we would fall asleep, and wake up in a ditch (or worse). Within a week we went to Pat and said he had to go. Pat told his friend, and we dropped him off at a mid-western airport. We suggested to Pat that we take the driver's wages ($200 a week) and divide it between the remaining six roadies. Then cocaine or crystal (known as "crank") was purchased with the money so we could "stay up" while driving. I chose not to take any share of the drugs, but I drove my share of the time any-way. Shortly after that change, we played a show in at home in Rochester. I was to see Patty again after our short separation.

When I saw her, I realized I had missed her even though the tour was less than half over. After the show Patty, one of her girlfriends, most of the crew, and myself were in the motorhome. I was getting ready to say my good-byes again, and head out for the remainder of the tour. Patty was enjoying my "share" of the week's buy, and then we had a terrible fight. She made some kind of crack about whether I had gotten laid by any groupies yet. I honestly answered, "No" (the truth was that once on the road, I found I really missed her, and didn't want to cheat on her). She stunned me by casually admitting two new sexual "encounters" since I had been gone. I was furious; I hadn't meant for her to cheat on me, I just wanted the option of cheating on her. We had now started a fight that I didn't have time to finish. She was right of course, I had set the rules, and now I was upset at losing the game.

She stormed out of the motorhome minutes before we were to leave for another 20 days. I should have gone after her, but I didn't. As we drove away, I made at least two classic mistakes. The first was channeling my anger into revenge. The second was bending to peer pressure. I couldn't get any instant revenge by sleeping with a random female; there just weren't any available right then. My roadie brothers had been patiently waiting for an opening to show me all the marvelous benefits of cocaine, and here was their opening. It didn't take much to convince me that the best way to "get even" with Patty was to snort cocaine. As I write the preceding sentence today, I can't believe I made that illogical leap twenty years ago.

Predictably, I did like cocaine and eventually crystal meth (speed). It was the dark turning point in my roadie career, and it is one of the biggest regrets in my life. Since I am alive, and writing this book, my story obviously has a happy ending, but you'll have to wait for the final chapters to hear more about that. I must mention a few other things here. Understand that the potency of the coke twenty years ago is estimated to be only 10% of what it is today. For those of you that may be "math impaired" that means that the drugs today are at least TEN TIMES more powerful than the drugs of my time. As hard of a time as I had stopping, it would probably be impossible to quit without help today. That is why it is a matter of life and death that you never ever ever experiment with drugs. If you are already under their spell, put this book down right now, and go get professional help. Another thing I want to mention here is that I never once saw any heroin or IV drug usage during my time on the road, although I'm sure it was out there with me somewhere. I also never saw "crack" cocaine used, since to my knowledge it hadn't been invented yet. Finally, we are dealing with potentially serious criminal acts perpetrated a very long time ago. Back then; possession of even a very small amount of cocaine was a felony in every state (and still is). With that in mind...

No specific illegal drug usage, possession or sale, or any accusations of illegal drug usage, possession, or sale by any character in this book should be inferred or implied except for my own personal drug experiences, which I freely admit.

Of course the statutes of limitation on all these illegal events have been expired for quite some time now.

And now back to your regularly scheduled "tour tales".

Mistake by the Lake

◆

During the fall of '78, we played a town in Michigan named Muskegon. It's on the Western side of Michigan about 200 miles from Detroit. It sits on the Eastern shores of Lake Michigan. We were playing a small theatre in the center of town. It had probably been (or maybe still was) a movie theatre and the cultural center of the town. As I exited the motorhome in the narrow alley just outside the stage door, I noticed a young girl was sitting by the backstage door. I don't recall her name now, but it was something ending with a "y" like Tammy or Cindy. She was probably 15, give or take a year, and unlike the girl at the KC & the Sunshine Band show or the one at the Rick Nelson show, she wasn't dressed in fancy clothes. She wore faded blue jeans and an old tight tank top. She was attractive, but in kind of a farmer's daughter way, innocent but not so innocent. Shyness wasn't a problem for her as she initiated conversation almost immediately. "Welcome to Muskegon, the mistake by the lake, nothing exciting ever happens here, are you with the band?" She didn't waste any time. "Yea, I'm the sound man." "Wow", she replied genuinely impressed. "My name is {Tammy, or Cindy, or something ending with a "Y"}, can I watch you guys work today?" "Sure," I said wondering why she wasn't in school. So she hung around with me for a couple of hours, staying out of the way, asking good questions ("what's that thing do?") and all the time explaining why her life in Muskegon was so boring and horrible. After everything was set up and we were waiting on the band for sound check she asked me if I could take a break. "Sure, it'll be about a half an hour before I am needed again, why?" "Let's go to your motorhome and screw!" I should have been expecting it from the signals she had been sending all day, but it caught me speechless never the less. Now I know I just wrote about the big fight I had with Patty and the revenge I was seeking, but that was months ago and Patty and I had worked out our difficulties at that point. I had already decided I didn't want to chop any wood on this tour, so I said, "How old are you anyway?" "What's that got to do with anything?" she retorted, confirming for me that she was jailbait. "Everything," "I'm sorry, you can watch us work, even come to the show, but I'm not going to the motorhome with you." She looked like I had just "grounded" her for a week or something. "You're no fun", as she turned and walked away.

About an hour later I asked one of the band roadies if he had seen that girl I had been talking to earlier. He smiled and said "Yup, but she's gone now." By the devilish grin on his face I knew immediately that there was more to the story than that. "What did you do?" I grimaced not really wanting to hear the answer. "He made several thrusting moves with his hips and said, "Pop'd her in the motorhome about twenty minutes ago." "She had a nice skinny ass."

I never saw her again, and she didn't come to the show that night. I guess in Muskegon, that was enough excitement for one day.

The Fix

◆

Have you ever had a really bad nightmare? Ever wake up in a cold sweat because in your dreamscape you were late for the final exam of a class you had never attended (while naked)? Ever had a sound system stop working ten minutes before the show for no apparent reason?

You probably answered yes to the first two, here's the story of number three.

It was a perfect day. A beautiful hall in the mid west, great crew, easy load in, showers, perfect. The sound check is behind me and I've had supper and a hot shower. I've changed into freshly laundered clothing and settled in at the main board for the show. The doors are opened, and the seats begin to fill with enthusiastic fans. I heard the show was a sell out, about 5,000 Jazz fans ready for a great show. Why couldn't every day on the road be like this?

It's about ten minutes until curtain. You sit at the board taking in the crowd while listening to the "walk up" music, Steely Dan. "Get it on, Get it on Kid Charlemagne, Get it on Kid.........................." Silence, that's strange, it stopped in the middle of a song, better check the tape deck. Hmmmm…, the play button is still depressed, it must have "eaten" the tape. Nope, the tape's fine. The mixing board is still lit; the VU's are even bouncing to the beat of the silent tape, that's not the problem. Shit, the power must be down backstage. Pick up the intercom box and flash your partner. "Hey Dave, the power go down to the stacks?" "Nope, lit up like a Christmas tree." "Is the signal still connected to the amps?" "Yup" "Are the monitors up?" "TEST TEST TEST, (the sound reverberates into the silent hall, and the audience stirs) "Yup." By now it's eight o'clock, and the road manager is looking for the OK to get the band and start the show. You wave him off, "Give me a minute Tim, I got a little problem out here." Now the severity of the situation begins to sink in. The crowd, usually calmed by the walk up music, starts to become restless. The fans closest to me can see from my actions that there is a problem and I hear a cascade of whispers rippling out from the board. It feels like 5,000 sets of eyes in the house are staring at me, but I block that distraction out. Now it's time to figure this out, and fix it quick. I've eliminated all the simple stuff, something is very wrong here. As I start to use logic to narrow down the possibilities, I start to also run through my contingencies. If it's the board or the amps, I could always use the monitor system, turn it around and mix from the stage. Yuk, there would be no monitors, the sound would be marginal at best and it would take a good half hour to recalibrate if I started now. We could cancel the show, and refund the money to 5,000 fans, give the promoter back his money, and…not a chance in hell. I have to fix this now. OK, the board works, the amps work, it must be between the two. What's between the two? Equalizers and crossovers. Ok patch around the EQs, bypass them. No effect, still silence. The crowd was creating its own noise by now, a low buzz probably talking about me. That leaves the crossover, it has to be the crossover. Now the crossover takes the sound that comes out of the board and it splits it into low frequencies, sending them to the amps hooked to the bass cabinets, mid range frequencies sending them to the amps hooked to the mid range horns, and finally the high frequencies to the high end horns. It had to be there. No problem, pull the spare crossover out of the case, hook it up and it will be all fixed. Here it is, wait what's this gaffer's tape on the face, something's written on it, it's my handwriting and it says, "BAD". Shit! It went bad a couple of weeks ago, and I was waiting to get home to repair it. OK plan B, you could steal a crossover from the stage monitor system. No, that won't work they are bi-amp crossovers, I need a tri-amp crossover. The only thing to do, and this is a long shot, repair the crossover. The intercom light starts to flash again, "Yes" I said in an irritated tone. "What's wrong?" Tim asked. "Got a problem here, tell the band to hang loose, I'll have it fixed in five, gotta go." I tossed the headset to the side and headed for the dresser. The dresser was a rolling cabinet with everything needed to fix any of our equipment (theoretically). I grabbed a Phillips, a needle-nose, and the little plastic case with the spare IC chips. I got back to the board and I heard random questions being asked as I went back up the aisle. "Hey you, what's wrong," "Is there going to be a show?" "What's the problem?" I gave no eye contact, grabbed a security guard on the way and posted him near me at the board. "No interruptions!" I instructed. I unplugged everything (no need in sacrificing myself to electrocution, although it may have been more merciful). I unmounted the crossover from the rack and dropped it down so I could open it up and work on it. I unscrewed the cover and using a flashlight and looked inside. OK, there are six chips, and luckily they are installed in sockets. If they had been soldered into place it would be "game over". Now, here's the $64,000 dollar question, which chips are bad? Damn, there are only two spares! I figure each pair corresponds to each frequency split, so I should replace a pair that are next to each other. I stare at the six chips and decide which two to replace, it's a wild dumb ass guess at best (Roadie Rule # 11 Never under estimate the value of dumb luck) After staring at the crossover's schematics for about a minute, I choose the two on the left hoping they represented the bass frequency split. I reach down inside the casing and pull the two chips out of their sockets with the needle-nose. They come out clean. Getting the new ones in is more difficult. If the contacts of the chips aren't lined up correctly when inserted they could bend over destroying the chip, then there's static electricity to worry about. My five minutes is up, and I successfully put the chips in the sockets. No time to put everything back together, just fire it up and see if it works. Volume down, power back on, volume back up, push the play button…

"Before the fall, when they wrote it on the wall, when there wasn't even any Hollywood." The familiar voice of Donald Fagen fills the hall.

It worked.

I actually then got a small ovation from the crowd nearest to me in the hall. They must have sensed that they had almost missed a great show. I flashed the intercom and told Dave to go get the band, we had a show to do.

Cold Shower

―――――――――――◆―――――――――――

Late during a fall tour, we pulled up to a sports facility in Duluth Minnesota. It was very cold and windy (as it usually is in the Northern edge of Minnesota. Duluth is actually as far North as Fargo North Dakota, and we all know how cold it gets there. The temperature was about zero, with the wind chill factor, it was probably 20 below.

It was about 30 minutes until load-in, and I hadn't showered in three days. What a stroke of luck! An arena like this would have a locker room, and locker rooms have showers. I grabbed a bar of soap and a semi-clean T-shirt. The locker room door was unlocked, no wasted time finding someone with the key. Turn on the water and wait for the warm water, a cold shower would be a bitter victory. Warmer, warmer…, here it comes…, hot! Blessed hot water! The water runs down my face and for several minutes I stand there in the spray forgetting that I have a bar of soap. After snapping back to reality, I wash all four quadrants of my body, finishing with my face and hair. A final rinse, and it's time to dry off, get dressed and head for the truck. There I stood, dripping wet, when I realized I had no towel. A quick check of the locker room yielded nothing but paper towels. I was down to about five minutes until my presence was required inside the trailer, so I grabbed a handful of paper towels and attempted to dry off. I was successful everywhere, except my hair. So I left the warmth and humidity of the locker room and entered the winter wonderland on the dock.

The wind hit my face like a hundred razorblades. I scurried to the open door of the trailer, noticing the looks of disbelief on the stage crew's faces. They all were wearing heavy coats, fur hats, and had donned lined work gloves. I was wearing a light jacket, no hat, and had very wet hair. I ignored the teamster steward as he said "Kid, you're gonna get pneumonia." I couldn't think about anything except unloading the truck, that was my job, I had to do it. The first ten minutes were the worst, since we were out in the open on the dock. Later the wind subsided, as we moved deeper into the Kentucky air ride. By the time we were halfway done, my hair had frozen solid. I'd sure that if I had bumped my head on something, parts of my hair would have broken off. Eventually, the trailer was empty, and I moved back inside the venue. The blast of heat hit me as I began the process of defrosting. I continued to work on the stage, working up a sweat while unpacking cases, and getting ready for the day's next scheduled event, the sound check a mere three hours away.

I don't actually remember anything unique about the show that night, I'm sure it was uneventful. I do remember how I felt the next morning, I was sick as a dog. I had a bad cough, sore throat, and probably a low grade fever. I took aspirin and decongestants, every four hours and kept going. My condition deteriorated over the next week or so as we moved south. By the time we got to Normal, Illinois, I was far from normal. By that night when we loaded out from Illinois University I definitely had a fever, and almost no energy. I was given an exemption from driving that night, and thought that after a good night's sleep, I'd be OK.

By the next morning when we got to Carbondale, I was only semiconscious. They tried to wake me for the load-in to no avail. I missed the entire setup that day, which ended up being the only time in my career that happened. Somebody took me to the campus clinic where an intern diagnosed me with acute bronchitis, and borderline pneumonia. The Union Steward back in Duluth had been clairvoyant. He gave me a ten day supply of antibiotic pills that were apparently designed for a horse, and some various other meds. He advised me that my condition was bad enough that I should fly home for several weeks of bed rest. I assured him I would do just that.

I lied.

I had no intention of abandoning the tour half way through. Besides, since taking over the front mix at the beginning of this tour, there was no one left on the crew that even knew how to do the house mix. That left the Carbondale show that night at Shyrock auditorium. I would have to mix the show, there was no other alternative.

The drugs hadn't kicked in yet, that was to take at least two more days. They had, however, made me nauseated, and that was not a good combination with the dehydration I was already experiencing. I rested all day, skipping the sound check. Jean-Luc and my partner Dave (on monitors) muddled through it, getting the settings as close as they could. When the time arrived for the show, Louie and Dave came to get me from my suspended animation in the motorhome. They helped me to the board and asked if I needed anything. "Water," I managed to utter, "Lots of water." They gave me a gallon of spring water from the dressing room, I sat it next to me at the board. As the fans flowed in, I found that standing up was better than sitting. This was possible since thankfully the board was in the back row, so my standing didn't block any views. As the show approached I tried to concentrate on the task at hand. I was still feverish, and drank water constantly. The show started and I made the needed adjustments by the end of the second song. I then looked at Louie stationed next to me at the light board and motioned that I'd be right back. I stopped at the security guard near us long enough to tell him that he shouldn't let anyone touch the sound board. While Jean-Luc spoke to the crowd, and the band prepared to play the third song, I was in the restroom, throwing up. I hurried back to the board as the song started, and then replaced the fluid I had just lost by chugging a large amount of spring water. At the end of the next song, I repeated the process. By the end of the set I had consumed the entire gallon and was asking for another. According to Louie, the show actually went perfect. I'll have to take his word for it, since I really don't remember much about the show, just the ping ponging to the restroom. At the show's conclusion, they helped me back to my bunk, and I missed my only load-out in four years. My prescribed three week bed rest lasted a total of about 48 hours. By the next show, I was much better, but to this day I have recurring problems with my respiratory system.

I can't imagine why.

Turn it up

◆

After making a switch in 1978, graduating from the stage monitor mix to the main mix, I had the chance to work with Pat Metheny. The first show was at his alma matter Berklee College of Music in Boston. He was to open for Jean-Luc that night, with his original quartet that included Lyle Mays, Mark Egan and Dan Gottlieb. His band was virtually unknown at that point, but to jazz fans around the world today he is a very familiar name.

Pat played the six and twelve string guitars (still does), while Lyle was on keyboards, Mark on bass, and Dan was the drummer. Pat's style was a form of traditional jazz but with a modern flavor. If Ponty's music was Classical Jazz Rock, Pat's music would have to be Jazz-Soft Rock. Lyle's use of autoharp gave the songs an open "airiness", while Pat's style of playing the guitar reminded me very much of Larry Coryell. The album they had just released was simply titled "Pat Metheny Group" and sported a plain white cover. Among others, they performed the classic Metheny tunes, "Jaco," and "San Lorenzo" that night.

I discovered that this fledgling band didn't have a sound man yet; I don't even think they had a band roadie (I vaguely remember the band setting up their own equipment at the Berkley gig). I was to mix their sound at the performing arts center that first night, and I was thrilled. Pat came out to the board, and supervised the sound check. He seemed pleased, and reminded me several times to use as little volume as possible. "Just amplify it so everyone can hear, don't overwhelm them with volume," he said. "Whatever you'd like, it's your show," I replied.

They were very well received at that show and the many others that they opened for us during the tour. Word of Pat and his group had started to get out to the true jazz fans, and his new following was evident during the ovations he got with us. During the last show we were to play together during 1978, and after his band had already played their set; Pat asked me if he could watch Jean-Luc's show with me from out at the main board. "Sure." As Ponty and the band took the stage, the power of the opening song "Cosmic Messenger" had Pat concerned. At the end of the song he whispered to me, "Does Jean-Luc know you mix the sound this loud?" "Yes", I said confidently, "he likes it to be powerful like this". Pat sat there the whole show, watching and listening, as I subtly raised the volume an imperceptible amount each song. By the encore the hall was rocking. The fans were on their feet stomping and clapping to the beat of "New Country." Pat thanked me for allowing him to sit there with me, and congratulated me on a great show.

The following year Pat opened for us on the "Taste of Passion" tour. Things would be different.

An entire year had gone by, and Pat had grown in popularity. He was still the opening act for Ponty, but arguably could have headlined in some cities. As the sound check approached, I was truly excited about mixing one of my favorite artists. I was completely deflated as an unfamiliar roadie walked up to the board, and announced himself as Pat's sound man. "Oh," was about all I could manage to say. Upon collecting myself I continued, "I'm Karl, Ponty's Production Manager and Sound Man, if you need any help let me know since I used to mix for Pat as well." "Thanks, but I've got it, Pat is very particular about how he likes his sound." I silently watched as the sound check for Pat's group took shape. Near the conclusion, as the entire band played a song together, I couldn't help but notice that it was every bit as loud as when I mix Ponty. "It's a little loud, don't you think?" I asked the new sound guy.

"Pat likes it this way, he wants the music to be powerful." "Really?"…I asked with a smirk, "I wonder where he got that idea from?"

Do Not Disturb

♦

Getting from "Point A" to "Point B" was sometimes the biggest adventure of all. We frequently had impossible all night drives, and coped with this situation by resorting to various drugs. The drug of choice was of course cocaine, but if it wasn't available, "crank" would do nicely. One creative (but stupid) way of delivering the powder to the driver was a variation of the "driver switch" I described in a previous chapter. Remember, the new driver would sit on the old driver's lap, while a third person held the wheel and watched the road? In this maneuver, the driver wanting to "do a line" would need help to prevent pulling over. Another roadie would prepare a line by chopping the coke with a razor blade or the edge of a credit card, forming a "line" several inches long that would be inhaled. The "tooter"(a straw or rolled up hundred dollar bill) was given to the driver. The second person would then hold the tray with the "line" under the driver's face, while also taking hold of the wheel. The driver would say, "go," and look down to snort the line while the second person would temporarily steer the motorhome, and watch the road. When finished a few seconds later, the driver would take back control of the vehicle (within the parameters of being able to control anything while doing hard drugs). Again let me reinforce that I am not glamorizing what we did, but am rather pointing out some of the incredibly stupid things a human being will do, endangering himself and others, to get the high associated with a powerful illegal drug. I am glad to report that we were very lucky; we never had an accident while doing this maneuver. I cannot, however, report that we never had any accidents.

During one tour we were short one bunk, even assuming that one person was always driving. There was, however, a pull down bunk over the driver's chair, but that rendered the motorhome undriveable since it pulled down to the middle of the chair. Roadie rule number 4, "When confronted with an insurmountable odds, improvise." After several attempts we finally figured out that if we used a pair of two by fours, cut to exactly the right length, these boards could be used to hold the bunk up high enough that the driver could still drive. The bunk would actually touch the top of his head, and there was so little room in the bunk that turning over was impossible. As you may have guessed, I was nominated for the "sandwich bunk". I have no history of claustrophobia, but I am sympathetic to that aliment after spending many nights wedged into that contraption.

One morning after freeing myself from the human toaster, I joined everyone for breakfast. I assumed the motorhome had gone through some kind of terrible storm the previous night since the side of the home was caked with dark mud. As we ordered breakfast at a Denny's or IHOP or equivalent restaurant, the conversation turned strange. "I think I bruised my arm in the fall," one said. ""Your arm, hell, my whole body is bruised" said another. I was still a little sleepy so it wasn't sinking in yet. "Good thing that heavy duty wrecker happened by when it did," said a third roadie. Now I was starting to regain coherency, and I asked, "What the hell are you guys talking about?" Six faces went blank as they realized the same fact simultaneously. "You don't know do you?" one offered. "Know what," I was getting irritated. "My God, didn't anyone check on him?" someone whispered. Again, six blank looks. "Karl, I fell asleep at the wheel last night, and dumped the motorhome over on its side into a ditch." "Everyone tumbled out of the bunks into a big pile, and later a wrecker had to pull us out."

I had actually slept through a serious accident. Being held in place by my cramped bunk, I had slept right through it. To this day, I still don't know if I was stood upright or on my head, but I've always assumed that if I had ended up on my head, the blood rushing south would have awakened me.

If this is Tuesday, this must be Cincinnati

◆

One morning during a lengthy tour, I woke up to find myself in an empty motorhome. I could find no signs of life, no driver, no sleepers, only empty bunks. I pulled a clean T-shirt over my head, and journeyed out to solve this mystery. I locked the door to the motorhome, and found myself in a bustling downtown area. It seemed to be mid day, probably close to load-in time. Where was everyone? At breakfast? Probably. I'd look around and find the hall. I wandered up the sidewalk, weaving in and out between men in suits and ties. After making my way to the corner, I turned around not wanting to lose sight of my mobile home. No evidence of a venue, and I couldn't quite remember details of where we were supposed to play. I decided to determine the time, which would give me an indication of when I could expect the crew to return. I imagine that I was quite a sight in my roadie garb, with my unwashed hair, as I approached the businessman and said, "Excuse me sir, what time is it?" "Eleven forty", he replied automatically. (Good, it was only twenty minutes until load-in, but load-in where?) As he turned to walk away, I imposed again, "Sir, excuse me again." "Yes?" he said now seemingly concerned. "What city is this?" "Why…It's Cincinnati," came the confused answer. "Thank you very much," I cheerfully exclaimed. He hurried off, and I'm sure he still wonders if he ran into an escaped mental patient on that day.

Now I remembered, this was Cincinnati, so I just needed to find the Taft Theatre.

A few minutes later, I found the hall, and my crew. By the way, they had found a restaurant for breakfast, and decided to let me sleep.

Hot fun in the Summertime

◆

It's the middle of summer, and we are driving from San Diego to Tucson. As we approach Gila Bend, Arizona, following the two roadies in a rented six-wheel truck, we pull over to the shoulder as the truck sputters to a halt. The gauge confirms that there should be over a quarter of a tank of gas in the truck, but the truck's engine does not agree. It is HOT; in fact Gila Bend is at that moment the hottest spot in the United States (well over 100°). This is big trouble, if the truck and the motorhome don't start moving soon, the load-in will be late. And then there's the heat.

Let's try adding some gas to the tank just in case the gauge is broken, I say. Everyone agrees, but no one is willing to do the siphoning. "Wimps," I mutter, as I find a tube and a container. This is easy, I said to myself as I sucked on that tube, moving gasoline towards my mouth. Now imagine my surprise as I was carefully timing this procedure, when I received a mouth full of unleaded gasoline. I had enough presence of mind to stick the end of the tube down into the container, successful in my attempt to initiate the siphon. I then spit the mouthful of gas out on the ground, trying in vain to neutralize the taste. "Water!" I gasped. "All out," came the dreaded answer. "Perrier, Dr Pepper, anything wet," I pleaded. "Here's a Heineken," someone offered. I took a big swig, and realized it was warm. I swished it around my mouth and spit it out, repeating several times. It didn't help. Anyway we now had the precious gas. We pour it in the truck's tank, and start it up. Nothing. The transfer of fuel was a waste of time. It must be the fuel pump, or something else more serious. Now we need a new plan, and I have a mouth that tastes like gasoline, and it's HOT. We drove the motorhome into Gila Bend, and found a Truck Rental franchise. We rented a 24 footer, and hot footed it back to the disabled truck ("hot" footed, get it?). The new truck was then backed up to the dead one. Imagine if you can the amount of heat contained in two trucks backed up end to end, on the side of the road, in the sun, in the hottest spot in the nation. It took about an hour to transfer the load over to the working truck, and then we abandoned the disabled one where it sat (the second vehicle that I had abandoned on an Arizona highway).

We finally got to the hall about four hours late. Despite the late load-in, and no sound check, the show actually did get started on time. The taste of 87 octane gasoline was still alive and well in my mouth during the entire show.

Today, I have a special appreciation for weather reports that announce where the hottest spot in the nation today was, whether it's Death Valley, or Gila Bend, or wherever. Also, I've never been able to bring myself to siphon gasoline again.

Road Clichés

━━━━━━━━━━ ◆ ━━━━━━━━━━

Sometimes a phrase will take on a life of its own during a tour. Words that are meaningless to an outsider can crumple a roadie to the floor in hysterical laughter when uttered at precisely the right moment. Pearls of wisdom like "Ching, ching, bye, bye," or "Nice talkin to ya'" seem benign enough but speak volumes to the members of the tour.

My favorite phrase has a history dating back to Vietnam. Tim, the Road Manager for most of my tenure with Ponty, had been a gunner on an evacuation helicopter in "Nam". He told us the story of one day while on a mission; they had drawn heavy fire after picking up some stranded G.I.s. One of the other pilots (that had a reputation for being sort of a whiner) was chatting with Tim's chopper, when a new distress call came in not far away. The unit commander got on the radio and ordered the "whiner" to go back and attempt the rescue. After a short silence the disgruntled pilot with the whiney southern accent replied, "Ever F****in' time,…Ever F***in' time."

Needless to say, anytime it was appropriate, like when a job was assigned that was less than enviable, the unfortunate recipient would let loose with, "Ever F***in' time,…Ever F***in' time."

"War is hell."

Turning Japanese

◆

In February of 1979, I flew to Japan to mix sound for two JLP shows. Louie and I considered it a vacation since we wouldn't even be touching any gear. In some ways it was a new high point in my roadie career, in others it was a new low point.

The first low came on the flight over. I had brought a small quantity of coke in my briefcase for the long trip. We knew we had to finish it before we got to Japanese customs (notorious for finding drugs just ask Paul and Linda McCartney). The only problem was that we didn't have anything with us to discreetly do the coke with. Part of the way over the ocean, I found the answer. I ordered a Jack Daniels and coke (the cola not the powder) from the stewardess (they weren't called flight attendants yet). After emptying the booze into the glass, I utilized the square bottle as a suitable surface the lay out a miniscule line. A rolled up hundred provided the tooter, and we were off to the races. Luckily, the jumbo jet was too sparsely populated for anyone to really notice what we were doing, and the contraband was soon gone. One more matter to take care of, my little brown coke jar still had illegal residue inside, and I didn't want to throw it away. A Pat Traver's song gave me an idea. "Snorting whiskey, and drinking cocaine," is supposed to be about somebody so messed up they get the words backwards. We were so messed up we thought it might actually work. I took the remnants of the Jack Daniels and poured it into the coke vial. After a proper shaking, we actually snorted the liquid formed by dissolving the cocaine into the bourbon. It burned our nostrils (Duh!), as we laughed out loud at our cleverness. I cleared Japanese customs with no trouble, but I soon discovered I wasn't quite so clever after all.

Due to the drug, I hadn't slept during the twenty hour flight. Jet lag now kicked in, and while most of the band and crew were spending the first two free days shopping and sight seeing, I spent it hibernating.

Once I woke up I had a marvelous experience in Japan. Here are a few random memories from my Japan trip.

I found myself fascinated with Pachinko. I played it constantly when we weren't working. They award you silly little prizes (like the ones you would get at a carnival midway) for a certain number of points scored. I didn't care about the prizes; I just liked playing the game.

The name of the sound company we used for our shows translated into English as "Birdsong Planning." No one, including our assigned interpreter, could explain the significance of the name. He just explained that it was a Japanese name that didn't translate to English very well.

A young Japanese girl assigned to us as an interpreter, told me her dream was to come to America, and work for a big record company someday. Her short term goal was much more humble. She was on a waiting list for a telephone number in Tokyo, and felt confident she may be assigned one in about three more years.

I did learn a few words in Japanese, which I retain to this day. Itchy, knee, sun, she, go (1,2,3,4,5), Domo Arigato (Thank you very much), and Hi! (which can mean different things, but basically is Japanese for "what's up?")

Flying to Osaka from Tokyo was one of the scariest airline experiences in my life. As you approach Osaka, it looks like you are going to crash into the peak of a mountain. At the last minute you clear the top (barely) and then you drop like a rock down the far side of the mountain until you finally hit the front edge of the tarmac and the pilot throws the engines into full reverse narrowly avoiding driving off the end of the runway and into the ocean. And you thought O'Hare was bad.

We took the bullet train from Osaka back to Tokyo. The ride was very cool, but the only thing available to eat on the train was curry shrimp, and it was horrible. Later one of our Japanese hosts told me "nobody eats on the train." Now they tell me.

When people ask me what Tokyo was like I say, It's like New York City, but with mostly Japanese inhabitants. There were Dairy Queens, Hardee's, and McDonald's, all with signage in Japanese. Also, I don't think I ran into one native of Japan that didn't speak at least basic English. We all felt right at home.

At the airport waiting to go through customs, we ran into Steve Allen and Jayne Meadows. A couple members of our band, along with Louie and I talked to Steve and his wife for quite a while. He was there doing some sort of show, and was on our flight returning to L.A. The things I remember about him vividly are how tall he was, and that he looked rather old. A few days ago I saw a special television tribute to Steve on the occasion of his 75th birthday. Happy Birthday Steve.

(UPDATE…Steve Allen passed away in his sleep on October 30th, 2000. Sleep well Steve.)

A Familiar Journey

◆

In the spring of '79, an old friend would come to town. Steve Smith, the drummer for Ponty during my first tour, was going to play the Rochester Auditorium. He was now the drummer for Ronnie Montrose's new self-titled jazz rock band. They were the opening act for Journey and Toto. I collected my pass at the stage door, said hello to the familiar stage crew, and looked for my old road buddy. I found Steve, and we picked up where we had left off. He introduced me to the then current members of Journey that included Steve Perry, Neal Schon (sporting a full length afro), and the drummer Aynsley Dunbar. While relaxing out in Journey's tour bus, Steve confided in me that he was about to join Journey as their drummer, replacing Dunbar. I found that hard to believe, Aynsley Dunbar was a rock drumming legend dating back to his work with John Mayall and the Bluesbreakers, Davie Bowie, Frank Zappa, and Jeff Beck. But I had no reason to doubt Stevie, so I kept my little secret to myself until it was announced later in the year. For that show Steve was still the drummer for the reinvented Ronnie Montrose Band. Ronnie had given up popular Rock & Roll, opting for a hard driving Jazz-Rock. The current album was "Open Fire," and is to this day one of my personal top five favorite albums. (It's now available on CD, but only as an import) If you can find a copy, check out the title song "Open Fire"…it rocks. The headliner that night was Toto, a studio band that had made it big, and they were supporting their "Africa" album with this tour. Journey was promoting "Infinity", and "Wheel in the Sky" was the current hit. I spent several hours backstage, and in the bus with Steve, it was good to see him. The show was great but I think Montrose was the highlight, Journey a close second, and Toto was a disappointment (basically an upside down show). When Steve said goodbye and left after the show, I never saw him, or heard from him again. Steve was of course correct. Aynsley Dunbar did leave Journey later in that tour, and eventually ended up as the drummer for "Starship" (formerly Jefferson Starship/Airplane). Steve replaced Aynsley and stayed with Journey through some of their most successful years. Later he started his own group called "Vital Information", was briefly a member of "The Storm", and even rejoined Journey again in 1997 for the comeback CD, only to leave again in early 1998. He continues to pursue his solo career, and is still one of the most accomplished Jazz-Rock drummers in the world.

More Quickies

---◆---

Natalie Cole: During April of 1978, I provided sound for several shows in upstate New York for Natalie Cole and her opening act Lou Rawls. They were very easy shows compared to a rock or funk gig. The monitors were more than adequate at low volumes, and both performers had very capable sound engineers, that were anything but demanding. All we had to do was set up, get everything working correctly, and watch the show. My interaction with both of these artists was limited, I don't remember anything specific about the conversations that I'm sure took place during sound check. They probably went something like…"That microphone OK for you Mr. Rawls, or would you rather have a different one?" "Please call me Lou, and this one here will do just fine, thanks." "Is that monitor level loud enough for you Ms. Cole?" "It's fine, thank you."

What I didn't know at the time I was working with her was that Natalie Cole was struggling with a serious substance abuse problem, which is well documented today. I didn't notice anything unusual during my brief dealings with her, but then I didn't have access to the dressing room areas. Also it was before my own problems with drugs started so I wasn't tuned in to what to look for yet.

The shows were very successful, and the artists well received. The only specific song I remember either artist singing was Lou Rawl's rendition of "Tobacco Road."

Head East: The "one hit wonders." They were the brunt of jokes in the music industry, and constantly struggled for that second hit. Sometimes the one hit was enough to afford the group the opportunity to do some concerts, usually in conjunction with other "one hit wonders." I guess the theory was if you put two or three "one hit wonders." together it would actually form a show worth going to.

Such was the case for an outdoor show I did in May of 1979 in Rochester that featured Head East, Wet Willie and several other "lesser" bands. I had just returned from a tour in Europe and Patty was at my side all day. Wet Willie had produced one real hit, "Keep on Smilin'" in 1974, the year I graduated high school. I remember seeing them perform it live that year on ABC's "Midnight Special" hosted by Wolfman Jack. Now here they were five years later, just a few feet away from me, as I mixed their stage monitors. The lead singer, Jimmy Hall, would lick his lips between the lines of lyrics with his over sized tongue. They of course did other songs besides "Keep on Smilin'," I just don't remember most of them. The only other song I do recall is a version of the old blues classic "She caught the Katy, and left me a mule to ride" that I had grown to love having heard Taj Mahal play it many times.

By the time the Head East hit the stage, the crowd was ready to party. Most of the kegs allocated to the festivities were already dry, and the heat had caused virtually every male in the audience to discard their T-shirts. Frisbees were zooming through the sky, looking for unsuspecting targets, while several "wasted" students tried in vain to climb a large tree for a better view. The show started with renditions of their limited selection of songs from the only original Head East album "Flat as a Pancake." From the first chord of the first song drunken fans were screaming, "Save my life," or "Going down for the last time," both attempts to get them to play the one recognizable Head East song, "Never been any reason." At the shows finale they got their wish as the band offered a carbon copy of the four year old hit.

There's never been any reason...for me to think about you

Save my life I'm going down for the last time

We had to load quickly after the show as we had a long drive to get to another show in another town. Patty said goodbye and was to get a ride home with her girlfriend Colleen. I would find out much later, that instead of going home Colleen and Patty went to "party with the band," back at the local hotel. Her version blames the entire misadventure on "Red," (Colleen's nickname & hair color). Patty did admit to partaking of nose candy with the Head East keyboard player, and then later that she had to fend off his aggressive sexual advances, eventually escaping unsoiled.

I'm not sure I ever accepted her version.

Also, I can't imagine where that keyboard player got the idea that just because he invites a couple of "backstage" girls back up to his room, and provides them with cocaine, that he should expect them to "put out."

Billy Cobham: If the name is unfamiliar to you, let me start by saying this man is quite probably the greatest "pure drummer" of our generation. His jazz-funk work is legendary, including the years he spent with the great keyboardist George Duke. He is, in my opinion, the strongest and most accurate drummer ever to lift a drumstick. Pretty bold statement considering some of the percussionists I have seen, right? I'll prove it.

Billy is an innovator who experiments with his art. He was the first drummer I know of to use "rocket tubes", those small diameter tom toms that opened up new tonal possibilities to drummers. He also was the first to use electronic "effects" on a drum kit. He had an entire rack of state of the art electronics placed near him as he drummed. Between songs he could make adjustments, like "more delay," or "less reverb." One night from my perch at the monitor board I saw him execute a long drum solo. His hands were a blur, as it seemed he was hitting them all simultaneously. I noticed him trying to get the drum roadie's attention who was preoccupied repairing a kick pedal. Apparently one of the settings on one of the pieces of electronics was in the wrong position. After about ten seconds he gave up using his facial expressions to correct the problem, and took matters into his own swift hands. During a blink of an eye, his drum solo was interrupted as he spun to his right, and accurately hit the offending switch with the drum stick, flipping it to the correct position, and then spun back resuming his solo without anyone knowing that anything had happened. Not a single beat was missed. That is accurate.

During another show a drum company representative came by the sound check and offered Billy a free set of drums (they were fishing for an endorsement). Billy was reluctant, but finally agreed. The new drums were set up for sound check as Billy prepared to give them a workout. He sat down and after making some adjustments, started to wail. Within about fifteen minutes most of the major components of the kit had failed. He broke both kick pedals, and snapped one of the tom toms from its mounting. By the end of the sound check, his original kit had replaced the newcomer, which was discarded in a mangled pile at the side of the stage. As Billy headed for the dressing room to get some food he told his roadie, call that drum guy, and tell him to come get what's left of his stuff. Now that's strong.

Blood Sweat and Tears: Here's an example of a sixties and early seventies super group that refused to roll over and play dead. I would provide lights for them many times in 1976. Believe it or not they could still pull in a crowd, and belt out a decent show. David Clayton-Thomas was still the lead singer, but a lot of the band varied from show to show. They played all the songs I had enjoyed in grade school, including "Spinning Wheel," "God Bless the Child," and "You make me so very happy." I actually looked forward to BST gigs, they were always well executed and the crowds, although older than the normal fans I was used to, were always enthusiastic.

One night after a successful show somewhere in the Carolinas, we were trying to decide what to do with a night off. We all had rooms and were in no hurry to leave since there was no gig tomorrow. The hotel clerk was about to give us directions to a local club when David bopped up sporting a loud leisure suit, and said, "Where are we going guys?" We all answered with blank looks. He continued, "Hey, let's go out and find some chicks!" "Whadda ya say?"

"No thanks David", I responded, "we were all too tired to go out, but you go ahead." "You sure?" came his disappointed plea.

After his cab left the front of the hotel, we all piled in another one, and went out to a different hot spot. I never heard whether David was successful in his chick quest.

Not long after the shows with BST, they began an extended engagement in Las Vegas. I think they are still there (just kidding).

LaBelle: Long before there was a Patti Labelle, there was LaBelle the group. We did the sound and lights for this innovative group in 1976. Patti Labelle, the group's namesake, who later would make a statement with her wild hair designs, would instead make waves with the groups futuristic costumes. Nona and Sarah completed the group that wore skintight silver spacesuits, while fog machines clouded the stage enhancing the surrealistic effect. Their big hit was "Lady Marmalade" featuring the lyrics "Voulez-vous coucher avec moi, ce soir? Which of course is loosely translated into "Do you want to sleep with me tonight? The LaBelle shows were always full of energy and a lot of fun to work.

Patti Labelle started her solo career about the same time I left the road, and the rest is history. (C'est la vie!)

Parlez-vous Français?

◆

As I revisited the land of my birth, I was determined to disprove the people back home that had warned me how rude the French really were. Certainly not, I thought to myself as I walked off the jet-way at Charles De Gaulle Airport. Now don't get me wrong, I wasn't expecting the mayor of Paris to greet me as I de-planed and kissing me on both cheeks, welcoming me back to Mother France. What I didn't expect was direct evidence to prove that it's not only the Americans that are ugly, it's also the French.

We arrived in Paris on the 28th day of February 1979, and then we were bused to our rehearsal hall in Cambrai (home of the cheese of the same name). The next day while the rehearsal was being organized, I walked into town to convert some traveler's checks into French Francs. I located a large commercial bank and entered the spacious lobby. It could have been a bank in New York or Chicago or even Houston. Large marble columns, oversized counters, and lots of bold vertical lines to give the architecture a powerful and safe appearance. This was the place I was looking for, they looked like they could handle a billion dollar international trade deal, certainly they could cash my hundred dollar traveler's check.

I confidently walked to the window, and presented the suited man behind the counter my endorsed check. I smiled, and expected the man to speak English, sounding something like Jacques Cousteau. "Oui?" he said obviously not realizing I was an American. "Francs, Sil vous plais," I said proud that I remembered enough sixth grade French to put a four word sentence together. "Je ne'comprone pas." He said with a disgusted look on his face like he had suddenly bit into a lemon. I don't understand he says, OK, let's try this a different way. "Je suis American, Je parle Francais un peau." There that should do it. "Je n parle Engalis."As he crossed his arms daring me to speak French. I really didn't have time for this. I had to get back to rehearsal. I turned to the other suited tellers at the adjacent windows. "Tu parle Englais?" "Non" came the unanimous answer in stereo. I started to give up, and turned to leave. I could sense that the tellers were probably all smiling, having won the sparing match. Then it came to me.

I turned and forcefully said, "Je suis Francais!" The smiles were replaced by looks of disbelief. I continued, "C'est Vrai, Je suis Francais." I then pulled out my passport and pointed to the Birthplace-Lieu De Naissance: FRANCE.

Things then changed very quickly.

In perfect Queen's English, the banker (that ten seconds earlier couldn't understand a word I was saying) spoke, "You were born in France, why didn't you say so?" "Where were you born, near here?" "Yes, La Chappelle St. Mesmin." I must have mispronounced the name of my birth town because several of them laughed, but only for a second. "Welcome to France, please let me take care of your transaction." He cashed my check, and I thanked him for his help. As I walked out the door, I'm pretty sure he didn't hear me as I said under my breath, "you son of a bitch."

I kind of wish he had.

My Paris Vacation

◆

After the rehearsals and show in Cambrai, we had a complete day off in Paris. As we entered Paris in a rented tour bus with the band, Jean-Luc found the microphone used for the tours, and became our impromptu guide. "And on your left the world famous restaurant and club, Moulin Rouge which means Red Windmill." He was very funny that afternoon, and seemed to be very happy to be back in Paris, where he had studied music so many years before. We pulled in to our new temporary home at the Hotel Lotti. After settling in, Louie and I hit the streets of Paris. Now it had been over 22 years since I had been to Paris, and since I was less than six months old when I left, I didn't remember much about where to go or what to do. That problem was remedied almost immediately as we crossed a busy street and Louie collided head on with a French girl. Louie was occupied looking around at the sights and the girl was trying to read something, and BLAMM, she ended up on the pavement. Louie helped her up, as she started to curse him out in French. "I'm sorry," he said very genuinely. "You are Americans?" she smiled. "Yeah, just a couple of clumsy tourists." "Hey, lets get out of the street."

From the safety of the sidewalk, she brushed herself off, and said she needed to be on her way. "So what's it like living in Paris?" asked Louie struggling for something to prevent her from walking away. "I work here for an airline, I'm American too." To answer your question, "I love living here in Paris, I been here over two years." She was an attractive young woman, probably about twenty or maybe twenty one years old. She had dark hair, and dark eyes and had a look that could either be a European Princess, or a Long Island Princess. "Would you two like me to show you Paris?" "That would be great, but don't you have somewhere to go?" Louie asked. "I just decided to take the afternoon off," she smiled, looking at Louie.

We started by going to the top of the Eiffel Tower. The day was so clear I could see everything for several kilometers around (of course I'm using kilometers, I'm in France aren't I?). We didn't have time to go in the Louvre (someday soon I will go back), but we saw just about everything else in Paris that afternoon. We saw the Notre Dame Cathedral, Le Rivé Gauche (the left bank), the Arc de Triomphe, and the Place de le Concorde. Towards sunset, she took us for a ride on the Metro (the Paris subway), which we took out to Sacré Coeur. The sight of that old cathedral lit up at night was spectacular. We had to hurry to get back to our hotel before the Metro shut down for the night. She came back to the Hotel bar, predictably hinting to Louie that she didn't want to end the evening. Louie and I were roommates in the $200 a night room, but we already had this kind of situation pre-arranged, as it had happened many times before. Since I was the one without female companionship, I would pretend to be tired, and go up to the room first. Then after a reasonable period of time Louie and the tour guide would make their way to the room, with the assurance that I was now sound asleep. When they arrived, I had the option of sleeping, or pretending to be asleep while taking in the show. Sometimes Louie would leave the light on, but tonight he wouldn't, so I fell asleep shortly after they started having sex.

We left the next morning for a show in Strasbourg, at the Palais De Congress. That show turned out to be a technical disappointment. Then back to Paris for one of the best shows of the entire tour. We played the Paris Pavillion, and the show was nearly perfect. It would have been perfect with a full house of fans, but with such a large venue a sell-out would have been a long shot.

There was enough energy in the house that night to light Paris, as the road manager made the introduction and the black stage blossomed to life with colored lights. "Madams et Messieurs…Jean-Luc Ponty!"

I smiled at Louie (his Paris airline babe was at his side) as the band launched into "Cosmic Messenger"; it just doesn't get any better than this.

Four nights later in Nice I would be proved wrong.

Very Nice

◆

We pulled in to the Theatre De La Verdure at Nice (pronounced niece), as the smell of the ocean competed with the smell of money. We were in the French Riviera, near Cannes, the setting for the Cannes' Film festival. We could see the beautiful people playing on the beach from the load-in. A large banner spanned the street near the hall. The banner read Elton John Ray Cooper under which it read Jean-Luc Ponty. We were playing there on a Wednesday; Saturday night would be Elton John. We had both sold-out the 3500 available seats. As good as the show in Paris was this show was even better. The acoustics made the sound as cooperative as I'd ever remembering vibrating air being.

On my itinerary for that night I simply drew four stars (the only show that received that score on this entire tour) and I wrote the word "Great!"

I never heard how Elton's show went a few nights later (as we were already in Switzerland by then), but I can only hope that anyone that saw both shows was at least slightly disappointed with his.

The British are Coming!

◆

During the European tour in 1979 we contracted for sound, lights, and trucking with a British company. It was more cost effective than trying to ship our own equipment overseas. The crew consisted of two sound roadies, two light roadies and a truck driver. This was in addition to our own two band roadies (Art and Allen), Louie on lights, and myself on the sound and as the Production Manager. Two of the British roadies were from Manchester, the other two were from Liverpool, and the driver was from London. We all crammed into a VW microbus in Cambrai and headed out for a six week experience together. It took a while to get used to their lingo and their culture. For example, they loved to "get pissed." Now in the states, that phrase meant to "get mad." In England, it meant to "get drunk," and they were very good at that. I was never one to pass judgment on someone that wanted to have a beer before noon, but these guys would drink a six pack each for breakfast, and then want to drive the micro van really fast. I was the only American insured to drive overseas, so considering the usual condition of the UK boys ("pissed")…I drove a lot.

Once on the Autobahn in Germany, a road that has no speed limit, one of them was driving (very fast) and another one had to urinate. The driver thought it was funny that the other one was begging to stop, and so he refused to pull over. "Go out the bleedin' window Lad," he said laughing loudly. The other one stunned us all by saying, "Right! I will then." I doubt you'll be able to picture this, but try anyway. We are cruising along at somewhere over 70 MPH (of course in the equivalent KPH over there) and the Brit in the front passenger seat rolls down his window and attempts to urinate out of that window. We all were yelling to stop since we could all predict that it wouldn't work. Luckily, we did have rooms that night and were able to take our second "shower" of the day. By the way if that didn't gross you out too bad, our UK friends later figured out a way around the obstacle of wind preventing them from a high speed urination. They "went" into a plastic bag and then threw it out the window, and this was before there were zip-lock bags, so this wasn't exactly a perfect plan either.

Some of the other English terminology included "suss it out" (figure it out), "torch" (a flashlight), "a fag" (a cigarette, imagine my shock the first time one of them told me he'd be right back, he was going to "smoke a fag."), "bum" (a buttocks), "bollix" (part of the male genitalia), "earth" (an electrical ground), "a lead" (a cable), "football" (soccer, can you imagine?), "Lorry" (truck), "lift" (an elevator), and poofter (a male homosexual).

The really strange thing about being around the Brits for those six weeks, is that to this day I can hear someone from the United Kingdom speak, and I can tell you whether or not they are from Manchester, Liverpool or London.

Border Crossing

◆

The microbus and its eight inhabitants left Zurich, and headed for the next gig in Zagreb, Yugoslavia. We cut through Italy and made our way to the Yugoslavian border. Now before we cross, I've got to reset your time clocks again. Yugoslavia was still a communist satellite controlled by Marshal Tito and under the influence of Mother Russia. The iron curtain was still down, and we were technically the enemy. I was the production manager so it was my responsibility to get the crew over the border safely. I gave a speech in the van about an hour from the crossing, "If anyone is "holding" (drugs) you need to lose them now, before we are in sight of the border. It's going to be bad enough, lets not give them any reasons to lock us up." There I made my case and I got everyone's assurance that we were clean. The movie Midnight Express about an American detained in a hellish prison in Turkey had been released the year before and since Turkey and Yugoslavia were right next to each other, we assumed there would probably be a similar treatment of Americans in the communist state.

At twilight, we approached the border complex. Nothing could have prepared me in advance for the scene I now viewed. Spot lights, perched on top of guard towers sweep around the perimeter of the area. Dozens of uniformed military police with heavy coats and classic Russian fur hats patrolled the area with Belgium Shepherds on leases. Every guard had a menacing automatic sub-machine gun slung over his shoulder.

We cued up (got in line) to cross, and waited our turn. The temperature had dropped greatly since we had left Southern France earlier in the day, and we had all left our heavy jackets in our suitcases with the truck. As long as we stayed in the warm interior of the mini-bus, that wasn't a problem. As we approached the checkpoint, I felt like I was in a bad spy movie, as a guard dog started barking. We finally got to the front of the line and an overweight guard, walked up to the driver's window and tapped on it with his metal flashlight. It was rolled down, and the flashlight quickly probed the interior of the bus. "Passports!" Came the abrupt order. We collected the eight documents, and surrendered them to the soldier. He examined the passports and I saw a smile come over his face. "Americans." Was all he said in English. He turned to two other guards, barking something in a language I can only guess was a Yugoslavian dialect. They hurried over and took up strategic positions around the van. After he was satisfied he had sufficient back-up to repel any potential American invasions, he spoke again. "May I see your Visas?...just the Americans." Sure I thought, I've got a VISA, and a MasterCard, but I hope they don't need an American Express. "The Americans will now exit the van and obtain visas. "What about the Brits?" I asked out loud. "European Common Market," no need from them to obtain visas.

We exited the warmth of the van, and headed for the long line to get visas. We stood in that frigid line, with what I would later find out were Turkish workers, for about two hours. We finally got to the window and attempted to communicate with the lady behind the glass. "Visas" I said, "Four," as I put four fingers up to reinforce the number. We had no Yugoslavian currency, but luckily they accepted Italian Lire. I was afraid I didn't have enough, and that we'd be subject to summary execution due to a violation of some international treaty. I actually had plenty of local currency, the visas were the equivalent of less than a dollar each U.S. All this red tape for less than four bucks! We rejoined the van and after another search of the interior by the comrade we were finally allowed to cross into what was then known as Yugoslavia.

After we were pulling away from the border station I noticed that one of the band roadies was as white as a ghost. What's wrong I asked, it wasn't that bad. He didn't answer, and the reason became clear to me from the look on his face. "Are you holding?" I demanded. After a long pause he finally said, "It's only a gram, it was in my boot." "You stupid son of a bitch!" I screamed. I never threatened another human being with his life until that moment and I haven't since, but in the heat of the moment I said, "There are two things certain if they had found that drug." "We all would have spent the rest of our lives in a communist prison, but you wouldn't have to worry about that, because you'd have never made it to that jail alive."

No one ever spoke of this incident again, but I made damn sure nobody carried anything over a border again.

Yugoslavia

◆

As we traveled across Yugoslavia, I never in a million years would have guessed that this country would be the location of one of the world's most devastating civil wars in just a few short years. If I had, I may have paid closer attention to the beautiful countryside, and the centuries old architecture. The parts I do remember were breathtaking.

We were to do three shows, in three days, in three cities. The first gig was at the Dom Sportova in Zagreb. The hall's acoustics weren't the greatest, and we didn't have a full house, but the fans that were there made up in enthusiasm for what was missing in quantity. I asked our state provided interpreter why the low turnout. His answer didn't really surprise me. The price of a single ticket to our show was roughly equal to an amount of currency that a comrade worker would have to save every spare ruble for a period of six months to afford. One thing they did have plenty of was labor. I don't think I ever had as large of a stage crew as that night. One thing about a communist country, there are plenty of workers available. After the show, I noticed another large crew apparently cleaning the parking lot. Some were sweeping, others were using high pressure steam cleaning devices as they sanitized every inch of the asphalt surface. Again I asked our interpreter to explain what those men were doing. "Cleaning the parking lot," he said confused why we were asking. "Why," I probed. "Because it's their job", came the logical answer.

We also did shows at the Hala Trivoli in Ljubljana, and at the Hala Pionir in Belgrade. Like Zagreb there was low attendance. As I look back on the Yugoslavian shows I can't help but wonder several things. How many of the people that attended our shows, or worked backstage are dead now due to over a decade of civil war? Are the three halls still standing (probably not), and what of that perfect parking lot? I'll bet it isn't steam cleaned nightly anymore. My final two questions are for all the people of the former Yugoslavia. How could you have destroyed your beautiful country? And why?

It was time to head to Germany.

Iron Curtain Call

◆

I was still mad at the crew for missing the load-in Hamburg, so I decided to ride in the truck cab for the trip to Berlin. The memory of the Yugoslavian border crossing ten days earlier was still fresh in my mind, as we approached the first East German border.

This was still the days of the "Cold War", the "Iron Curtain", and the "Berlin Wall." The only access to West Berlin (by land) was to drive up the "Berlin Corridor". This was a narrow strip of land that had a Communist guard station at each end, and miles of guarded road in-between. At the end of the corridor, on the other side of the East German guards, were American soldiers and as much safety as possible in this very dangerous part of the world. Like the Yugoslav border my memories of old black & white films featuring exchanges of Soviet and British Spies on the Berlin Bridge come to mind. As we rolled to the first checkpoint, I was expecting a real life version of Boris or Natasha, the greeting we got surprised me.

"Passports please," came the firm but polite demand in perfect English. The British driver handed the guard our two dissimilar passports. After a brief amount of time while he studied the documents he said, "You are an American?" For a split second I was tempted to say, "No kidding Comrade, I guess you know how to read." Instead I chickened out and said, "Yes sir." And the purpose of your visit to the DDR?" The German Democratic Republic, what a joke! Its name should be the

Commie Stooges that used to be German, I thought, as my German blood was a few degrees below boiling. "We are traveling to Berlin to do a show." The British driver gave me a side glance silently telling me I was volunteering too much information. "Really, what kind of show?" He asked obviously pleased with himself that he was now on to something important. "A concert, Jazz-Rock music." "You will please wait here," again in perfect English, as he turned and went into the guardhouse.

We waited there in the truck for about fifteen minutes wondering if we would be late for the load-in a few hours from now. Eventually, the English speaking guard returned (with two more identically uniformed guards) and calmly announced that they would now search the truck. Search the truck I thought, we've got nothing to hide. After the high drama in Yugoslavia I was sure we were clean. I guessed they would use dogs. I was wrong.

"Please unload your truck now." smiled the guard. "Excuse me?" I said in disbelief. "We are going to search your truck, please unload it." "But there is only two of us, it will take hours to unload it." "Then you better get started," came the predictable response. The British driver turned to me and said, "Stay here." The look in his eyes added the unspoken words, "and shut-up."

I sat there in the cab for about five more minutes as the driver and the three guards disappeared behind the trailer. I tried to see what was happening in the side mirror, but I couldn't get the right angle. About then, the driver side door opened, the driver jumped up, and started the diesel engine, then threw the rig into first. I sat there in silence until we had cleared the red and white striped gate that had been lifted out of the way. As we gained speed and entered the mouth of the corridor I turned to the driver and asked him one question. "How much did that cost us?" "Only a case of albums and a case of T-shirts." "Tim gave them to me last night in Hamburg, in case we needed them." I smiled as we headed towards the gig in Berlin, finding it mildly amusing that capitalism was alive and well behind the "Iron Curtain." As the world would discover about ten years later, capitalism would be successful in knocking down the Berlin Wall, and East Germany would reunite with West Germany. Communist Russia's crushing grip on the region would finally be released.

By the way, in an anti-climatic side note, the show in Berlin was horrible. The load in was late due to the unprepared promoter (we were actually there on time). The hall was atrocious, the crew worthless, and the crowd uninspired. The note I wrote in my itinerary that night tells it all..."The worst gig of my life so far".

We then drove for the next 24 hours straight as we headed for Stockholm.

Scandinavia

◆

It took over 24 hours to reach Stockholm in the minibus, including the first of several long ferry rides across vast fiords. It was now the 30th day of the European tour, 11 more days to go. My morale was beginning to deteriorate for several reasons. One was that I was beginning to really miss Patty, I talked to her several times by phone, but it wasn't enough, I wanted to go home. Also, now that we had no more communist countries to worry about, I was using lots of cocaine to help improve my attitude. As is always the case with this drug, any improvement it gave me was only temporary and perpetuated the need for more of the drug (this is what is known as a "downward spiral"). To make matters worse, I had broken a tooth that had become decayed, and it was starting to hurt. I knew where to buy drugs in a strange land, but not where to get professional dental care there. Then when we finally arrived at the Hotel Anglais in Stockholm, I received the final straw. A telegram awaited me from Duffy. In eleven days (at the conclusion of this tour), Instead of flying home to Rochester, I was to fly to somewhere else in the states, and join the Patti Smith Tour in progress. It would be a three week tour. Normally I would be thrilled at the prospect of extra work and working with PSG, but considering my mental condition at that point I was devastated. I sent a cryptic telegram back to my company as follows…

"Received and understand message, have a broken tooth, and in severe pain, if possible find replacement for me or have pain medication available at first gig". "Special K"

Of course the pain medication I mention is a request for coke, but I really hoped they'd find someone else. By the way, my nickname on the road was "Special K."

By the time I got to London, I got the message that I had been replaced on the first three gigs. I also got word that it was "snowing" in Rochester (there was cocaine waiting for me).

We played the show in Stockholm, and then one in Gothenburg. The next night was in Norway at the Chateau Neuf in Olso. All three of these shows were good shows, and good crowds, but I just wanted to go home. We had a day off to get to Denmark to play the Musiktheatre in Aarhus. That show featured a load-in up a flight of stairs, another great morale booster for me. Another day off...then back to Sweden (who does these schedules anyway?). That show took place at the Olympen in Lund. Then back to Demark for a show at the Falkoner Theatre in Copenhagen. With one more show in London in two days, and with British customs to get through tomorrow, we all pooled our resources. We found a large wall mirror, and after removing it from the wall of the dressing room, everyone dumped all their nose candy together. We stirred and mixed the white powder, eventually laying out nine lines for the nine contributors. They were long lines probably each over a foot long. We polished them off just prior to the show.

The Rainbow at the
end of the tour

◆

We made our way back to the French coast near Dunkirk, and caught the hovercraft to England. I've got to say this was very cool. I know that today there is a tunnel that allows you to travel under the channel between France and England (the "Chunnel"), but in 1979, the hover-craft was the state of the art way to get across the channel.

We arrived in London with about 48 hours left until we were to fly home. We had a day off to see London, then a final show at the world famous Rainbow Theatre. The first stop was customs. We queued up for our turn to be admitted to Great Britain. I ended up in front of a boyish looking female inspector who started with the interrogation. "Passport please." I complied. "Business or pleasure?" "Excuse me?" I asked not exactly understanding her accent. Couldn't they have given me some-one from London, Manchester, or Liverpool? Where was this chick from…Dover? "What is the purpose of your visit to the UK?" "Business." This time I had my work permit arranged in advance, which she diligently verified. "Is this your suitcase?" I was tempted to say "It depends on what you find in it," but I could see that she had been born without any sense of humor, or perhaps had it surgically removed. "Yes, it's mine." She then proceeded to empty the contents out on the table. "Anything to declare?" "No," I offered confidently. Ouch, I forgot about that magazine I bought in an Amsterdam adult bookstore. She (of course) found it immediately, and brought to my attention the United Kingdom anti-pornography laws. She said she could confiscate the contraband or levy a fine against me for my attempt to bring it into the UK. Instead she surprised me by telling me to make sure I took it with me, when I left the country in two days (like I'd leave it there). I may have misjudged her; maybe she was really a party girl under that stuffy uniform. I gathered up my possessions and moved on. Joaquin was right behind me in line, and his shoulder length hair won him a special prize. They opened his suitcases and having not found anything illegal or illicit, they proceeded to rip the linings out of his luggage. Upon thanking him for his cooperation and telling him he could go, he protested, "Hey what am I supposed to do about my suitcases?" "I'm afraid you'll have to suss that out yourself," came the less than sincere answer.

We took the chartered bus (sorry only a single decker) to the Hotel.

Louie and I got a chance to see a little of London, but everyone was pretty much out of steam (and drugs) so we took it easy. Back at the hotel I found a new type of entertainment that I was fascinated by. It was something called a video game. I played the "Space Invaders" game for hours, instead of viewing the changing of the guard at Buckingham Palace. Today with the US stranglehold on global technology, it's hard to imagine that in 1979 the English had Space Invaders before we did. The final show at the Rainbow Theatre was inspiring. I couldn't believe I was in the hall that was played by all the great rock bands. The Who, Cream, and Led Zeppelin were all there before us. I walked around the foyer, and the dressing rooms before the show, and wished that the walls could talk. Jean-Luc and the band put on a show worthy of the venue that night.

I boarded the plane for Rochester the next morning; my tooth had stopped throbbing, perhaps sensing that home was only about six hours away.

I finally saw my first "Space Invaders" game in the United States about a year later.

Lana

———————————— ◆ ————————————

Shortly after the European Tour I came home only to turn around and go back out with Patti Smith Group again. Being away from Patty (my girlfriend, not the singer) for six weeks took a great toll. My drug usage had made the leap from recreational to a problem. I knew in my heart that something was going to have to change. Before I left for PSG, Patty and I agreed to stop doing coke. We also started to come up with a plan that included getting out of Rochester, moving to Texas, getting married, and getting off drugs. I had already had discussions with JLP management about working directly for Jean-Luc during the upcoming fall tour. (Please note this is in direct violation of Karl's Roadie Rule #2, "Never work directly for a band.") Going out on a short tour with Patti Smith was not exactly the right environment to be in to stay off drugs and stay faithful to my now fiancée.

There were several shows, but the one I met Lana at was Minneapolis. As we pulled up to the load in at the gig, she was sitting on the pavement near the backstage door. She wore a long dark dress that clung to her slender shape like an extra layer of skin. She had an expensive 35MM camera, and introduced herself to me as an aspiring photographer. "I have a degree in photography," I offered trying and succeeding in impressing her. "From where?" "R.I.T., but I quit after two years, I like mixing sound better." As impressed as she was by the photographer stuff she seemed even more impressed by the sound man declaration. "For Patti?" she was obviously a fan. "Well, sort of, I mix monitors for her sometimes." "Can I watch you work today? I promise I won't get in the way." For a minute I thought this through to its logical conclusions. Possibility one: she'll use me to get to the drummer, or guitar player, or hell, maybe even Patti herself. Possibility two: we'll end up having sex, and Patty will find out, and the wedding will be off. Possibility three: We could become friends. After a quick mental calculation of the "risk vs. reward" on each scenario, I agreed to get her backstage all day to see us work. There was one unusual aspect about the gig that is different than many of the other stories I've told you so far. This was a two night gig. First day was set up and show only, the rest of that night and the entire second day was off, until near the second showtime, then a load out before heading to the next city.

Lana was wonderful. She had a full time office job but had taken the day off to see one of her favorite artists. Actually I believe she wanted to get backstage, and party with famous or semi-famous people. Instead she ran into me. She paid attention to no one but me all day. Even introductions to various band members had no effect on her. She could have "traded up" at any point but chose to stay with me. Closer to showtime I knew that my resolve would be tested. Eventually she maneuvered in close and attempted to kiss me. I averted her lips, and explained that I was recently engaged and that her friendship was as much as I wanted, I just didn't think it was right for me to "start" with her. She smiled and said "Don't you think you deserve one last fling?" I didn't answer the question; I was too busy thinking about it. She kept her word and stayed out of the way all day. She must have been backstage a time or two since she seemed to be pretty knowledgeable about backstage etiquette. At one point she produced some above average quality cocaine, and I broke the first of many promises to Patty, by indulging in a line. We talked about photography, rock & roll, her life across the river in St. Paul, and artists I had worked with. By the time the show started I was beginning to re-think my allegiance to Patty, while trying to rationalize any events that probably were going to happen after the show.

The show was vintage Patti; she had seemed a lot happier this trip, compared to previous tours. This was due to her new courtship with Fred "Sonic" Smith. They had been introduced at an earlier show in Detroit, and they had become an item. Fred had been the part of the notorious "MC-5" group that was busted for drug possession in Detroit many years earlier. Now he fronted The Sonic Rendezvous Band, and he seemed to be just what Patti needed. I could tell being around Patti that she had many demons inside her that she needed help with. If you listen to her lyrics you will see hear an angry and bitter woman (like Jim Morrison of the Doors, Patti always considered herself to be a poet first, and a musician second). She seemed to be more alive tonight than I had ever seen her in the dozen or so shows over the past year. She was focused on the show. Candi Slice would not be making an appearance tonight.

She took the stage wrapped in the American flag, wearing a black wide brimmed hat she had taken to wearing lately. She dove right into "Babelogue," (a free form poem that she would basically ad-lib every night)…

"*I don't f*** much with the past, but I f*** plenty with the future…I wake up! I am lying peacefully, and my knees are open to the sun, I desire him, and he is absolutely ready to seize me.…In heart I'm a Moslem, in heart I'm an American artist, and I have no guilt. I seek pleasure, I seek the nerves under your skin. The narrow archway, the layers; the scroll of ancient lettuce. We worship the flaw, the belly, the mole on the belly of the exquisite whore, he spare the child and spoil the rod, I have not sold myself to God.*"

As the crowd cheered, and the band built the volume, she exploded into the first song.

"*Baby was a black sheep, baby was a whore, baby got big and baby get bigger.*

*Baby get something, baby get more, baby, baby, baby was a Rock n' Roll
N****r*

...Do you like the world around you, are you ready to behave?

*Outside of society, they're waitin' for me. Outside of society, that's where
I want to be!"*

She wasted no time launching into other crowd pleasers off the new
"Wave" album like "Dancing Barefoot," "Frederick" (written about
guess who?), and "So you want to be a Rock & Roll Star". There was also
a good mix of songs from her other albums, including ones from
"Radio Ethiopia," "Easter," and "Horses." The show closed with a "kick-
ass" rendition of the Who's "My Generation." Lana loved the show, and
the more I was around her the more I was actually considering cheating
on my soon to be bride. At the conclusion of this show, unlike most
shows, there was no load-out, only a brief securing of valuables like
mics. After that was done, Lana organized a night out for the crew. "I
know a place we can all go," she offered. Most of the crew agreed, and we
all went back to the hotel after arranging to meet in the lobby in about
30 minutes. She followed me to my room so she could "change", since
the club we were headed to was a blue jeans kind of place. She went in
the bathroom, not bothering to shut the door. We continued to talk, as I
tried not to look in the open door. "What do you think?" she said exit-
ing the bathroom. I turned expecting to see her in jeans and a T-shirt,
but she was completely naked. "Let's make love now, before we go out so
that we'll be ready for round two when we get back." I turned away and
said, "Lana please go back in there and put you clothes on, you know
I'm getting married in a few weeks." "I won't tell Patty if you won't."
That actually made sense for a split second. Before I could answer she
came up behind me, and held me, "Are you sure you want me to get
dressed?" It was painful, as I heard my mouth say, "Yes,...I'm sorry" I
had done the right thing. She didn't seem put off by my rejection, she
probably took it as more of a challenge. She finally put on the jeans and
T-shirt and we went to a club with several others from the crew. At the

end of the night she suggested that we spend the day together tomorrow. "OK," I said, "Sounds like fun".

She knocked at my door the next morning. I answered the door in disbelief since I never really expected her to show up. We drove all over the twin cities that afternoon, even spending time at the zoo. We also bought some more cocaine, which we polished off prior to that night's show (breaking my promise to Patti). Late in the day she surprised me again. "Hey, if this thing with your girlfriend doesn't work out, why don't you give me a call, and then come spend some time up here in St Paul with me?" "OK," I said, "If things don't work out I'll do that." She gave me her phone number (which I cleverly added to my address book "in code"). I never really thought I'd use it, but it was a huge ego boost to know I had it. The day ended too soon, and she returned me to the theatre. She took a backstage pass, and told me she'd see me at show-time. I half thought she wouldn't show, but there she was with minutes to spare. She said "Hi", kissed me on the cheek, and sat next to me at the monitor board for the entire show. She had given up trying to seduce me, and seemed a little distant tonight, which was understandable. Tonight there would be a load-out, but no drive. We were to spend the night in the same hotel. As we started to pack up, she told me she would say her good bye to me now. I was too busy for a long dramatic send off, but I think she knew that, and selected this moment to break clean. A minute later she was gone.

I didn't sleep well that night. I almost called her several times, but I couldn't bring myself to pick up the phone. As I packed my bag the next morning, and got ready for a trip to the airport and a flight home to Patty, I went down the hall to get a coke (the soft drink) from the machine. Guess who I ran into there in the hallway?

Lana.

Before you think she was there for one last tearful goodbye, or to make one last ditch effort to get me to stay in Minnesota, she was actually there to spend the day with the PSG drum roadie (who had the day off). "I'm sorry Karl, you more than had your chance."

She was right, so I boarded the plane and went home to my future ex-wife.

I wonder if Lana took him to the zoo?

Upon my return, my fiancée immediately found the coded number in my address book (the code was pretty lame), and confronted me about it (it turns out she had all the entries memorized, and looked for new ones when I came home). I "fessed up" to the whole thing, and assured her that nothing irrevocable had taken place. She, of course, canceled the wedding and moved out, because she didn't believe me. It took me a solid week of begging, pleading, and apologizing to get her to set this incident aside.

Patti Smith eventually retired and left the road later that same year (shortly after I did). She married Fred "Sonic" Smith in 1980, and had two children, Jackson and Jesse with him. I can only assume that they chased off each other's demons and had a happy life together.

After her retirement, at least two of Patti's songs have been re-released by major artists. "Because the Night" was recently remade by Natalie Merchant, and "Dancing Barefoot," has been covered by U2, and various other bands.

Sadly, the demons that Patti had finally slain back in the eighties were reincarnated in a new form during the nineties. Fred died suddenly in 1994 of an apparent heart attack, and as she was still coping with that grief, a mere month later, her only brother Todd (her one time stage manager), died of a heart condition as well.

I've seen Patti twice recently on "Late Night with David Letterman" promoting her new CD. I find it kind of odd that "Patti Slice" is now mainstream enough for CBS.

Breakfast in Canada

◆

As Patty and I made plans for our eventual escape to Texas, and my move to work directly for the JLP band, we got word of an upcoming event that was unbelievable.

I had just seen one of my favorite bands "Supertramp," when they played Rochester during their "Breakfast in America" Tour. I had obtained the eighth row tickets from a local DJ friend of mine that arranged for me to "win" them in a call-in radio contest. (I also got to be a guest DJ on his radio station for a one hour show that was supposed to be determined by a random drawing of postcards and believe it or not I "won" that too!). Anyway, with the memory of the Supertramp concert still fresh in my mind, I found out that we were going to open for them during a 15 day swing through Canada. Jean-Luc wanted me to mix the sound, and Louie to do lights, so he contracted our services directly from our company. Little did my company know that this was to be my last gig while I was in their employ. The tour would be known as the "Breakfast in Canada" Tour.

On July 14, Louie and I flew to London Ontario after clearing customs in Toronto. We both had done a lot of work in Canada, in fact we both had Canadian Social Medicine cards, so obtaining work permits was relatively easy. The next day we had rehearsals at Centennial hall in London. (Which we badly needed, since we hadn't performed live since April 4th). We woke up the next morning wondering what to expect.

The massive stage was already erected on the football field of the University of West Ontario Campus as the load-in started at 10 AM promptly. The PA stacks were about three to four times the size and power of what I was used to carrying on tour, and should be more than adequate to cover the outdoor venues planned for this leg of the tour. The lights were incredible and included some good old fashion "low tech" special effects that I'll get to during the show. To cut down on confusion and speed up the change over from JLP to Supertramp, I was given my own 36 channel Midas mixing board. Russel (the long time sound man for Tramp, and the acknowledged "sixth member of the band" on most of their albums) had a 48 channel board in front of mine. There was no need to change any settings between sound checks, they simply unhooked my board, and hooked the cables to his board. The sound check was to start at two, and I doubted it was possible. I was right.

We finally got our shot at the stage after four o'clock, which was the time the gates were supposed to open. We managed a short sound check, but I wasn't at all happy with the way the PA sounded. After a wonderful catered meal and a chance to meet some of the band and crew for Supertramp, at 7:30 I climbed my scaffold, and took my place at the board.

There were probably between 10,000 and 15,000 fans waiting for Supertramp to start playing that night in that stadium, and the only thing between them and that show was our band. As Jean-Luc took the stage and Tim made his intro (in French again), I gave Louie one of my "here goes nothing" looks. The audience gave Ponty a cordial welcome, and by the third song seemed to be really getting into his music. The PA was powerful, but my top volume was limited on purpose by the headliner. I didn't need any more gain however, the amount they gave me was more than enough. I had a hard time with the bass frequencies (there was too much bass), a problem that shouldn't be happening outdoors. I spent most of the show trying to compensate for it. All too soon we played our encore, and then Jean-Luc said "Thank you and Good night!" We were done for the night.

After a very long change over, the stadium lights were finally extinguished. The sound system stirred from its slumber, awakened by Rick Davies' harmonica piercing the night. The lighting system obviously startled by the sudden noise, joined the fray by warming the stage with several rows of par lamps. The familiar lyrics of "school" fill the stadium...

I can see you in the morning when you go to school
Don't forget your books, you know you've got to learn the golden rule

Interesting, start the show with a song off "Crime of the Century," instead of one off "Breakfast." The tactic worked as the crowd was whipped up to a proverbial frenzy by the end of song one. The sound was still not quite right, Russel was having the same problems with the "muddy" bass as I had experienced during sound check. I'll save you a trip back to the glossary now and explain what I mean by "muddy." When there is plenty of bass (low frequencies), but they seem muffled, that's classic "muddy bass." You know it's there working in the background, you just can't distinguish any of the notes. It can be very distracting, almost like there is a background hum to the music that blurs together into one long note. So that was what was happening now, Dougie's bass guitar, and Bob's kick drums were all kind of blurred together. Even though my ear caught the shortcoming, most of the crowd was screaming too loud for it to make much of a difference. Plus, when you've heard songs as many times as Supertramp's, your brain knows what to expect, and generally fills in anything not actually picked up by your ears.

What was lacking in sound was more than made up in lights. The lighting design was inspired. In 1979 there were no computer controlled lighting systems, these lights (probably over 300 of them) were controlled by a human being, in conjunction with a half a dozen Super Trouper spot lights. One of the most unexpected special effects I've ever witnessed at a concert was during "Dreamer." When dreamer started, the stage was dark. As Roger sang the first few lines of the song, he was lit only by a narrow spot light. What the audience couldn't see was that on either side of the stage there were two large star shaped structures on hinges, covered with stage lights pointed straight ahead. Under the cover of darkness, invisible roadies swung the structures out parallel to the front of the stage, pointing the banks of lights directly at the unsuspecting fans. By the second verse, the effect was ready. When Roger sang, "Dreamer, you stupid little dreamer" The lights snared their prey, and lit up the crowd with artificial daylight. 15,000 voices all squealed in unison. Every time the word "Dreamer" was used for the remainder of the song, those lights would again blind the crowd, and they would respond like they didn't know it was coming. It was a great show enhancer.

Another "low tech" effect (by today's standards) that was incredibly well done was their rear screen projection. Now this wasn't a high tech video projection system like the kind used today, this was a simple 35 MM movie projected on a large screen at the rear of the stage. The most effective use of this oversized movie theatre was during the song "Rudy", where every member of the audience boarded a train that took us on a high speed tour of the British countryside. I can verify that by the final line of the song, as the train is pulling into the station, everyone is physically dizzy.

During the show they rendered flawless versions of every major hit from every one of their albums including, "Crime of the Century," "Even in the Quietest Moments," "Crisis what crisis?" and of course, "Breakfast in America." The show was not only exciting, it was remarkably consistent. I saw Tramp do the same exact show eight times, and it didn't vary at all.

The next shows after Ontario were in Toronto. Three shows in three nights at Canadian National Exposition Park. Most of the time this was a venue for soccer.

Patty drove up from Rochester to be with me, and see the show of course. She had finally forgiven me for the Lana incident although to this day I doubt she believes me that nothing happened.

As had been the case in Ontario the set up in TO was a huge effort that took place effortlessly due to great organization and tons of man power. The sound check wouldn't be that effortless.

Once again, Russel had difficulties with the bass while fine tuning Supertramp. No matter what he tried, the bass frequencies refused to cooperate. After an extended sound check, they yielded the stage to us. Our sound check went about like theirs, the bass was all mush. I was beginning to think the sound system itself was the problem, but I couldn't do anything about that. I concentrated on fine tuning the instruments that created the most bass. The first thing I did was to stop using the mic on the Ralphe's bass guitar, utilizing 100% of the direct connection instead. I figured I would sacrifice the control I was getting from that mic, to cut some of that low frequency garbage. I also had Ralphe turn down his stage amplifier; it could only make things worse. As the check progressed I had a visitor. Russel came and watched me as I tried to adjust for the over bearing bass. "Any luck?" he asked cheerfully. "A little," I replied not really sure if it was the truth. We debated the cause of the dilemma, as I attempted solutions. My final play was to use parametric equalizers to isolate and suppress as much of the offending frequency as possible. By the end of the sound check, I had a small measure of success. Russel made written notes of some of my settings, and retreated back to his board, I assume, to simulate them.

The show was much better than the night before from a sound perspective. The bass was still not perfect, but was almost acceptable compared to Ontario. There were over 20,000 fans in attendance on each of the three nights, equally appreciative of the show as their counterparts in London.

By the second day in TO I was beginning to make friends with the crew of Supertramp. I even spent some time talking to Bob, the

American drummer. He seemed like the odd man out of a band that had two British singer song writers (the stars of the group), a British bass player, a British keyboardist & saxophone player, and an American drummer. I don't remember what we talked about, but I do remember that he was interesting (and fun) to talk to.

One road souvenir I still have and cherish is a T-shirt given to me by the Tramps. It features the artwork from the Breakfast in America album, but is titled "Breakfast in Canada." They were sold to the public at the seven Canadian shows, and must be a collector's item today.

After the third show in Toronto, I said goodbye to Patty, and we flew to Montreal. The next two shows were in Jarry Park, the abandoned baseball park of the Montreal Expos. The park had never been used for a rock concert, so this was kind of an experiment to see if there would be life after baseball for old Jarry Park.

The first night in Montreal fetched about 30,000 ticket holders. The problems with the sound persisted, which in my mind was a conviction of the system. Not all these venues could have the exact same acoustic failing. I again did the best I could to faithfully reproduce the sound of our band, and again it was less than favorable. Russel had his most difficult time of the tour in here as the "Montreal Star" newspaper account of the first Jarry Park show points out.

"The concert was alright, but the light system gets a full three points as far as I'm concerned," said Lorraine Désert. Marie Lirette agreed, adding: If it hadn't been for the sound problems, it would have been really good." "The problems with the sound were a little annoying and I would have liked to have heard more songs from the Breakfast in America album," said 16-year-old Pierre Lebrun. "But all in all the concert was very good."

Well, you can please some of the people, some of the time; just don't screw with the sound.

The final show was in Ottawa. It was final in more than one way.

It was of course the final show I worked with Supertramp.

It was to be the last show I worked with my longtime partner, Louie.
It was to be the last time Louie would do lights for Ponty.
It would be my last show working for the sound company.
It would also be my last show as an unmarried man.

As you may have guessed a lot happened during this two week tour. On the visit from Patty in Toronto, the final decision was made to move to Texas. We would be married at my parent's house in less than three weeks. I had made arrangements with Ponty's management company to work directly for the band. This was in direct violation of Roadie Rule number 2, "Never work directly for a band." I had also arranged for Patty to come along on the tour as the T-shirt sales manager. (You can't expect newlyweds to be separated can you?) This is in direct violation of Roadie Rule #1 "Never under any circumstances take your spouse or significant other on the road with you for more than 24 hours." I had set myself up to break rule number 1 & 2, and there is a reason they are at the top of the list (more on that soon). I also knew that JLP's company was going to hire a new sound and light company for the fall tour starting October first. This would make me a hated man at my former employer. Even though I had nothing to do with the selection of a new sound and light provider, I would be blamed. I headed back to Rochester, and resigned my position. To quote my old friend Loudon Wainwright "then the feces hit the fan."

As I predicted, everyone at my former employer blamed me for the loss of a lucrative account. No one would even talk to me, I was a pariah. Patty and I loaded (by ourselves) my 1976 Toyota Celica, and a rented U-Haul trailer, with all our worldly possessions, and headed for Texas. I never got to say goodbye to Louie, or Dan, or JC, or Dick, or Duffy, or Fred, or Ronnie, or either of the Carl's (big & little). I did see several of them during the fall tour when we played Rochester, but they barely spoke to me.

One of the reasons Patty and I left Rochester was our mutually stated desire to quit doing coke. I had already made the decision to quit after the Lana incident. Patty claimed she also wanted to stop. I figured that by going to Texas, where we had no available source for "blow", it would be easy to quit. The only flaw to my plan was that we were about to go out on the road, where cocaine is as easy to find as a cup of black coffee.

Does anyone else see the word "disaster" stamped on this plan?

The Final Tour

◆

So Patty and I moved to Texas, and on a sweltering day in August we were married in my parent's house in front of our family and friends. Several things had changed besides Patty's last name. She now wanted to go by Pat instead of Patty, and we had both stopped doing drugs. Within a couple of weeks I was flown to California to sit in on the rehearsals for the upcoming fall tour. Ponty had released "A Taste for Passion," a light and airy album, that remains my personal favorite of his. The entire band returned including Jamie, Casey, Joaquin, Allan and Ralphe. A new lighting designer named Bobby, from the new light company in Houston, was to take over the lighting duties. There was also to be a new sound company, and I could tell from the beginning that they weren't thrilled with me being there. Phil was part owner of the company and would be joined on the tour by his wife. From the beginning they would plot to over throw me as the sound engineer. After the rehearsals were over, I returned to Texas. A few weeks later the tour started in Omaha.

Home Grown

◆

It was ironic that the first show of this final tour (of course I didn't know at the time that it would be my last) would be in Omaha. I had grown up in Nebraska, and had attended grade school there in Omaha. Many of my relatives on both sides of the family lived in Omaha and Lincoln (50 miles away), and would be attending the show. These were straight laced grandparents, uncles, aunts and cousins that didn't really know what I did for a living. They also didn't know what to expect from the show. For some of them it was their first time meeting Pat.

The show's setup was chaotic, normal for the first show of a tour, but made worse by the fact that we had a new sound and light company. The new sound system was acceptable, but not as good as the one I was used to with my old company. Even though we had an extra four hours to setup (we had made arrangements to load in at 8 AM) we were barely ready at show time.

As the crowd filtered in, I said hasty hellos to my grandparents, and various other relatives. Their VIP tickets put them in the row next to me at the board, and everyone settled in for the show. After an annoyingly long delay, the show finally started. At that exact moment, hundreds of marijuana joints fired up as well.

Unlike a typical rock show, like say Patti Smith or the Outlaws, where the smell of burning cannabis was a given, this was rarely the case at a Jean-Luc show. Tonight would be the strongest concentration of pot smoke I had ever seen at one of his shows. Perhaps the ventilation system was broken, or the hemp crop in Nebraska was exceptionally good that year, but this was something I really didn't need tonight.

The show was only about half over as my relatives started to leave. "Grandpa has a headache, it was good to see you, but we have to go." "It's a little loud, we're afraid it will hurt your cousin's hearing, maybe we'll see you at Christmas." By the end of the show most of them were gone.

I was not at all happy with how I had mixed the sound that night. The new system was more "harsh", than the previous one. Also I had started a new bad habit to replace my now conquered cocaine habit. The new one wasn't illegal, but it was a big problem. I was hooked on volume.

I mixed the sound louder and louder as the tour went on, ignoring the suggestions from Phil that I back down. At the time I blamed the sound system, but having the last twenty years or so to reflect on it, I now believe it was an unbridled ego.

I had always enjoyed the feeling of power derived from controlling the volume of a show. During this tour the need for that feeling grew with every show. Perhaps the euphoria and sense of invulnerability promoted by my recently discontinued cocaine use needed to be replaced. For whatever reason I felt compelled to seek ever higher volume levels. Eventually this would be my "Waterloo", or in my case it would become my "Palladium".

Union Dues

◆

By the forth day on the road Pat was beginning to appreciate my obses-
sion with showers. As we pulled up to Kiel Auditorium in St. Louis, she
had gone an excruciating 36 hours without a shower. I reassured her
that I knew for a fact that Kiel had showers.

Kiel was a multi purpose facility that included an ice arena, meeting
rooms, and a traditional theater. The good news was they were a union
house; the bad news was that the load in was a bear. The equipment was
off loaded on a dock, and then had to roll down a long hallway, up a
freight elevator, down another long hallway, and then find its way on to
the stage. There were always plenty of stagehands so the movement of
the gear wasn't the problem; it was the security of that equipment. The
other thing about Kiel was that the union was difficult to deal with at
times. They were a "by the book" union shop, which meant that if you
played by their rules you were fine, if not, they made your St. Louis
experience pure hell. They also (like most crews) were aggressive in trying to get freebies like T-shirts or albums.

Pat was in charge of the T-shirt and program sales for the band. In
some cities she actually sold them at a booth or table in the lobby
before, during and after the show. Other cities (like here in St. Louis)
this was handled by union vendors. She just counted shirts, collected
the money, and settled up with the "house" at the end of the night. One
of her biggest responsibilities however, was the security of all those

valuable shirts and of course the cash. I wasn't able to help her much with her duties, I was the production manager and had other more pressing issues like coordinating the load-in and set up, and in union houses like Kiel, kissing the union steward's ass.

We backed the truck up to the dock, and I greeted the union steward I had dealt with many times before. I used caution since once about a year ago he had shut down the setup because the Road Manager had questioned why the sound check was late. The band got there at four, expecting to start the check, but we had gotten a late start due to another event in the complex, and were playing catch up. I told Tim that we needed about another half hour and he exploded. "You had four hours to set up, what's the problem isn't this stage crew helping you?" That did it, the union steward yelled, "BREAK," and came over to tell me to inform my Road Manager that the union will be on a fifteen minute break. Nothing on his stage is to be touched, by anyone, or he will call for an early supper (an hour). He had effectively taken control of the situation. Tim started to protest and I simply said, unless you want to explain to Jean-Luc why our show in St. Louis is canceled you will shut up now. In fifteen minutes I had convinced Tim to leave the stage area, and I sweet talked the steward and his crew into resuming the setup. With that memory fresh in my mind, I greeted that same union steward. "Hi, good to see you again, load in is at noon right?" "Yup, you guys got shirts this time?" as he craned his neck trying to look in the now open trailer. "Yes, but the band won't let us give any away, {forced laugh}, they even make us pay for ours." This was essentially true but the steward was displeased by the answer. "Remember this is a union house, your guys don't touch anything, right?" Great, he was going to enforce the "no touch" rule, which would slow everything down today. "Sure, by the book." I grimaced. As I started to unload the truck, I looked around for Pat, but saw no sign of her. She would be in the first hallway waiting on her boxes of shirts, no need to worry. I unloaded the truck with two burley stagehands, sending the cases one by one into the darkness of the corridor where more crew would continue their journey to the stage. Near the nose of the trailer I thanked the two men and headed for the stage. By the time I got there about two thirds of the gear was already on the stage. I started to "suggest" directions to the crew (they didn't take kindly to direct orders). "I think we should move the bass cabinets over there now, OK?" "Did you want to help the light guys with the truss now or would you rather help me wire the stack?" The stage was starting to take shape as I saw something that stopped my heartbeat dead in its tracks. Up walked Pat brushing her wet hair. What did you do?" I asked frantically. "I found a shower, and I figured I had time before you got to the shirts, where's the dock?" "Shit!" was all I could manage as I ran for the elevator. When I got there I confirmed what I had feared. Several of the large cardboard boxes were ripped open, having obviously been pillaged. "This is bad." I said to my bride who hadn't quite grasped the seriousness of the situation. "Count them and let me know how many are gone…do it now." We moved the merchandise to a secure area and she started her inventory. I went back to my duties wondering why I had brought her with me in the first place, and wondering if I had enough clout with Ponty to save her job.

Within an hour or so Pat reported that a little over a hundred shirts were missing, but all the programs were still there (of course). We were selling the shirts for $9.00 each, and even though they didn't cost us that much, there was no way to get any replacements. We were out about a thousand dollars. I asked the union steward for help. "Sorry, we didn't see anything, my men say the boxes came off the truck that way." "The crew in Kansas City must've hit you last night during load-out." "Too bad about losing all those shirts, since you guys are so stingy with them and everything." There it was, my notification that this wouldn't have happened if I had given them all shirts to begin with. I put my tail between my legs and went to go tell Tim.

Tim was a great Road Manager, always fair and in control at all times. He let me run everything regarding the show except the two things he managed, the band and the money. Needless to say he was livid. The tour had certain budgets, and a loss of a thousand dollars in revenue would dent that budget. "I'll talk to Ponty and let you know," came the ominous response. I let Pat know that she may be on a plane home by tomorrow, but to do her job, and hope that the worse wouldn't happen.

The incident wasn't mentioned before or during the show, but just before the band left for the hotel, Tim approached me. "We discussed all our options, and Pat can stay, just make sure she never does anything stupid like this again."

She never did.

It would be her husband that was to come down with a severe case of stupidity.

The Palladium

◆

I returned to my favorite venue one more time. The Palladium, located on the island of Manhattan, which had been the location of previous shows by Ponty, Patti Smith, Carole King, and Stanley Clark. It was like a familiar old friend with its tiny dressing rooms, and grizzly union crew. As we neared today's load in time I remembered an incident here a year or two earlier.

The stage door is at street level. There is no dock, so the trucks park along the side of the street, off loading by using the truck's ramp. On this particular day, as the load in time approached, a car had illegally parked at the spot we needed to park the truck. There were "no parking" signs in place stating that this was an unloading zone, but the driver of this car either ignored the sign, or thought it didn't apply on weekends. The union stagehands waited until noon, and then they calmly took care of the problem. Eight of them gathered around the mid sized vehicle and proceeded to drag it about twenty feet out of the loading zone, and right in front of a fire hydrant. They then "hailed" a police car that was driving by, pointing out the serious infraction. The cops called for a wrecker, and the unsuspecting owner's car was hauled off to an unknown impound lot within a few minutes. They were still laughing about it as we unloaded the truck.

This time there was no car illegally parked and the load in went normally.

The familiar musty smell of the Palladium stage filled my nostrils as the stage door opened. It was the essentially the same smell as other old stages like the Auditorium in Rochester, the Capital Theatre in Passaic, and the Agora in Cleveland where my roadie career began. I immediately asked about the condition of their house electrical system, since my only bad experience at the Palladium had involved a bad hum at a Stanley Clarke show that I had suspected was electrically related. The union electrician told me they finally isolated and corrected the recurring problem, and that it was now fixed. One less thing to worry about.

The sound check was a who's who of New York musicians and record industry big shots. They paraded through all afternoon to greet Jean-Luc and the band. They would all return that night to hear the show; it would have to be a good one. I felt at home in that hall, it was truly an old friend. The best part of our friendship was how easy of a mix it provided me with, aside from our one electrical disagreement. As a bonus treat, the opening act that night would be Maria Muldaur (Midnight at the Oasis), who I was looking forward to finally hearing. I was beginning to think Phil from the sound company was finally starting to think I knew what I was doing, and would stop trying to undermine my credibility with Ponty. Whether that was the case or not, tonight would tip the scales against me for good.

During load in Phil and I disagreed on how much PA to bring in. I wanted it all, stacked as high as needed. He wanted a small stack for the small footage allowed to not encumber the audience sight lines. "Just go higher," I demanded. What is this guy a "Wuss"? I remember thinking. We compromised and he brought in more than he thought I needed and less than I wanted. In the back of my mind I probably was planning the night's outcome before the stack was even wired. My out of control ego looking for a sonic "fix".

The sound check went great except I should have known there was something going on because Jean-Luc asked me if I thought the sound had been too loud lately. In all the time I had been doing the front mix he had never directly challenged my overall levels. Well the system is a little "harsh" so I'm sure any reports you've received about excessive volume are related to that. I'll keep it in check tonight and be more careful. That was good enough for him.

The show went flawlessly. The electrician, true to his word, made good on his promise to not have any hum in the PA. Maria Muldaur put on a great show, not disappointing me, or the sold out house full of fans. By the time our band took the stage the crowd was ready for a show. Jean-Luc and the boys gave them one. As they worked their way through the new tunes of "A Taste For Passion" while mixing in selections from Cosmic Messenger and Enigmatic Ocean, the crowd got more and more appreciative. I yearned for more and more volume as the night went on, responding sympathetically to the crowd. I was cursing Phil since I was running out of available gain due to the reduced stack and fewer amplifiers. I kept pushing the PA for all it was worth, only an encore or two to go. Several fans got near me and encouraged me by saying things like "Turn it up man!" or giving me the "thumbs up." One member of the audience however, did come up to me and say, "Hey man, it's too loud, you should turn it down." He was not at all pleased with the mix. I shrugged my shoulders as if to say, "If you don't like it you can leave, these other people are digging it."

Then as Ponty came out for his second and final encore, I pushed a little to far. I had been dangerously close to the edge for the last three songs but now I tried to tweak a little more gain out for the final tune. About halfway through it I noticed a drop in the volume that I didn't instigate. The sound was also not quite right from the stage left side. I had probably caused some speaker damage due to my zealousness. I limped through the end of the song and thankfully there wasn't a third encore.

Immediately after the show I discovered I had severely damaged the PA. Many blown bass cones (woofers) and several blown horns. We would be repairing the PA tomorrow during setup and those parts aren't cheap. Phil was hot, he knew it was my fault that his PA was trau-matized. He quickly disappeared from the stage, I can only presume to complain to Jean-Luc himself. I began to rationalize the night's events in my head. But the show, the fans loved the show; I was just giving them what they wanted, "louder" and "louder". Every fan said "louder" except that one crackpot that wanted it turned down. Then as I turned around, there was that crackpot, standing next to our very irritated drummer. Casey spoke, "Karl, this is a good friend of mine, and he's the drummer for Carlos Santana's band." (Oh Shit) "He says you ruined the entire show tonight by mixing it too loud." "Was it too loud?" The best defense is a good offense, so I proclaimed, "The fans loved the show, they wanted more volume and I gave it to them." "The show kicked ass, I know what I'm doing." I then walked away to make my point, and to avoid any further discussion.

This was not the last of this discussion, just the last of anyone dis-cussing it with me. After a few more shows I thought it had all blown over, when I got to Cleveland I found out I was wrong.

The Cleveland Massacre

◆

Pat had been looking forward to the Cleveland show for the entire tour. Her parents lived in Solon Ohio just outside Cleveland, and they would be attending the show that night as our guests. We had just seen them a few months ago in Houston at our wedding, and now they were going to see what it was their daughter and son-in-law did for a living.

We pulled in to the Cleveland Music Hall just like hundreds of load-ins I had pulled into over the last four years. Nothing was to give me any clue as to the finality of this show. The Palladium incident had apparently blown over, and Pat's management of the T-shirt concession was now back on track. I had started to tone down my nightly "quest for volume," and the shows were (in my opinion) going well. We had even gotten word that the West coast leg of the tour was to be extended. Shows were added in Denver, Seattle and several cities in California. Pat had always dreamed of going to California, and now in a few weeks she would be there with me. We also heard that Jean-Luc had been signed to do shows in South America after this tour was over. Buenos Aires, Brasilia, and Lima, among others were on the itinerary, and I would surely be going as his Production Manager and sound man. It was a quiet day, almost too quiet. The sound check went normally until at the very end when Jean-Luc turned to me and said, "I'd like to try something new tonight, Phil is going to mix the sound." I was too stunned to speak as he finished. "This is just an experiment, he says he

250

can do a better job than you, and I want to see if it's true." "If not, you will be back on the board tomorrow night." I responded with silence. Phil smiled as he escorted Jean-Luc to the dressing room extracting last minute advice from him while they walked. I went to find Pat.

Pat, however was nowhere to be found. Nobody had seen her, or knew where she was. Nobody from the crew would talk to me, apparently everyone knew the thin ice I was on except me. What were my choices? I was still Production Manager, at least technically. I would be allowed to remain for at least this leg of the tour if I found some humility and accepted the situation. Maybe I could go back to mixing monitors, that had always been a less political job anyway.

During that second or two that I was considering the alternatives, I made my decision. Nobody mixes Ponty but me, period. I have to quit, it's the only way. I can't sit and watch the show with someone else's hands on the board. I can't relinquish the control I've earned. What about my in-laws, "I'm sorry Mom and Dad but they've decided to let someone else mix the sound tonight because I tend to use too much volume." Unacceptable. Where's Tim, I need to quit.

I found Tim lurking nearby, apparently anticipating my move. "I can't stay here." "I understand," came the compassionate response. I'll get you and Pat tickets home and arrange for your final checks. And that was it, no good byes to the band members I had grown to love like brothers, no tears, no regrets. My roadie career was all over in an instant. Ironically, it had started and ended right there in Cleveland. My final act of defiance was to reset all the controls on the mixing board to zero, negating the day's entire sound check. "Let Phil try to mix the f***ing show from scratch," I remember thinking. I gathered up my belongings from around the board, including my Andrew Lloyd Webber "Variations on a Theme" cassette tape that had greeted the fans to the venues on this tour. With my now newly retired "Anvil briefcase" in tow I went to find Pat. I was busy packing our suitcases in the motorhome, when she showed up along with Phil's wife. "What's going on?" she asked looking at the cases with confusion. "Where the hell have you been?" I retorted. "We went to do some coke," came the startling answer. So this disappearance had been premeditated, by Phil and his wife, a divide and conquer tactic. Pat was sequestered during my ouster, using cocaine as the bait. I was numb, as I told Pat what had transpired only ten minutes earlier. She held me tightly, and after a moment simply said, "Let's go home." We finished packing, and waited in front of the theatre to greet her parents with the cheery news that we were now their unemployed houseguests.

So the real reason I quit the road was because somebody had stepped on my pride.

We stayed in Cleveland for about a week, celebrating Thanksgiving with them. Eventually we flew back to Houston to start a new life, and to find new passions. I never did hear how the show went that night, it probably went fine. I did hear that Phil became the new sound man until they got to Peru (during that South American Tour) where he allegedly ended up staying, because the cocaine was so cheap. As far as I know, he may still be there today. Many years later, I heard that Tim (the Road Manager) got fired for stealing not long after I quit. I have no way of knowing if he uttered "Ever F***kin' time" when he was caught.

During my years on the road, I ended up traveling to 45 states and 17 different countries. I worked on approximately 500 shows working with more than 200 different artists.

I never saw or heard from Jamie, Casey, Ralphe, Allen, Joaquin, Art, or Bobby again.

I did see Jean-Luc and Claudia one more time at a show in Houston in 1984. I was recently divorced from Pat and I bought tickets to the show for my new alcoholic girlfriend and myself. After the show I asked the sound man if he could get a note backstage to Jean-Luc, and that I was an old friend. While I waited for him to come back I saw Claudia headed backstage and I called to her. "Claudia, do you remember me?" "I'm Karl, Jean-Luc's sound man a long time ago." She looked at me for a long second and said, "Of course, come with me, he's very sick tonight but I'm sure he will see you." So I went backstage for a brief and awkward meeting. Jean-Luc was indeed very sick, almost as sick as Bill Cosby was so many years before. He looked at my semi-conscious date and asked, "Where is Pat?" "Pat and I got divorced, this is Angela." At that very moment another familiar voice behind me said, "Hello Jean-Luc, it's good to see you." It was my ex-wife Pat and a "girlfriend". She had the same idea I did about coming backstage to say hello. I hadn't seen her in many months, and now I was standing there in front of her, holding my current girlfriend up, and praying she didn't get sick right there in the dressing room. Jean-Luc broke the pregnant pause, "I'm very confused, but it's good to see you both." "I'd love to talk longer, but I need to go back to my room and try to sleep, goodnight." And in a flash Jean-Luc and Claudia were gone again. I mumbled an introduction of Angela to Pat, and then quickly left the theatre without a single shred of my dignity.

I had intended to tell Jean-Luc I was sorry for how it all had ended, for my out of control ego and my foolish pride, and for my thinking that I was as important as the show, instead of being part of a team that made up a successful show. I had intended to make amends.

I didn't quite get any of that part out, considering the surprise that ambushed me that night in the dressing room. When will I ever get to tell him these things?

Maybe someday, I'll just write a book.

Epilogue

◆

"All that I need to know about life, I learned on the road." Actually that's not completely true, life is one long learning experience. I did learn a lot on the road, and I've learned a lot every day since then as well. I've learned what's important, and what's unimportant in life. I've learned some, but not all of the secrets of success in life, and have actually instituted some of them in my daily habits. Here's a brief wrap up of my life as it is, along with some of the people in the book.

Upon arriving in Houston with no jobs, Pat and I moved in with my parents. With that as a starting point we went out and started looking for "real jobs". She found a job at a department store as temporary Christmas help. I had a tougher road since several electronics sales jobs I applied for wouldn't hire me because of recent drug use. Now back then they didn't have drug tests, but they did have polygraphs (lie detectors) and I couldn't get past them without admitting the coke. I finally found a job that looked the other way and I was their top salesperson in stereo sales that Christmas. Pat was kept on after the holidays and eventually became a buyer at that department store. I became a store manager at my job, and eventually branched out to sell video equipment, appliances, cellular phones, and even waterbeds over the years. Pat and I grew apart and as I already discussed we were divorced in 1983. I haven't talked to her since 1984, a year or so after that last meeting backstage with Jean-Luc.

During the eighties I was engaged at least four times, never making it to the alter because I would choose women that either abused cocaine or alcohol or both. I hadn't learned my own lesson yet.

In December of 1990, I had what is known as a "moment of clarity". I was out drinking with two good friends until they made us leave the bar at two. The next morning I woke up with such a bad hang-over that I called in sick. This was to be the first and last time I would ever let that happen. I had gone to work with hang-overs, but I had never missed work before. I decided to quit drinking that day. Later that day, I found out one of my two friends had been pulled over on his way home and had spent the previous night in jail for DWI. My decision was then cemented.

As soon as my "leap of faith" was made, good things started to happen to me. I met my wife Christine about five months later. I got a new job working for a cellular phone company and made more money than I had ever made in any year previously. In that same year I got involved with a local Houston charity that benefits multiple handicapped children. In 1992 I joined the board of directors of that charity. That same year, while selling cellular phones, a customer of mine convinced me to consider the financial services industry, and I obtained my securities and insurance licenses. Since 1994 I have been working for a large regional bank in Texas.

As of this writing I have not used cocaine or any other illegal drug for over twenty years. After quitting the road, I substituted alcohol, and serial dating of "troubled" women, as my new addictions. I'm happy to say that I've been free from alcohol since late 1990, and I have been happily married to my wife Christine since 1992.

How, you may ask, did I walk away from drugs, alcohol, and dangerous random sex so easily?

I went through a self imposed two step program.

Step One: I decided to quit.

Step Two: I quit.

Actually, it can be that simple. Please don't confuse simple with easy, they are totally different. Some people struggling with addiction need extra support in the form of support groups, counseling, church, friends, family, or in severe cases, "detox". All of the "programs" and support in the world won't matter though if you don't want to quit. You have the ability to walk away from any substance or situation that you WANT to walk away from. Then (and only then) you can use your support systems to help you keep your demons away.

Jean-Luc Ponty continues to write music, release CDs, and perform concerts worldwide. During the 80's, Jamie Glaser was frequently featured as his guitar player. With the launch of my website (www.roadie.net) on July 4, 1998, I have been able to locate many of the players in the story you just read. I am happy to say I have found my old partner Louie, and believe it or not he is still in the business, but now much older, wiser, and like me, happily married. I also located Jamie, still playing and teaching guitar out in LA. The big story for me is that Jean-Luc and I have rekindled our friendship and correspond frequently. Jean-Luc and Claudia's daughter Clara, who I knew as a very young girl, has now released a CD of her own piano compositions. Clara and her sister Valerie were still in grade school when I visited the Ponty's home during some rehearsals in LA. I remember Clara playing us a song on the baby grand piano in the study. I see that she is now frequently the opening act for her father's concerts.

Life has truly come full circle, as the next generation now takes the musical spot light.

About the Author

◆

Born at La Chapelle-St. Mesmin, Loiret, France to American parents in 1956. Attended grade school in Lincoln and Omaha, Nebraska, attended high school in Windsor, Connecticut, attended college in Rochester, New York (Rochester Institute of Technology, studied Photographic Illustration), became a full time a roadie in October 1975. Worked with over 200 artists providing sound reinforcement and lighting design. Traveled to 45 states and 17 countries before retiring from the road in November, 1979. Started a sales career in Houston, Texas. Sold stereo and video equipment, major appliances, waterbeds, furniture, and cellular phones. Now married, works as a sales manager in a large regional bank marketing life insurance and investments.

Appendix

◆

KARL'S ROADIE RULES

1	Never under any circumstances take your spouse or significant other on the road with you for more than 24 hours.
2	Never work directly for a band.
3	Never turn your back on anything of value on the road.
4	When confronted with an insurmountable situation, improvise.
5	All headliners started out as opening acts, in most cases, they will be opening acts again someday.
6	Anybody can go see a band that's popular; it's only special when you see a band before they are popular.
7	Have your salary sent home, live off your per diem.
8	Plan for the worst, hope for the best.
9	Everything happens for a reason.
10	Get the money before the show
11	Never under estimate the value of dumb luck
12	Always trust your first instinct
13	Never try to predict which artists will be stars, you will be wrong well over half the time.
14	Whenever given an opportunity to take a shower, do it
15	Never Assume... Never

Glossary

◆

A frame	Very tall step ladder with an additional straight extension ladder sticking out of the top of the "A"
Accom	Pronounced A-Kom, accommodation (hotel/motel room, bus, tent, whatever) provided for the band and crew on tour. Varies in quality from heavenly to diabolical
air ride	Type of air cushioned trailer used in transporting fragile electronic equipment
Anvil briefcase	Brand Name: briefcase of choice for Roadies
Anvil case	Brand Name: road case fabricator
apron	The very front edge of the stage
Arno	Brand Name: Gaffer's tape (reputed to be the best)
Arp	Brand Name: Keyboard related products, now out of business
Ashly Audio	Brand Name: Amps, EQs, mixing boards.
ax	Slang: An electric guitar, bass or almost any musical instrument
B-3	Model of Hammond organ. Distinctive sound caused by a spinning high frequency horn in speaker cabinet
backstage pass	Usually a colorful printed self adhesive cloth patch that allows certain access and privileges during or after the show. Highly sought after, and has a high trade value (see also "groupie")
balanced line	Refers to audio outputs, inputs and cables where the signal is carried on two wires instead of one, the two signals being identical but opposite in phase. Balanced circuitry has much better hum & noise rejection than unbalanced (single wire) circuitry
ballink	A chain device that can hold up to 4 lights, mounts to lighting truss
bar bands	Bands that primarily play in local bars, lounges and pubs. Sometimes they "open" for a touring band
Barcus Berry	Brand Name: Musical equipment including electric violins
barn doors	Metal doors hinged on the front of some lighting instruments to block off light that would otherwise hit off stage
"beach"	Slang: refers to where something will stay at. Its proper position. "That rack goes over to dimmer beach." See also "lives"
Bi-amp	Use of two amplifiers to reproduce bass and treble separately after electronically splitting the highs from the lows by use of a crossover
"bit"	Slang: To get hurt by a piece of equipment. "John got bit by the truss"
Blinkie	Slang: Lighting Director (see also "squint")
blow	Slang: To play an instrument. "Who's blowing lead?" Taken from old horn player lingo
board	Refers to a control panel typically situated somewhere out in the audience (e.g. sound board, light board)
bobtail	Semi Trailer Truck with a short trailer
bog	Slang: The toilet on a tour bus

book of lies	Slang: A tour itinerary, which are notorious for being incorrect/out of date
boom	Type of microphone stand, used to get the base of the stand away from something (e.g. the singer, the drum kit)
bootlegger	Someone illegally taping a show. Roadies are always on the look out for this vermin, bad things can happen when they are discovered
bottom end	The low frequency range of a sound system's frequency response curve
brand name act	Headliner act playing large venues, with a major record in heavy rotation
Brits	British Roadies
Cali Cab	(California Cab): The extended-type cabs driving the 53 foot trailers used to haul the show from venue to venue. Usually driven by IBT (Teamster) drivers
cans (1)	Slang: for headphones
cans (2)	Slang: for Par-Cans (lighting instruments)
catering	Under-cooked, over produced meal-type substance (...usually)
cattle	Slang: derogatory term for the audience (e.g open the doors, let the cattle in)
center stage	Middle area of stage
changeover	Time period where removal of an opening act and set up of the next act or the headliner is done
channels	Refers to the number of separate audio controls available to the sound man or the monitor man. Note: more than one microphone could be connected to one channel. Each channel typically controls the sound of one instrument, or one vocalist (e.g. 32 channel, 24 channel)
Cheeseburger	Slang for a cheesbourgh clamp
Cherber	Cheap multi-tool from K-Mart
click track	A timing sequence sometimes used to coordinate the music with the light show. Pink Floyd's drummer, for instance, listens to a click track on headphones so the movie of the hammers walk in time to the nazi part of the Wall
club mode	Scaled down version of normal band set-up due to space limitations (like in a nightclub)
coil	Wire wrapped around the base of the cone or diaphragm that moves when motivated by an electrical current within the magnetic field of the speaker
Compression Driver	Kind of loudspeaker used to reproduce high frequencies
condom (1)	Slang: refers to the think vinyl that covers a stage's roof (aka "skin")
condom (2)	Slang: A cover placed over speaker cabinets to prevent damage in transit, because owners are usually very vain
condom (3)	What any roadie better have on hand, useful in many (MANY) ways
condom (4)	Foam wind-screen placed over the end of a vocal mic'. i.e., put a condom on that thing to take some "pop" out

cones	(Speaker cone) Paper piston that pushes air in or out of the bass cabinet. When a speaker quits working it probably needs to be re-coned
console	Mixing console (see board)
Crew chew	Slang: fast food sandwiches whose mayo has turned clear and meat sports a mysterious rainbow sheen, often accompanied by chips and Snapple®
crossover	An electronic device, either passive or active, used to split an audio signal into the appropriate frequency ranges for the loudspeakers in the system. Sophisticated active crossovers may also "listen" to the amplifier outputs, providing useful things like phase compensation and loudspeaker protection
cross stage stack	Small PA stack set up off stage left and off stage right to supplement the stage monitors. Used with very loud bands to help raise monitor levels on stage
Crown	Brand Name: PA Amplifier
curtain	End of the show, or in some cases an actual fabric curtain that drops in front of the stage signifying the end of the show
curtain call	Encore, additional song or songs. Usually the first encore is automatic and pre-arranged
Dave Clarks	Brand name: Headphones
dB	Abbreviation: decibel: a measurement of sound levels. Technically, the decibel is used to describe the *ratio* of two power levels, a known "reference" power and the power level being compared to it. It is also used to describe electrical signal levels (e.g. "line level")
dB meter	Electronic device for measuring sound levels (in dBs)
DDL	Abbreviation: Digital Delay
dead head (1)	A run on a truck or bus that is needed to begin or end a tour without freight or passengers.. ie: from home base to first stop on tour or from last gig to home base, p.s. bands still have to pay for fuel, lube and driver for these
Dead Head (2)	Grateful Dead fan
Desk	Mixing desk (see also board)
DFA	Label on fake knob installed on mixing console to deceive bands when they wanted more treble/bass/volume or whatever, and turned it to full at their request. "DFA"? Well, it means "Does F*** All"
DI box	Abbreviation for Direct Injection. DI boxes are used to connect instruments, e.g. bass, keyboards, directly to the console, i.e. without using a microphone. They can be passive (containing no powered electronics) or active (with powered electronics) and they are usually fitted with ground lift and pad switches
diaphragm	Mid range and high frequency equivalent to a speakercone. Usually made of a phenolic resin or aluminum. Not related to a preventive device used by some groupies
Digalo Relay	slang: Digital Delay

digital delay	Digital device creates an echo or endless repetition of a recorded sound by using digital circuitry Aka: DDL
dimmer	Electronic controls that allow stage lighting to fade up or down slowly, as opposed to being on or off only
dimmer beach	Area where Dimmer racks are located, usually as far off stage as possible, as to prevent a visual obstruction, and to make the lighting peoples work extra hard running feeder
down stage	Portion of the stage closest to the audience. Comes from old stages that were "raked" or inclined , and were actually lower at the audience edge
dulcimer	Stringed instrument used by Blue grass bands. Can be played with a pick or small cane like devices called hammers
dykes	Diagonal wire cutters
Echoplex	Brand name device: creates an echo or endless repetition of a recorded sound by using a tape formed in a loop. Replaced later by digital delays (DDL)
EQ	Equalizer, critical to a good mix it raises or lowers the volume of specific frequencies to compensate for problems with the acoustics of the venue
E.W.O.T	Extreme Waste of Technology
feedback	Sound of amplified sound recycling and re-amplifying itself very quickly causing a loud shrill tone. The Sound man's Moby Dick. Can be worse in some venues due to poor acoustics, and be partially controlled by use of equalizers
feeder (1)	High Voltage power cable
feeder (2)	Those nice people in Catering
Fender	Brand name: Guitars and amplifiers including infamous "Stratocaster"
fills	Small PA stack set up off stage left and off stage right to supplement the stage monitors. Used with very loud bands to help raise monitor levels on stage (aka side fills, cross stage)
flash pot	Pyrotechnical device that utilizes photographic flash powder to produce a blinding explosion, can be as simple as a coffee can with a thin wire and battery ignition system
floods	Wide angle lighting instrument, could be a par lamp
Flying	The activity of suspending equipment from the truss or scaffolding (usually done with motorized chain hoists), e.g. loudspeaker clusters. "We spent two hours flying the stacks". Usual variations - flown, flew, etc apply
F.N.G.	F*****g New Guy, When something goes wrong blame it on the F.N.G.
fog machine	Device to deliver large amounts of dry ice fog to a stage. Typically a 55 gallon drum full of heated water with a large blower and dryer vent hose
follow spot	A spot light on a swiveling and tilting stand, so called because it can "Follow" an artist around the stage. See also "spots," "Trouper," and

"Super Trouper"

FOH (1)	"Front of House" - Sound Engineer that "mixes" the sound heard in the audience
FOH (2)	"FOH only" pass.: Stands for "F*** Off Home". A special award to a crew member no longer required backstage. They can watch the show for the last time from the front and saves the production from buying a train ticket
frequency	Measurable amount that air vibrates at to produce certain tones. Audible range for human beings is generally considered to be 20 Hz to 20,000 Hz (but somewhat less for veteran roadies)
fresnel lamps	Pronounced {"fra-nell"} Traditional stage lighting instrument with fresnel lens and "barn doors" for fine tuning. They are also rarely used in live touring situations
fusion	Music genre part rock part jazz, fused together. Rarely include vocals
gaff	Verb: To gaff or to gaff something. Use of Gaffer's tape to attach, fix, secure, repair, waterproof, seal, rig, stabilize, stick, mummify, or generally make semi-permanent
gaff tape	Abbreviation: same as Gaffer's tape
gaffer's tape	Special kind of colored tape (usually matte black) similar to duct tape, but more expensive due to the non reflective surface and special adhesive that doesn't leave gummy reside behind. Used for everything from securing mic cables to the floor, to holding speakers in place on the stack. Roadies know that gaffer's tape can fix anything
gain	Volume: the amount by which an amplifier circuit amplifies or attenuates a signal. Usually expressed in decibels
gate (1)	Proceeds of ticket sales
gate (2)	Short for noise gate
gel	Colored cellophane used to make stage lights produce various colors. A numbering system is used to identify them
Genie Lifter	Heavy duty lifting device lifted by a hand crank that resembles a huge car jack, typically used in pairs to lift trusses
Genie Tower	Pneumatic pole raised using compressed air used to elevate racks of lights to a pre-determined height
Germ	Slang: A fan or someone who meets you one time and is your "best" friend. The one who calls you when the Stones come to town, for tickets
Gibson	Brand Name: Guitars and amplifiers
gig	Slang: same as show or performance
gig butt	That burning sensation caused by wearing your underwear way too long on the road
gig meat	Generic catering (cold cuts, bread, soda)
G.I.G.O	"Garbage In Garbage Out" - term used when confronted about the bad sound, blaming the band

Gladiators	The massive Gladiator III is the largest and most powerful spot light in the entertainment industry. It is a must for larger venues and jobs requiring maximum performance
gonk	One who stands among men at work, without really working. Merely "posing" as a worker (common at most college gigs) a.k.a "poser"
"GP"	GP stands for General Public. "Let in the GP"
graphic	type of equalizer
graphic EQ	type of equalizer
green room	Aka dressing room, where the band (and sometimes roadies) hang out prior to the show. Sometimes they're even painted green
grid	what you hang your lighting from
groupie	A girl (usually fairly young) that wants to "meet" the band. Sometimes will settle for a road manager or roadie. (The Most famous groupie is Sweet Connie from Little Rock AK, but that's a whole different story)
Hammond B3	Brand name model of organ. Distinctive sound caused by a spinning high frequency horn in speaker cabinet
Harpo	Old BBC slang for toolbox
hat	Slang: high hat cymbals
Head (1)	Marijuana smoker
head (2)	Membrane of a drum, frequently needs replacing during some shows
head (3)	amplifier part of a guitarist's amp/speaker combination (e.g. Marshall stack)
head (4)	Sometimes traded for back stage passes (see "groupie")
headliner	Main performer of the show, usually controls the sound, lights, and staging decisions
headset	Headphones with a noise canceling mic, used as an intercom between roadies during the show
Helpensticl	Brand name device attached inside a grand piano to pick up sound like a microphone
high beams	Slang: Super Trouper
hit	Slang: The time the show begins. "Hey man what time do we hit?" Concatenation of "hit the stage"
horns	Mid range or high frequency device used in sound reinforcement
Hot Spot (1)	Brand name: tiny little monitor speakers positioned close to drummer and keyboard player's ears
Hot Spot (2)	Where two or more spot light paths meet, creating a "brighter" light
house	Where the audience sits (even at an outdoor show)
house lights	Lights in the audience
"Hum Head"	Slang: Sound Roadie
Hz	Hertz (cycles per second) a measurement of sound frequency
IATSE	The International Alliance of Theatrical Stage Employees, Moving Picture Technicians, Artists and Allied Crafts of the United States and Canada, AFL-CIO, CLC (Union)

Ibanez	Brand Name: Guitars
intelligent lighting (1)	Programmable lights, also known as wiggles or movers, such as Vari-Lites, Studio Colors, Techno-Beams or Martins
intelligent lighting (2)	An oxymoron
Intern (1)	Free Labor
Intern (2)	Presidential Groupie
Iron Bitch	Slang: Barricade
jack	Standard 1/4" (6.3mm) audio connector, often used on line-level and instrument cables. Just be damned sure you buy good ones - to spare expense here is to buy trouble
JBL	Brand Name: Speakers
kak	Slang: general equipment or gear. Used in a derogatory way as an alternative to calling the gear "Sh*t". For instance, "Hurry up, let's get this 'kak' off of the truck so we can start setting up."
Kel-light	Brand Name: Aluminum flashlight favored by roadies. Sometimes used alternately a an impromptu weapon (originally designed for police use) See also "Mag-Lite"
kick	Slang: for bass drum
kit	Slang: for drum kit
laminate	Permanent plastic laminated stage pass given to road crew and band for an entire tour
lammie	Slang: see laminate
lammy	Slang: see laminate
lavaliere	Small microphone hung from the neck with a string
LD	Abbreviation: Lighting Director (the person who controls the lighting for the show)
lead	Wire or cable (imported term from UK)
leko	Traditional stage lighting instrument with lens and "shutters" for fine tuning
Leslie	Organ speaker made by Hammond for its B-3 and M-3 organs. Featured a whirling horn that is impossible to reproduce with synthesizers
Liger	People who hang out backstage, act like they are best friends with the band, and eat and drink all the goodies
Ligger	Same as Liger
Lighting Designer	Person who often never sees more than one show, and is sometimes exclusively the designer of the show.
Lighting Director	Person who runs and co-ordinates the various elements of a light show, frequently including controlling the lighting console.
Lighting Guy	Derogatory comment made usually by an audio engineer...can be replaced with: Truss Tart, Gobo Geek, Squints, and any combination of the above)
"live(s)"	Refers to where something will stay at. Its proper position. "Hey Jim, Where does this amp rack live at?" "That rack lives on stage right, over there"
load in	Unloading and set up of all equipment prior to sound check

load out	Packing up and loading in trucks all equipment after the conclusion of the show
locals	Crew hired in each town to help unload trucks and set up gear
mains (1)	Slang: for the main sound system
mains (2)	Common term for AC power. (i.e. "The mains went out and the whole gig went dark.")
Mag-light	Brand Name: Aluminum flashlight favored by roadies. Sometimes used alternately a an impromptu weapon (originally designed for police use) See also "Kel-Lite"
Magic Touch	When you touch a knob/fader/pot without moving it when the artist asks for "Just a touch"
Magic Wave	Moving the hands over the console (usually the monitor console) to make the artist think that you're actually doing something instead of messing with your perfect settings (related to "Magic Touch")
Marshall	Brand name: guitar amplifier
mic check	Verification that every mic is wired correctly and functioning (Test 1,2 3,Check 1,2,3, it can get boring)
mirror ball	Rotating ball covered with small mirrors. Popular during the disco era
mix	Delicate balance of sound controlled by the front sound man. Within the limits of the acoustics of the venue, a sound man can make or break a successful show by his ability to mix well
monitors	Separate sound system maintained to allow the performer(s) to hear themselves on stage. A special sound roadie typically mixes the sound on the stage
muff (1)	Cover for mic, cuts wind-noise and pop
muff (2)	Sometimes traded for Backstage pass (see Groupie)
"Multi"	Slang: Multicore
Multicore	A cable with multiple wires used to connect the stage to the mixing boards (both sound and light) See also "Snake" and "Multi"
"Nail Bender"	Slang: Carpenter
"Noise boys"	Slang: same as audio crew
"on top"	Part of the mix that is slightly louder or "in front" of the other channels. Typically the vocal or the featured instrument
one night stand	Single show usually picked up between tours. Several could be stringed together in a mini tour of unrelated bands
One Off	Slang: Same as "One night stand", a lot of times working for local production company
O.N.S.	Abbreviation: one night stand
opening act	First band to perform in a show. There could be many opening acts but only one headliner
Orange	Brand name: Guitar amplifier
overhead(s)	Microphone(s) positioned high over drum kit to capture the sound of a cymbal or cymbals
PA	Public address, slang for main sound system
P.D.	Short for "Per Diem" or "Power Distro"

P.S.D.	Short for Professional Sh*t Deflector / Slang for Monitor Engineer
pad	Device used to reduce the level of a signal. Pad switches are often found on console channel strips and DI boxes. Very useful if you have to deal with a particularly "hot" signal
par cans	Same as par lamps (stands for Parabolic Aluminized Reflector)
par lamps	Common lighting instrument, essentially a car headlight in a black tin can. Much cheaper and sturdier than traditional stage lighting
parametric	Type of equalizer
Pass Line	A line of roadies between 2 points in which gear is passed along from one to the next one in line
per diem	(Latin: Per Day) Allowance paid every day (on the road) to the to band and road crew. Not taxable (up to certain limits) since it is supposed to pay for food expense. In reality most days there is more food provided free than you can possible eat
Phantom power	Microphones that have built-in active electronics usually require an external power source, called phantom power, which is supplied by the console and fed to the mic via the mic cable. Most decent active DIs may be phantom powered as well. Standard voltage of 48V DC is universally used
Phase (1)	Slang: Phase linear amplifiers, originally made by Bob Carver.
Phase (2)	Hefty AC supplies are usually multi-phase. i.e. The fat black power cable coming from the generator has 3 "hot" wires, each of which is called a Phase. "We lost a phase and half the lighting went down."
Philishave	Slang: Name for the electric razor shaped mid speakers on split pa systems like martin audio.
pickle	Slang: Name for the controller for the motors that lift the rigging for the lights and speakers
pig	Slang: term for a large, heavy roadcase such as one containing cables or mic stands
Pig's	Pig´s ear (Beer)
Pignose	Brand name: Little baby guitar amplifier about the size of a large clock radio, used to tune guitars backstage. Can run off batteries
pink noise	Pink noise is a random noise source characterized by a flat amplitude response per octave band of frequency i.e., it has equal energy, or constant power, per octave. Since pink noise has equal energy per octave band, it is the sound source of choice for many acoustical measurements
pit	Slang: orchestra pit. Usually a good place to stash empty road cases, or form a buffer between the audience and the band
plugs	Slang: for ear plugs, not commonly used except by truck drivers. Sound men can't use them and light guys tend not to
pop filter	Foam bulb around the business end of the vocal mics. supposed to prevent wind noise and "pops".
poser	One who stands among men at work, without really working. Merely "posing" as a worker (common at most college gigs) a.k.a "gonk"

pot	Wrong!, not the drug, it's an abbreviation for a potentiometer: the technical name for a volume control
power distro	Slang: electrical box where the stage AC power distributes from
Prevost	Brand Name: (pronounced "Pre-Voh") "the Cadillac of tour busses."
prod tabs	Cigarettes paid for by Production
Production Manager	Person in charge of everything (sound, lights, staging, trucking, effects) except the band and the money, usually a working roadie
Production meeting	Usually held just outside the venue building prior to the show, usually downwind. Also held after a show, before returning to bunk in bus or room in hotel. Usually involves back lounge (bus) or bar (hotel). Dress code = whatever you were wearing at the show.
Promoter	Person or company that is bank rolling the show. They stand to make or lose the most money depending on show attendance and ancillary sales
rack (1)	A self contained roadcase with components for sound effects, lighting dimmers, or amplifiers inside. Usually pre-wired.
rack (2)	Slang for your bunk on the tour bus. (i.e. "I'm going to hit the rack...G'night.")
rack (3)	Toms mounted on the kit as opposed to those resting on the ground ('floor tom) referred to numerically, ie 'rack 1', 'rack 2'
rack (4)	See Also "breast augmentation"
raked stage	Old stage built on an tilt towards the audience. Very rare, but a roadie nightmare if you run into one
RCA	Abbreviation of Radio Corporation of America - kind of audio connectors found on domestic CD and video players
"Redneck Laser"	Slang: A mirror ball
RFL	"Roadie For Life" Professional designation ONLY available from www.roadie.net (e.g. Karl Kuenning RFL)
R.T.L.	Random Tie Line; cut pieces of black tie line that you find on the deck
rider	The document details the performer's requirements regarding food, drink, etc. Also known as "the wish list"
road	Anywhere (except your hometown) where a show can be promoted
road case	Protective case for virtually every piece of equipment carried on a traveling concert tour. It is typically made of plywood covered in a skin of colored plastic called Kydex. They usually have heavy casters for easy movement, and metal corners and edges along with foam lined interiors for added protection (see Anvil)
Road Manager	Responsible for managing the artists while on the road, while attempting to keep them out of "trouble". Generally handles all the money as well. The man to see to get a supply of backstage passes.
Roadie	Technician that travels with a musician or musical group typically providing sound reinforcement, lighting design, instrument support, staging, special effects, wardrobe, security, production management or all of the above for the artist(s)
Roadie billfold	Large leather billfold with chain attached to belt (to prevent pick-

	pockets I guess) Same as a biker billfold or trucker billfold
RTA	Abbreviation for "Real Time Analyzer". This device is used to graphically display audio frequency spectra and is commonly used as an aid in the fine-tuning of PA systems. A "pink noise" source is connected to the PA and a mic connected to the sound which the RTA picks up the sound which the RTA then displays as a frequency/level graph. Very handy tool for accurately identifying problem frequencies, but it's no substitute for an experienced pair of ears
scaff	Slang: Short for scaffolding, which sucks, no matter how far you have to move it.
scrim	Thin fabric backdrop, used in conjunction with front or backlighting effects. Could be white or black depending on effect
set	Part of a show. If there is an intermission (rare) there is a first set and a second set. More common in "bar bands"
Sharpie	Brand Name: permanent marking pen (writes great on gaffer's tape) Roadie's choice...don't leave home without it
shed	An outdoor amphitheater where the stage and part of the audience is covered by a roof. Usually features some grass seating...(e.g. Pineknob, Wolftrap)
shop	Workshop back at the company headquarters
show	The actual performance as in the show must go on
shower slides	Special shoes for in those strange venue showers with the sketchy looking shower floors
Shure	Brand Name: microphone, commonly used for vocals.
side blows	Another term for cross stage stack or fills
side fills	Small PA stack set up off stage left and off stage right to supplement the stage monitors. Used with very loud bands to help raise monitor levels on stage (aka fills, cross stage)
Silver Eagle	Brand Name: a deluxe tour bus, and all that implies.
skin (1)	Slang: refers to the think vinyl that covers a stage's roof (aka "condom")
skin (2)	Slang: Small rectangular pieces of paper used to hand-roll the <ahem> tobacco often smoked during "production meetings"
Slacker	One who works as little as possible, more than a poser, yes less than an actual stagehand/roadie.
SM-57	Shure vocal mic, sometimes used for drums.
SM-58	Shure vocal mic.
snake	Thick cable with hundreds of wires used to connect the sound and light boards to the equipment on stage
snare	Snare drum
sound check	Time allocated to "fine tune" the sound for the specific venue. May or may not involve actual musicians
Sound Nazi	You run into this poor soul when doing a gig at a venue with a decibel level he tells you that you can't go higher than a certain DB or the band will get fined (aka sound police)
"Spark Fairy"	Slang: Lighting roadie

Sparky (1)	An electrician
Sparky (2)	One whom has had a misfortunate incident with mother electricity
"special"	Anything that doesn't "go" (is broken), but is left in to make the set up/stage/whatever look complete. usually speakers or lights
Special Guest	Alternate name for the opening act(s)
special guest	Slang: Something left on stage in full view of the punters e.g. jacket on drum riser, someone's towel hung out to dry on keyboard stand etc
spin the bottle	Adjusting the bulb in a PAR can
spot op	Person who operates the follow spot
spots	Narrow beam light, could be operated by a stagehand (Trouper) or be a stage light (par lamp)
squint	Slang: Lighting Director
stacks	Wall of speakers at either side of the stage (modern stage shows suspend the sound systems high in the air
"stacks & racks"	A sound rental that includes everything except the mics and sound console. Common in bar or small theatre tours.
stage box	A junction box, typically allowing 6-12 microphones to be connected via one cable
stage crew	Local labor hired to help with load in and load out, and in some cities (union) actually perform some roadie duties like mixing sound or operating spot lights.
stage left	Side of the stage to your left if you are standing on the stage looking out to the audience
stage right	Side of the stage to your right if you are standing on the stage looking out to the audience
steel toes	Safety boots with metal reinforced toes, worn by some roadies to prevent injury. (e.g. Road cases are heavy and tend to crush things when they fall)
straight truck	Truck with 2 axles, 6 wheels, and generally an 18 to 28 feet long box
strike	To take down or disassemble (e.g. we started to strike the stage)
strobe	Rapid flashing light, popular in the disco era
struck	To have taken down or disassembled (e.g. we struck the stage)
sub	Shortened form of "subwoofer", a loudspeaker designed to reproduce very low frequencies, enhancing the "bottom end" of the PA sound
Suck button (1)	Slang: Any button or knob on a mixer that will make a band sound bad
Suck Button (2)	A switch, knob, fader, etc. on the mixing console that does absolutely nothing, but is used to threaten the band. (i.e. I'll push the suck button on your channel.) For a better effect, it should be labeled with a label maker
Super Trouper	Xenon arc spot light (incredibly bright), also a song by ABBA about their spot lights
supplemental sound	Extra Sound equipment brought in especially for large shows to provide enough power to cover the venue

"swag" (1)	A term that comes from the olden days in Australia... A salesman would walk for miles to sell his goods to the aboriginal people and those in distant towns.. he would carry his goods in a bag over his shoulder and by the time he got to town, he would have a definite "Swagger" to his step from carrying the weight all day.. Hence "Swag" means commercial goods, trinkets, souvenirs, clothing, .etceteras....
S.W.A.G. (2)	"Swag" also stands for "Stolen While At Gig" Can include collectibles, T-shirts, tools, underwear, etc...
S.W.A.G. (3)	"Swag" also stands for "Sh*t We A'int Getting"
S.W.A.G. (4)	Also known as a term used by the local hands as the local crew shirt: given out to the hands by the tour (if the tour co. is not to CHEAP!)
"swag" (5)	Term used in referring to slack in sound or lighting cable
S.W.A.G. (6)	"Swag" also stands for "Something We All Get"
S.W.A.G. (7)	"Swag" also stands for "Sex With A Groupie"
S.W.A.G. (8)	"Swag" also stands for "Scientific Wild Ass Guess!"
S.W.A.G. (9)	"Swag" also stands for "Sh*t Whiners Ain't Gettin"
Talent	A one-word oxymoron
Tech	Slang: Technician
Technical Hell	It's when everything that could go wrong, can - and does... but ONLY with the technical things. Technical Hell is NOT fun.
Tin-Ear	Slang: A sound roadie (usually a FNG) that mixes the sound with too much mid-range
tip (1)	To unload (e.g. to tip a trailer)
tip (2)	A cash bonus paid from a performer to an engineer and/or lighting tech. Almost unheard of.
toast rack	Slang: Guitar stand that holds 4 guitars
tom	Slang: Tom Tom drums
Tour Manager	The tour manager is usually the real boss and he co-ordinates all the road managers as well as the details and logistics of the tour itself. (see also Road Manager)
trainwreck	Slang: When the band drops the ball, the phrase "Trainwrecks are music too" keeps you sane
tri-amp	Use of three amplifiers to reproduce bass, mid range and treble separately after electronically splitting the highs and mids from the lows by use of a crossover
Trouper	A xenon spot light (the old ones used two carbon rods that would arc across a gap and create light, the current ones use a xenon arc)
TRS	Abbreviation of "tip - ring - sleeve". A jack connector typically used for balanced lines and console insert points
truss	Span of light but strong material (usually aluminum) that supports dozens of stage lighting instruments. (See Genie lifter and grid)
trussing	Same as truss, The gridwork of horizontal towers from which the Lighting and P.A hang.
Tweak (1)	To adjust, fiddle with, or fine tune equipment
Tweak (2)	Slang: Sound Guy

tweaking	When a roadie has too much party favor the night before a gig
union	Organized labor at certain venues, usually IATSE. (International Association of Theater and Stage Employees)
up stage	Portion of the stage farthest from the audience. Comes from old stages that were "raked" or inclined, and were actually lower at the audience edge
Van Hool	The Rolls Royce of tour busses
"Vej"	It is an attempt from German roadies to pronounce "Wedge". A "Vej" is either a "Wedge" formed loudspeaker cabinet placed on the floor with the loudspeaker facing up at an angle, or it's something which you can eat in catering if you don´t eat meat.
vendors	People selling ancillary products (T-shirts, programs, food, drink). Could be with the band or local
venue	Place the show takes place. (e.g.Theatre, gym, outdoor stage, Quonset hut)
VOM	Abbreviation: Volt Ohm Meter: used to identify and fix electrical problems
VU meter	The level meter on a mixing board, old ones used needles that bounced with the music, newer ones are rows of colored LEDs.
wedge	A stage monitor so named for its wedge-like shape, pointing the speakers up at the performer from the stage floor.
white gloves	Slang: A roadie that doesn't seem to get dirty, or doesn't seem to really do any work. (i.e. "He's strictly 'White Gloves")
"Wood nymph"-	Slang: Set Carpenter
World	Guitar World, Monitor World, etc. Anything World means an area. "That kaka lives over there in Monitor World"
XLR	Microphone connector (also called cannon connector, 300 ohm balanced, 3 conductor)
Zero Halliburton briefcase	Brand name briefcase of choice for Road Managers

References

◆

For the latest Roadie news, updates, job postings, top ten lists, stories, pictures, links to other Roadie sites go to www.roadie.net